Liberty, Property and Popular Politics

England and Scotland, 1688–1815

Essays in Honour of H. T. Dickinson

Edited by Gordon Pentland and
Michael T. Davis

EDINBURGH
University Press

© editorial matter and organisation Gordon Pentland and Michael T. Davis, 2016
© the chapters their several authors, 2016

Edinburgh University Press Ltd
The Tun – Holyrood Road
12 (2f) Jackson's Entry
Edinburgh EH8 8PJ
www.euppublishing.com

Typeset in 11/13 Adobe Sabon by
IDSUK (DataConnection) Ltd

A CIP record for this book is available from the British Library

ISBN 978 1 4744 0567 6 (hardback)
ISBN 978 1 4744 0568 3 (webready PDF)
ISBN 978 1 4744 0569 0 (epub)

The right of the contributors to be identified as authors of this work has been asserted in accordance with the Copyright, Designs and Patents Act 1988 and the Copyright and Related Rights Regulations 2003 (SI No. 2498).

The publishers would like to acknowledge the generous subventions towards the production of this book offered by the Enlightenment and Romanticism Research Network at Griffith University, Brisbane, and by the School of History, Classics and Archaeology at the University of Edinburgh.

Contents

List of Figures and Tables   v
Acknowledgements   vi
H. T. Dickinson: An Appreciation   vii
Frances Dow

Introduction   1
Gordon Pentland

Part I   Parliament and Political Cultures

1. 'The Press Ought to be Open to All': From the Liberty of Conscience to the Liberty of the Press   9
   Eckhart Hellmuth

2. 'Could the Scots Become True British?' The Prelude to the Scottish Peerage Bill, 1706–16   26
   Shin Matsuzono

3. Parliament and Church Reform: Off and On the Agenda   39
   Joanna Innes

4. Liberty, Property and the Post-Culloden Acts of Parliament in the *Gàidhealtachd*   58
   Matthew P. Dziennik

5. Political Toasting in the Age of Revolutions: Britain, America and France, 1765–1800   73
   Rémy Duthille

Part II   Beyond Liberty and Property

6. Edmund Burke, Dissent and Church and State   89
   Martin Fitzpatrick

7. 'The Wisest and Most Beneficial Schemes': William Ogilvie, Radical Political Economy and the Scottish Enlightenment   103
   David Allan

8. Thomas Spence and James Harrington: A Case Study in Influence 118
   Stephen M. Lee

9. Thomas Spence, Children's Literature and 'Learning ... Debauched by Ambition' 131
   Matthew Grenby

Part III The Long and Wide 1790s

10. British Radical Attitudes towards the United States of America in the 1790s: The Case of William Winterbotham 149
    Emma Macleod

11. Was there a Law of Sedition in Scotland? Baron David Hume's Analysis of the Scottish Sedition Trials of 1794 163
    Atle L. Wold

12. The Vilification of Thomas Paine: Constructing a Folk Devil in the 1790s 176
    Michael T. Davis

13. Nelson's Circles: Networking in the Navy during the French Wars 194
    Marianne Czisnik

14. The Posthumous Lives of Thomas Muir 207
    Gordon Pentland

Appendix: Selected List of H. T. Dickinson's Publications, 1964–2015 224
Notes on the Contributors 233
Index 235

Figures and Tables

Figures

3.1	English general acts concerning parishes and parochial clergy, 1689–1830	40
3.2	English local acts concerning church building, etc., 1689–1830	40
3.3	English general acts concerning non-Anglican sects, 1689–1830	41
12.1	Isaac Cruikshank, *Mad Tom's First Practical Essay on the Rights of Man* (1792)	181
12.2	Isaac Cruikshank, *Wha Wants Me* (1792)	182
12.3	Isaac Cruikshank, *The Friends of the People* (1792)	184
12.4	*The End of Pain* (1793)	188
13.1	Number of letters per year, 1777–1805	195
13.2	Number of letters per month, 1793–1805	196

Tables

8.1	Authors cited in *Pig's Meat*	122
8.2	Sources for Harrington citations in *Pig's Meat*	123
8.3	Comparison of *Pig's Meat*, I–III (1793–5) with *The Oceana and other works of Iames Harrington, with an account of his life by Iohn Toland* (1771) and J. G. A. Pocock (ed.), *The political works of James Harrington* (1977)	126

Acknowledgements

First and foremost, we would like to thank Harry Dickinson, who has been supervisor, mentor, colleague, role model or friend (and often more than one of these) to the contributors to this volume. The idea for a *festschrift* had its origin some time ago and gained momentum following Gordon Pentland's visit to Griffith University in August 2013, which was sponsored by the Enlightenment and Romanticism Research Network. The subventions offered by the Enlightenment and Romanticism Research Network and by the School of History, Classics and Archaeology at the University of Edinburgh are gratefully acknowledged. Finally, we would like to offer our thanks to Ellie Bush, John Watson and their colleagues at Edinburgh University Press for their assistance in the preparation and production of this book.

Gordon Pentland and Michael T. Davis

H. T. Dickinson: An Appreciation
Frances Dow

Harry Dickinson came to Edinburgh in 1966 and has made it his home ever since. Appointed initially as an Assistant Lecturer in the Department of History at the University of Edinburgh, he became Lecturer in 1968 and Reader in 1973. In 1980 he took up the Richard Lodge Chair of British History and held it until his retirement in 2006, whereupon he became Emeritus Professor and Honorary Professorial Fellow. During his long and productive career he has published with enormous regularity: his c.v. lists items for every year since 1964 and includes six single-authored and over twenty edited volumes. He has been an effective and popular teacher at undergraduate and postgraduate levels; and he has made important contributions to the development of history in schools and universities in the UK and across the globe.

Harry's academic success is testimony, first and foremost, to his intellectual abilities and his dedicated professionalism; but it owes something, too, to the encouragement he received from key figures during his school and university years. Born in Gateshead on 9 March 1939, Harry was the only one of five surviving sisters and brothers to continue his education beyond the age of sixteen: no mean achievement for a son whose parents had both left school at twelve. Happily, a teacher at Gateshead Grammar School recognised his potential and encouraged him to apply to King's College University of Durham, where he studied history from 1957 until 1960. He recalls being greatly impressed and influenced during his undergraduate years by the scholarly qualities he saw in J. R. Jones and Professor W. L. Burn. From Jones he learned sheer efficiency in organisation and presentation, qualities which have stayed with him throughout his career. From Burn he absorbed the importance of developing a deep appreciation of a period or topic, and his interest in the early eighteenth century was fired as a result of choosing a final year Special Subject on the reigns of William III and Anne, taught by Jones.

Jones's influence did not end there. After graduation, financial constraints led Harry to take a Diploma in Education at King's College and to become a schoolteacher. In retrospect the experience he gained then, and during his three years as history master at Washington Grammar School from 1961 to 1964, was to stand him in excellent stead as a university lecturer. But although he enjoyed teaching, he was conscious of an intellectual frustration and a desire for deeper study; this led to Jones, with whom he had kept in touch, recommending that he take an external MA, by thesis only. The thesis was to be on the War of the Spanish Succession in Spain itself, focusing on military and naval operations. In fifteen months, while studying part-time, Harry completed a 70,000 word dissertation which provided the basis for four peer-reviewed articles published in quick succession.

By the mid-1960s postgraduate opportunities and university posts were becoming more available. With support from Jones (who had moved to the University of East Anglia in 1963) and Burn, Harry embarked upon a PhD. King's College Durham – which had by then become the University of Newcastle upon Tyne – awarded him the full-time Earl Grey Fellowship for 1964–6. Under the supervision of W. A. Speck, he began research on 'Henry St John and the Struggle for the Leadership of the Tory Party 1702–1714'. The thesis was completed and the degree awarded in 1968, two years after his move to Edinburgh.

Harry's choice of PhD topic arose from his realisation, while exploring the War of the Spanish Succession, that the war had caused considerable debate and dissension within British domestic politics. He became particularly interested in the Tory criticisms of the war and chose to concentrate on Bolingbroke's role, rather than that of Harley as he had initially hoped, because he believed that Geoffrey Holmes, then the leading authority on the politics of Anne's reign, intended to write a study of Harley. Harry's work was particularly influenced by Holmes, whom he greatly admired, as well as by Speck. Although appreciative also of Lewis Namier's great work, he thought that Namier's conclusions, adopted by Robert Walcott, did not apply to Anne's reign, where party and ideological disputes were rampant.

The thesis developed into a full study of Bolingbroke's career. Published in 1970, *Bolingbroke* remains the standard biography to this day. In studying the later career of Bolingbroke, Harry had become interested in the political and ideological opposition to Sir Robert Walpole, in which Bolingbroke had been a leading figure. This led to a short, analytical study of *Sir Robert Walpole and the Whig Supremacy* (1973) and to an edited collection of primary sources, *Politics and Literature in the Eighteenth Century* (1974). Clearly Harry had come to the view that the Namierite approach to the politics of the eighteenth century had serious limitations. He was convinced that historians needed to study the political ideology, the political debates and the political press in the eighteenth century if they were to appreciate more deeply the nature of British politics of the period.

This was an important period in Harry's scholarly evolution. It resulted in the monograph on *Liberty and Property: Political Ideology in Eighteenth Century Britain* (1977), which he has described as the 'toughest assignment I have ever completed'. At this time intellectual historians, particularly J. G. A. Pocock and Quentin Skinner, were beginning to explore lesser-known philosophical works in an effort to understand the intellectual climate of early modern Britain. Harry's work, however, was focused more on linking political pamphlets and polemical literature, which often lacked philosophical depth, with the practical political issues of the day. While a few other scholars, such as J. P. Kenyon and John Brewer, were attempting this for short periods of British history, Harry's work offered an interpretation of British politics throughout the whole eighteenth century. Essentially, it related the ideological issues discussed in the political press with the major political divisions in national politics and was an explicit challenge to the Namierite approach to eighteenth-century British politics. Since then, no historian has been satisfied with the Namierite approach alone or willing to dismiss the importance of the press and the ideological debates of the period.

Harry's interest in political ideas, ideology and action was to find further expression in later publications, notably *British Radicalism and the French Revolution* (1985). Although much of his later work has been concerned with the 'age of revolution' of the later eighteenth century, after *Liberty and Property* his interest in politics across the whole eighteenth century did not wane. Increasingly, however, his concern was with the political world beyond the confines of the aristocratic or Westminster elites as he sought to develop an understanding of how elite and popular politics, as well as practical politics and political debates, interacted with one another. One of the major fruits of this was *The Politics of the People in Eighteenth-Century Britain* (1995).

From any brief survey of Harry's published work, certain things stand out which say much about the man as well as the scholar. Harry has tended to concentrate on big issues and long periods. His intellectual tendency has been to emphasise similarities and to establish relationships between people, ideas and actions, rather than to emphasise differences and to highlight incoherencies. To adopt the terminology used in the debate between J. H. Hexter and Christopher Hill in 1975, though without its pejorative connotations, Harry is much more of a 'lumper' than a 'splitter'. He has tried to build up an original synthesis about topics that have interested him, rather than concentrate on deep, forensic investigation of a very narrow or specific topic. Thus by doing justice to both Walpole and Bolingbroke, by exploring practical politics and political ideas, by linking elite with popular politics and by looking at radical and conservative responses in Britain to both the American and French Revolutions, he has produced new interpretations and insights into some of the major issues in eighteenth-century British politics.

Harry's scholarly excellence has led to many prestigious awards, fellowships and appointments. He was awarded the degree of DLitt by the University of Edinburgh in 1986 and was elected Fellow of the Royal Society of Edinburgh in 1998. He has been invited to deliver prestigious lectures, including the Anstey Memorial Lectures at the University of Kent (1987) and The History of Parliament Annual Lecture (2010). Throughout his career he has held numerous research fellowships, including several which have enabled him to work in major libraries in the United States: Fulbright Fellow, Huntington Library Fellow and Folger Shakespeare Library Senior Fellow, all in 1973; Ahmanson Foundation Fellow, Clark Library, UCLA, 1987; and Lewis Walpole Library Fellow at Yale University, 2004. An honour he particularly appreciated was appointment as Douglas Southall Freeman Visiting Professor at the University of Richmond, Virginia in 1997.

Harry's work has been published in fourteen countries and translated into seven languages. It comes as no surprise therefore that he has received dozens of invitations to speak at international conferences and to make academic visits for both research and teaching purposes within Britain and in many countries in North America, Europe and Asia. All academics welcome such invitations as evidence of peer esteem; but as an instinctive teacher and avid learner Harry especially valued those occasions which offered an opportunity for extended dialogue with both junior and senior scholars. For him, research is in the broadest sense a collaborative and cooperative enterprise in which all parties can learn from one another, whatever their position in the academic 'pecking order'.

One such contact, which blossomed into a fruitful exchange with the Ludwig Maximilian University of Munich, Germany, began through his association with Professor Eckhart Hellmuth. In 1997 the British Council gave him funding to develop research links in British history with postgraduates and staff in LMU. The focus was to be on the history of ideas in their cultural and political context during the long eighteenth century. Over the next four years small teams of faculty members and postgraduate students made week-long organised visits to one another's universities for seminars, discussion of student research projects, advice sessions and visits to museums and galleries. Harry maintained the connection with Munich, delivering Hauptseminars and giving research papers in later years. Another academic link, which was focused more strongly on teaching, was cemented with Dr Pascal Dupuy at the University of Rouen, France. For several years from 2002 Harry taught an intensive two-week course in Rouen on Britain in the period of the French Revolution to a group which included Masters students. Other links, with Poland and above all with China, were to achieve even greater significance, as we shall see below.

Working with postgraduate students is an aspect of Harry's career at the University of Edinburgh which he has much enjoyed, and for which he has gained an enviable reputation. He has been the formal supervisor of over thirty successful doctoral students and has given specific help and advice to countless others. He has also supervised many dissertations at Masters level, where a number of students (like Harry himself) have gained their first postgraduate degree by thesis only. The list of contributors to the present volume testifies to the excellence of several of his former doctoral students, and others who could not be included have also gone on to successful careers in universities across the globe.

His doctoral students have come from a range of countries, including Canada, China, France, Germany, Japan, Norway, Taiwan and the United States of America as well as all parts of the United Kingdom. He has felt a special obligation to help students from educational systems which differ from that in Britain, most particularly those whose first language is not English. In addition to his readiness to advise on methods and sources, he has devoted much time to discussing problems of structure and organisation in the writing of a thesis, and to helping his supervisees develop a clear writing style. His patience in this regard with international students is legendary. It is noteworthy that of the administrative roles which Harry has filled at the University of Edinburgh, two were concerned with postgraduate affairs. As Associate Dean Postgraduate in what was then the Faculty of Arts he played a major role in introducing the degree of MSc by Research; and as Convener of the Senatus Postgraduate Studies Committee from 1998 to 2001 he chaired the senior committee dealing with postgraduate affairs across the whole university.

Despite his interest in postgraduate matters, Harry never neglected undergraduate teaching. He always undertook a full teaching load and was a particularly effective lecturer to large classes, where his structured approach, clarity of presentation and sheer efficiency in covering the essential features of a historical problem gained the admiration of students of all educational backgrounds and abilities. His training as a schoolteacher undoubtedly benefited him as a lecturer and tutor, but so too did his memory of how much he, as a first-generation university student from a working-class family, had owed to the helpfulness of his teachers at King's College Durham. J. R. Jones and W. L. Burn had been scholarly role models, but it was a part-time lecturer, Mrs Elizabeth Fawcett, who had taken great pains to advise him on the techniques of writing essays and developing a prose style. Thereafter Harry always tried to offer similar help to students who most needed it. A belief in the responsibility of established academics to advance their discipline, encourage younger scholars and improve the quality of teaching and learning underpins another aspect of Harry's career, his distinguished service to the wider scholarly community in the UK. He was a Vice President of the Royal Historical Society from 1991 to 1995 and again from 2003 to 2007; he served on the history panel for the Research Assessment Exercise of 1992; and he has had a long association with the Arts and Humanities Research Council and its predecessor the Arts and Humanities Research Board. From 2002 to 2006 he chaired the history panel of the AHRB (which became a Research Council in April 2005), and was later involved with the AHRC's development of block grant schemes for postgraduate scholarships. Currently he is a member of the AHRC's Peer Review College.

Over many years Harry has been involved with various bodies set up across the UK to monitor standards and quality in teaching and learning in higher education. From 1987 to 1993 he worked with the Council for National Academic Awards, which validated degree-level programmes in those higher education institutions that had not yet achieved full university status. The later 1990s saw him acting as an academic reviewer with the Higher Education Quality Council. Two other appointments were particularly to his liking, because they focused directly on the teaching of history. From 1995 to 1996 he was appointed by the Scottish Funding Council as a team leader on its Teaching Quality Assessment Panel in history. This involved visits to several of Scotland's universities, where the lessons that could be learned from observing how others went about the teaching of history were of genuine interest to him. History Benchmarking was another challenge he enjoyed, following appointment to the UK-wide Quality Assurance Agency in 1998, because it involved consultation across the profession about the knowledge and skills required for a history degree. On a more personal level, Harry's commitment to reflecting on and improving his own teaching brought him membership of the Institute of Learning and Teaching in 2000; this later became a Fellowship of the Higher Education Academy.

Harry's interest in developing the curriculum and improving the standards of teaching in history was not confined to higher education. He was equally concerned with the study of history in schools, which he rightly saw as an indispensable foundation for the health of the subject in universities. His most notable contribution to history outside the academy came through his membership of the Historical Association, which he first joined as an undergraduate. The Association's broad aims – to further the study, teaching and enjoyment of history at all levels – reflected his own experience and outlook. He became a Council member in 1982, was Vice President from 1995 to 1996, Deputy President from 1996 to 1998 and then from 2002 to 2005 President. During these years the breadth of his commitment to history was shown in his willingness to give talks to many schools and local societies, as well as in his editorship from 1993 to 2000 of the Association's academic journal *History*. In order to bring to fruition plans which had been mooted during his presidency, he was re-appointed Vice President in 2005. He successfully promoted the Association's request to the Privy Council for a Royal Charter, which enabled it to award fellowships not only to those historians with distinguished publication records, but also to those who had advanced good practice in teaching and assessment in schools, and to others who had disseminated a love of history to the wider public.

Harry's expertise in assessing the quality of research and teaching and his commitment to the advancement of historical study was to find its fullest and most significant expression outside the UK. In 2003 his academic reputation brought an invitation to lead a team of international experts to assess the quality of research being undertaken in history and archaeology in two universities and three research institutes in Tartu and Tallinn, Estonia. A second visit a year later assessed the quality of undergraduate teaching in the three institutions in Tallinn. The team's recommendation that these bodies should unite into a new University of Tallinn was accepted, and in 2006 a team, again led by Harry, returned to Tallinn to evaluate degree provision in the new university. A more extensive visit to Tartu and Tallinn followed in 2008.

When Harry retired from his full-time position as Richard Lodge Professor in 2006, the Senate of the University of Edinburgh recorded in a Special Minute that 'without doubt ... Professor Dickinson's main passion has been to advance the teaching of British history throughout the world'. The most impressive examples of this have been the relations he has built up with Poland and, above all, with China.

The connection with Poland came about when he was contacted by a young Polish scholar studying at the Institute for Advanced

Studies in the Humanities at Edinburgh. Dr Pawel Hanczewski from the Nicolas Copernicus University of Torun, Poland was on a short-term fellowship at the Institute in the summer of 2001 and was keen to seek advice on developing the study of British history at his home university. Harry was particularly sympathetic to Dr Hanczewski's wish to promote historical study in an environment where there was limited autonomy for the individual scholar and inadequate resources for curriculum innovation or for research materials. There began a long-lasting exchange between the two on all matters related to research and teaching, with Harry on occasion also proffering advice to other colleagues of Dr Hanczewski and to graduate students. Most importantly, since 2003 he has made annual weeklong visits to Torun to teach intensive courses on eighteenth-century British history. He has given lectures and seminars on aspects of Britain in the age of the American and French Revolutions, devoting many hours to formal teaching and to informal discussion.

Undoubtedly the most sustained and significant expression of Harry's commitment to promoting British history worldwide has been his connection with China. It is no exaggeration to say that it is largely thanks to him that British historical studies now flourish in China. The link goes back to 1978 when, after a chance encounter with an Edinburgh alumnus, Professor Wang Juefei of Nanjing University wrote to Harry to ask for his help in reviving the study of British history. After the devastating effects of the Cultural Revolution of 1966–76, the priorities were to educate young scholars who could fill the shortage of university teachers and to replace resources, particularly books and journals, which had been lost or destroyed. Harry's response was twofold. In 1980, with the aid of a Winston Churchill Memorial Trust Travelling Fellowship, he accepted Professor Wang's invitation to give extended courses of lectures in Nanjing to about forty young Chinese scholars, drawn from universities from all parts of China. He went again in 1983. Several of these scholars now occupy leading academic positions across China, notably in Peking University. Harry was also assiduous in writing to publishers in Britain and elsewhere to ask them to donate books to Nanjing University, with considerable success. The British Council was also supportive. Professor Wang meanwhile organised the China-British History Association to coordinate the improvement in British studies across China. He himself made two lengthy visits to Britain in the early 1980s. In this way, networks were built up which drew in historians from other British universities and laid the foundation for Chinese scholars to visit the UK to work in libraries and archives.

An important milestone was reached in 1987 when Harry and Wang Juefei collaborated on the first international conference on British history to be held in China for many decades. For this, Harry secured funding from Cable and Wireless plc, which had business interests in China. He persuaded over twenty western experts from Britain, the USA, France and Germany to give papers to an audience which included over one hundred scholars from China's leading universities, among them delegates from Beijing, Wuhan, Shanghai, Tianjin and Nanjing. Many of the western experts forged lasting personal connections with their Chinese counterparts which facilitated later exchanges and collaborations. It was a fitting recognition of the part that Harry had played in these developments that in 1987 he was made (and remains) Concurrent Professor of History at Nanjing University, an honorary appointment which enabled him formally to supervise Nanjing students.

For some years thereafter the political climate was not conducive to putting British–Chinese links on a firmer, more institutional, footing. It was not until the end of the 1990s and, in many cases, even later that UK universities began seriously to engage with China. Harry's commitment to the development of British studies in China was nonetheless unwavering and earned him the gratitude and trust of his Chinese colleagues. Although he made only one academic visit in the 1990s, to Nanjing in 1994, he continued to offer what help he could to individual scholars and, often at considerable personal expense, sent books and other materials to assist their research. As funding became more available, Harry, with characteristic energy and determination, advanced the case for British history. Together with like-minded historians in other universities he secured opportunities for a succession of Chinese postgraduate students and postdoctoral workers to come to Britain.

Since 2004 Harry has made visits to China in every year except one, teaching at a total of twelve universities in nine different cities. His most frequent visits have been to Peking University and Capital Normal University in Beijing. On three occasions he has attended the multidisciplinary and highly prestigious Beijing Forum, delivering a keynote speech in 2008 and a special address in 2013 to mark the tenth anniversary of the Forum. This signal honour gave him great pleasure. So too did the graduation in 2014 of one of his Edinburgh doctoral students, the son of a young Chinese graduate (now a Professor) whom he had taught in Nanjing in the 1980s.

It is fitting to conclude this appreciation of Harry Dickinson's career with an account of his contribution to the study of British history in

China. Although there are many other arenas in which he has excelled as a scholar and teacher, this is undeniably the one in which his personal qualities and academic abilities have made the most difference. It is also, by his own admission, the achievement of which he is most proud and from which he has gained the most personal satisfaction.

Introduction

Gordon Pentland

Like all *festschriften* deserving of the name, this one might have been considerably longer. As Frances Dow makes plain in the preface, the range and depth of Harry Dickinson's influence and experience offered the editors a choice of scholars from across at least four continents working across the wide canvas of eighteenth-century studies. Many of the contributors have been taught and supervised by Harry; others have been influenced by his work or developed especially fruitful working relationships with him. For each of these categories, our 'pool' of potential contributors was wide and deep indeed.

The great (and often just) charge made against volumes of this description is that they are a hotchpotch – more or less idiosyncratic collections of essays by individual scholars whose professional and personal linkages are more tangible than their intellectual ones. If this volume is received as such, none of the blame lies with the scholar in whose honour it was commissioned. Harry's key works – in particular, *Liberty and Property* (1977) and *The Politics of the People* (1994) – were explicitly aimed at imposing some coherence on eighteenth-century ideas and politics.[1] Across a formidable and growing list of publications Harry has met the challenge laid down by the subject of his first monograph, *Bolingbroke* (1970), that the historian 'must rise from particular to general knowledge'.[2]

One purpose of both of the books alluded to in the title of this *festschrift* was to argue eloquently against a narrowing of scholarly ambition. Both also took issue with 'Namierite' approaches to the eighteenth century, while still maintaining a generous admiration for Namier's scholarship and the insights it afforded.[3] More generally they rejected perspectives which compartmentalised or isolated particular aspects of past politics. *Liberty and Property* aspired to examine principles and interests, political ideas and political actions. *The Politics of the People* similarly aimed to reconnect politics inside Parliament with the diverse political activities and cultures outside its walls. This ambition to capture politics in their full complexity remains the hallmark of Harry's scholarship. To take one example, this aspiration surely lay behind the concern to recover the diversity and creativity of popular conservatism during the 1790s, which now constitutes a major area of the scholarship on that tumultuous decade.[4] Few historians would now contemplate a serious discussion of popular radicalism that failed to examine its relationship with loyalism. We thus take these two books to provide the architecture for this volume. Contributors have mobilised their 'particular' knowledge to test it against our 'general' picture of eighteenth-century politics.

Before discussing how each contributor has chosen to do so, one thing further is worth highlighting: the presence of England *and* Scotland in the volume's title. While Frances Dow rightly dwells on the international scope of Harry's career and scholarship (duly reflected in the contributions to this volume), Harry's 'local' influence within the University of Edinburgh has had profound effects. Harry is a self-consciously *British* historian, something reflected in both his undergraduate and postgraduate teaching and in his published work. Whereas many of his contemporaries might have described themselves as such, but continued to research and write essentially English history, Harry's work pays close attention to the multinational and imperial contexts of eighteenth-century politics.[5] It forms an extension to that ambition to see politics 'in the round': a sensitivity to the interconnections of nations and peoples as well as those between ideas and actions and between different modes of politics. It made him a natural, indeed, a sought-after supervisor for many students of Scottish (as well as Irish and North American) history at Edinburgh. Over his long career, therefore, he has done much by supervision and example to change the shape of Scottish historical studies of the long eighteenth century and this is reflected in the contributions to this volume.

The first section, 'Parliament and Political Cultures', focuses on politics both inside and outside of Parliament and offers insights on that central theme of 'the way in which elite politics and popular politics inform, influence and interact with each other'.[6] The first two essays examine aspects of politics during the 'Rage of Party' before 1715. Eckhart Hellmuth examines a range of responses to one of the preconditions of this period of political contest: the lapse of the Licensing Act in 1695. His essay examines how a number of writers, both supporters and opponents of the 'liberty of the press', linked the issue of press freedom to liberty of conscience and increasingly employed an idiom of natural rights in doing so. Shin Matsuzono's essay is more resolutely focused on elite politics. He reconstructs the debates and contests surrounding the sticky question of the role of post-union Scots peers in the House of Lords, thus illuminating the interaction of political argument and party interests in the early eighteenth century.

Essays by Joanna Innes and Matthew Dziennik focus explicitly on interactions between politics inside and outside of Parliament. Innes explores the neglected topic of Church reform and establishes the complex route by which challenges to and changes within the Church of England translated into a concern to act among parliamentary elites. Dziennik approaches this relationship from the opposite end to examine how parliamentary legislation intended to 'assimilate' the Highlands to Whig and British norms was appropriated and adapted by local political actors. Finally, Rémy Duthille explores a key feature of 'the politics of the people' – toasting – in an Atlantic context. He vividly reconstructs a politics of conviviality, which acted variously as an integrative performance, a vehicle for ideas and a challenge to authority.

The second section, 'Beyond Liberty and Property', shifts the focus to another of Harry's preoccupations: 'the ideas, principles and assumptions of those engaged in the struggle to defend, amend or radically alter the political and social order'.[7] Martin Fitzpatrick's essay on Burke is a model of what can be achieved when historians take seriously the further aspiration 'to relate political ideas to political action'. Burke's shifting thought as well as his immersion in the political life of the late eighteenth century are both examined to explain how he moved from advocating toleration for Dissenters to become such a staunch defender of establishment as to have 'un-Whigged' himself.

Ideas are at the forefront of David Allan's essay on the fascinating figure of William Ogilvie. He offers an account of Ogilvie's *Essay on the Right of Property in Land* (1781), which demonstrates how an otherwise quite conventional product of the Scottish Enlightenment could reach startlingly radical conclusions. As Allan points out, Ogilvie often joined another figure, Thomas Spence, in later pantheons of 'agrarian socialists' or 'land nationalisers' and Spence himself is the subject of essays by Stephen Lee and Matthew Grenby. Both highlight the important role of Harry's own work (in particular his edition of Spence's writings) in stimulating wider interest in this important and rich thinker, and both provide sophisticated accounts around the theme of the 'influences' on Spence.[8] Lee's essay provides a detailed assessment of the evidence for the standard claim that the seventeenth-century writer James Harrington and his utopian text *Oceana* were the decisive influence on Spence's ideas about land. Finding the evidence wanting, he suggests a more nuanced account of the development of Spence's thought is required. This is, in part, supplied by Grenby, who focuses on Spence as a radical educationalist and finds synergies between his work and the non-canonical utopian children's literature of John Newbery.

The third and final section, 'The Long and Wide 1790s', narrows the chronological scope to a key decade, which provided the dynamic end-point for *Liberty and Property* and *Politics of the People* as well the focus for an exemplary and influential edited volume.[9] The 'width' to this decade is provided by contributors seeking to take account of the international contexts which are now such a familiar part of the increasingly globalised historiography of eighteenth-century Britain. The 'length' is provided by contributions considering the profound legacies of this unsettled decade in the early nineteenth century and beyond.

Emma Macleod's essay provides an eloquent reminder that, while events in France drove much political debate and action during the 1790s, radicals such as William Winterbotham continued to look west, both to monitor the ongoing 'republican experiment' in America and to deploy aspects of its experience (whether real or imagined) within their own struggles. As Macleod points out, Winterbotham's imprisonment for seditious libel was bracketed by contemporaries with the more conspicuous 'martyrdom' of five men sentenced to transportation by the Scottish High Court of Justiciary. Atle Wold takes up these notorious trials to reconstruct debates over whether the crime of 'sedition' had any meaning within Scots law. Radicals in the 1790s had clear practical and ideological grounds for arguing that it did not, but Wold dissects the more complex legal debates over this question, which was not settled until that revolutionary decade had long passed.

The final three essays examine three 'citizens of the world', whose actions and persons reverberated around the globe in different ways during the 1790s and beyond. Marianne Czisnik makes clear in her quantitative and qualitative study of the correspondence of Horatio Nelson that the French Revolutionary and Napoleonic Wars saw the decisive expansion of Nelson's 'network'. Her essay aims to assess how efficiently this network functioned to allow Nelson to navigate personal, professional and political challenges. Michael Davis's essay examines Thomas Paine as a 'folk devil'. As such, his focus is less on Paine the man and more on the ways in which stories and myths about Paine and his works were implicated in the tense politics of the 1790s. Finally, Gordon Pentland's essay looks to a similar range of myths and appropriations, those surrounding one of the 'martyrs' – Thomas Muir – who fell foul of the Scots law explored by Wold. Pentland explores the ways in which Muir was used by political activists, historians and writers in both Great Britain and Australia in the centuries following his death.

That the editors have been able to incorporate essays on themes as diverse as radical conviviality, naval networking, utopian literature and highland chiefs is testament to the breadth and richness of Harry's scholarship and influence. Readers will judge how far contributors have been able to do justice to another of Harry's great virtues as a historian, which has been frequently and justly praised: his pellucid prose and admirable clarity of expression. A number of contributors who studied under Harry have confessed that they all became used to that mixed feeling of embarrassment and gratitude on receiving draft chapters back from him, with every error and infelicity highlighted. All agree that we are infinitely better writers (as well as historians) for the experience; but all agree that we are still trying to live up to his high standards. Indeed, all of us who studied under him, or have otherwise benefited from his collegiality, intellectual guidance and friendship, owe him a signal debt. We hope that Harry and some of the many people whose interest in and understanding of the eighteenth century have been shaped by his writing and teaching will find something of profit in this volume.

Notes

1 H. T. Dickinson, *Liberty and Property: Political Ideology in Eighteenth-Century Britain* (London, 1977); idem, *The Politics of the People in Eighteenth-Century Britain* (Basingstoke, 1994). For a selected list of publications up to 2015, please see the appendix to this volume.
2 Henry St John, Viscount Bolingbroke, *Letters on the Study and Use of History* (2nd edn, London, 1753), p. 48. See also H. T. Dickinson, *Bolingbroke* (London, 1970), pp. 250–3.
3 Dickinson, *Liberty and Property*, pp. 2–4; idem, *Politics of the People*, pp. 1–4. See also his review of Linda Colley's short study of Namier in *English Historical Review*, 107 (1992), p. 1031.
4 H. T. Dickinson, 'Popular Conservatism and Militant Loyalism 1789–1815', in H. T. Dickinson (ed.), *Britain and the French Revolution 1789–1815* (New York, 1989), pp. 103–25; idem, 'Popular Loyalism in Britain in the 1790s', in Eckhart Hellmuth (ed.), *The Transformation of Political Culture: England and Germany in the late Eighteenth Century* (Oxford, 1990), pp. 503–33.
5 For examples, see H. T. Dickinson and K. J. Logue, 'The Porteous Riot: A Study of the Breakdown of Law and Order in Edinburgh, 1736–1737', *Journal of the Scottish Labour History Society*, 10 (1976), pp. 21–40; H. T. Dickinson (ed.), *Britain and the American Revolution* (London, 1998); idem, 'L'Irlande à l'Epoque de la Révolution Française', *Annales historiques de la Révolution française*, 342 (2005), pp. 159–83; idem (ed.), *Ireland in the Age of Revolution 1760–1805*, 6 vols (London, 2012–13).

6 Dickinson, *Politics of the People*, p. 1.
7 Dickinson, *Liberty and Property*, p. 1.
8 H. T. Dickinson (ed.), *The Political Works of Thomas Spence* (Newcastle upon Tyne, 1982).
9 Dickinson (ed.), *Britain and the French Revolution*.

Part I

Parliament and Political Cultures

CHAPTER I

'The Press Ought to be Open to All': From the Liberty of Conscience to the Liberty of the Press*

Eckhart Hellmuth

Among the most momentous insights in the modern history of fundamental rights is Georg Jellinek's thesis that individualism in religious matters was the real beginning of the Western understanding of freedom. He went on to argue that the demand for freedom of conscience necessarily brought with it a call for further freedoms.[1] Ernst Troeltsch pushed this further and arrived at the view that 'the demand for religious freedom ... tore up democratic constitutional guarantees'.[2] Jellinek's and Troeltsch's work must be seen in the context of attempts around 1900 to explore the relationship between religion and 'modernity' associated, above all, with Max Weber's name. Although the generalising nature of Jellinek's and Troeltsch's theses makes them problematic, they have retained a degree of plausibility and relevance. Most recently, Justin Champion – unaware of this older tradition – has written of the early modern world: 'The simple claim [...] will be that the relationship between citizenship and conscience was the critical starting point for definitions of *libertas*.' At the same time, he laments that 'the study of the history of civil liberty (as an aspect of the broader history of political thought) and the history of religious liberty (conceived of as the rise of the 'liberty of conscience' and ideas of toleration and persecution)' are still frequently treated separately.[3]

This essay may be read as an attempt to overcome the dislocation noted by Champion. Specifically, it deals with the liberty of the press.[4] Historians so far have not failed to notice that early modern authors created a close connection between the principles of independent, rational knowledge of God and free public reasoning, freedom of conscience and freedom of the press. Jellinek had already commented: 'The struggle for

---

* The title quote is from Matthew Tindal, *Reasons against Restraining the Press* (London, 1704), p. 6. This essay has been translated by Angela Davies.

another freedom, that of expression in general, is closely connected with that for the recognition of religious freedom. The history of the idea of freedom of the press points clearly to its religious origins.'[5] The classic example of this is Milton's *Areopagitica* (1644), which Nigel Smith, with good reason, has described as 'that most elusive of pleas for liberty of conscience and freedom of the press'.[6] Other seventeenth-century authors argued in a similar vein to Milton. Here Charles Blount's *A Just Vindication of Learning* (1679), William Denton's *Apology for the Liberty of the Press* (1681) and Edmund Hickeringhill's *A Speech without Doors* (1689) could be mentioned.

This essay examines a number of texts dating from a later period (the turn from the seventeenth to the eighteenth century) that took a new look at the problem of the freedom of religion, the press, and opinion. This represents part of the debate that was conducted after the abolition of the licensing system in 1695.[7] The essay traces the line that leads from Matthew Tindal's *Letter to a Member of Parliament* (1698) to Anthony Collins's *Apology for Free Debate and Liberty of Writing* (1724). These positions from the deistic milieu are contrasted with reflections on the liberty of the press from the camp of High Church orthodoxy.

I

The 1662 Printing Act was not renewed in 1695, which put an end to the licensing system. At the same time the Stationers' Company's trade monopolies came to an end. This was not the result of a protracted campaign in favour of the liberty of the press. Rather, the non-renewal of the Printing Act can be put down to the vagaries of parliamentary business and frustrations about the privileged position of the Stationers' Company.[8] The end of the licensing system, however, was not generally accepted and between 1695 and 1714 a number of bills came before Parliament aiming to reintroduce it.

Attempts to return to the strictness of the Restoration regime were not, however, limited to the parliamentary stage. Similar demands were heard from exponents of Anglican orthodoxy. The 1690s were a turbulent time for the Anglican Church.[9] Internal tensions were accompanied by attacks from outside. Among other things, the end of the licensing system meant that the Church was confronted with a flood of anti-clerical and heterodox writings.[10] Texts such as Toland's *Christianity Not Mysterious* (1696) and Locke's *Reasonableness of Christianity* (1696), in particular, set the alarm bells ringing in High Church circles.[11] The motive of their campaign in favour of the calling of Convocation was largely to find ways and means of putting a stop to these 'heresies'.

This was clear, for example, in Francis Atterbury's *Letter to a Convocation Man*, which concerned the relationship between secular and spiritual power. Beyond its immediate aim of questioning who had the right to call and dismiss Convocation, this text was also a declaration of war on all those who undermined the true faith with their scribbles: 'Deists, Socinians, Latitudinarians, Deniers of Mysteries, and pretending Explainers of them'.[12] The lament about these 'heretics', raised by Atterbury and other representatives of High Church orthodoxy, went along with pleas for religious writings to be censored by the competent 'experts' on faith questions, that is to say, the Anglican clergy.[13]

These demands for stricter control of religious writings brought the advocates of a 'liberal' press regime onto the scene. They included Matthew Tindal, a lawyer and Fellow of All Souls Oxford and an admirer of Locke, who, alongside John Toland, Charles Blount and Anthony Collins, is generally regarded as the central figure in English deism.[14] His reputation as a deist author is based largely on his work *Christianity as old as Creation*. Published in 1730, it quickly went through several editions, and was vehemently criticised by Christian orthodoxy. Tindal created a similar stir when, in 1706, with his *Rights of the Christian Church*, he ventured onto the controversial terrain of relations between church and state, offering a powerful argument for ecclesiastical supremacy lying in Crown-in-Parliament.[15] In 1698 Tindal's *Letter to a Member of Parliament, shewing that a Restraint on the Press is inconsistent with the Protestant Religion, and dangerous to the Liberties of the Nation* was published.[16] That Tindal's text contains 'only ... isolated remarks on the subject' of the liberty of the press, as Jonathan Israel claims, is simply untrue.[17] On the contrary, Tindal treats the subject in greater depth and breadth than almost any other author around 1700.

Like other heterodox authors before him, Tindal combined the question of freedom of the press with that of denomination. For Tindal it was beyond question that, as the title of his text indicated, 'a Restraint on the Press is inconsistent with the Protestant Religion'. In principle, it seemed to him that the Reformation had only become possible through the press, indeed, it was 'wholly owing to the Press'.[18] He saw Catholicism as a hostile power opposing the principle of press freedom. What is remarkable, however, is that he ascribed the same repressive attitude to a large part of the Protestant world.[19] He directed his charges mainly against the established Anglican Church, whose clergy he accused of being worse than that of the Catholic Church. In his eyes, the Anglican Church had fundamentally discredited itself during the Restoration by advocating the 'Doctrine of Absolute

Obedience'. And he vehemently rejected any claims by the Anglican clery to censor religious writings: 'The trusting not only the Pulpits but the Press in the hands of the Clergy, is causing the *Blind to lead the Blind,* because the generality of them are more likely to be guilty of a blind Obedience than the Laity.'[20] Tindal believed that the progress of the Reformation, which for him was essentially about the freedom of religious interpretations of the world, had ground to a halt and was awaiting completion.[21] And this required freedom of the press.

At the heart of Tindal's reasoning about the freedom of the press was the assumption that human beings have the capacity to seek rationally for religious truth. In his view, God had therefore imposed upon the individual the duty to think independently in matters of religion. Conversely, this meant that: 'He that neglects to do this, is disobedient to his Maker, in misusing his rational Faculties.'[22] In line with the Protestant principle of individual appropriation and interpretation of Scripture, certainty in matters of faith could only be achieved through personal efforts to gain knowledge. This presupposed a free exchange of ideas with others. God, he argued, had created humans as social beings with an innate right to enlighten one another: 'For a Man would be in a miserable state of Darkness and Ignorance, were it not for the Light that others afford him.'[23] Only when free communication was possible could humans fulfil their divine duty to gain knowledge of religious truth. Among other things, Tindal wrote:

> I think I may safely conclude, that Men, if they regard the employing their rational Faculties as God requires, and ... the discovery of Truth in Religion, and their being influenced by it as they ought to be, are obliged to allow one another an entire liberty in communicating their Thoughts, which was never forbidden but where Interest supplanted Religion.[24]

A determined opposition to any limitations on freedom of the press necessarily followed on from this idea. A general and public discourse, obeying the dictates of reason, on religious questions necessarily presupposed a free press, which, for Tindal, was the main medium for breaching isolation and exchanging ideas in order to promote the advancement of knowledge.[25] With the help of a free press, the correct religious views could be produced: 'An entire Liberty of the *Press* would by degrees establish religious Truth, because that is supported by better, plainer, and more cogent Proofs than any false Opinions are.'[26] The principle of press freedom was here embedded in a radical theology that was closed to all authoritarian views and focused on the process of individual cognition. For this theology, it was not crucial whether religious truth could, in fact, be found; rather, it honoured the *striving* for truth. This was a radicalisation of the principle of freedom of conscience, based on reason. But for Tindal, freedom of conscience was unthinkable without freedom of the press; he regarded both elements as the basis of the Protestant *lebenswelt*:

> Wherefore they who are not for destroying that just and righteous Law that allows Liberty of Conscience, ought to be very careful of the Freedom of the Press, as the only means to guard and defend the other; and both being built on the same foundation, cannot ... be destroyed but by striking at the foundation of the Protestant Religion.[27]

Tindal's view that freedom of the press was a complementary freedom to freedom of conscience was by no means new. It can be found in authors such as Blount, Denton and Hickeringhill, who, a number of years earlier, had argued in a very similar manner. What was new was that Tindal elevated the freedom of the press as an independent means of attaining knowledge of God and the truth to the rank of a natural right: 'Whosoever ... endeavours to hinder Men from communicating their Thoughts (as they notoriously do that are for restraining the Press) invade the natural Rights of Mankind, and destroy the common Ties of Humanity.'[28] One could speculate whether this reference to the idiom of natural rights was derived from Tindal's closeness to Locke. That Tindal did not, however, embed his maxim in a larger theoretical framework of natural rights renders this view questionable.

Tindal not only pleaded for a free discourse on matters of faith and religion, but also advocated free public reasoning in the civil sphere. Although brief, his thoughts on this subject were remarkable. He advanced the idea of the press as a critical instrument in the political process and as an anti-governmental force, a formulation later to be found in much eighteenth-century writing.[29] Tindal's view was based on the assumption that as a rational and sociable creature, man naturally also had a need to exchange ideas on political matters with the help of the printed word.[30] This process of communication, he argued, made it possible to make public the grievances of the people, and to expose the crimes of government. For this reason, most regimes had always tried to keep the press under control with the aid of 'State-Licensers'.[31] Tindal vividly conjured up the dangers that the system of pre-censorship could bring with it. 'For should a Magistrate arise with Arbitrary Designs in his head', he wrote, 'no Papers that plead the Rights and the just Privileges of the People would be stamp'd with an *Imprimatur*. Then the Press would be employed only to extend the Prerogative beyound all bounds.'³² As an example of this situation he pointed to what he saw as the tyrannical rule of James II, which had provoked the Glorious Revolution.³³ For Tindal, freedom of the press was the key right by which all other rights of freedom stood or fell:

> Secure but the Liberty of the Press, and that will, in all probability, secure all other Liberty; but if that once falls into the hands of ill designing Men, nothing that we hold dear or precious is safe. And experience manifests, that wheresoever that of the Press is denied, there no other is preserved.³⁴

These sentences describing liberty of the press as a special right of freedom were to be repeated thirty years later in the *Craftsman*, which in 1728 reprinted a long passage from Tindal's *Letter*.³⁵ Tindal's comments on the 'Jewel Liberty', as he called press freedom, had obviously lost none of their power of persuasion.³⁶

II

The advocates of Christian orthodoxy responded to Tindal's treatise. Under the title *A Modest Plea For the Due Regulation of the Press* the Anglican clergyman Francis Gregory published a voluminous reply that clearly breathed the air of High Church Anglicanism.³⁷ In the past Gregory had distinguished himself as a staunch Royalist. In 1660 he had preached the thanksgiving sermon in Oxford on the return of Charles II (*Davids Return from Banishment*). He had also expressed his undivided sympathy for the Restoration by publishing a celebratory collection of poems: *Votivum Carolo, or a Welcome to his sacred Majesty Charles II*. In 1672 Gregory had entered the royal service as a chaplain-in-ordinary.³⁸

Gregory's *Modest Plea* clearly expressed his irritation about the situation that had developed after 1695. He wrote of the 'dreadful Confusions, under which our Church and State now do'.³⁹ He evoked the danger of Socinianism, a current term often used for dismissing everything that might be suspected of deism, Arianism or atheism. This was the polemical side of Gregory's *Modest Plea*. On the whole, however, it was not merely polemic; long sections of the text provided a solid theological argument. And Gregory, like Tindal, linked his thoughts on press freedom very closely with his general understanding of religion.

Like Tindal, Gregory began by reflecting on the problem of human reason, but he clearly distanced himself from Tindal's assumption that human reason alone pointed the way to religious truth. As man was no longer in a condition of original innocence, Gregory argued, it could not be assumed that he was capable of moral self-determination by his own efforts. For Gregory, therefore, human reason was not absolute, but relative: 'The Common Reason of Mankind is become like the *Moon* lying under, though not a Total, yet a very great Eclipse.'[40] This relative reason allowed humans to recognise the existence of God and the need for divine worship; but it was not enough to be sure of salvation. This required a divine revelation in the form of the Holy Scriptures. Gregory described the relationship between human reason and Holy Scripture as follows: 'The Light of *Reason* is but the Light of a *Glow worm* ... but the Light of the Gospel is as the Light of the *Sun*.'[41]

For Gregory, the quest for religious truth had to be centred on Holy Scripture: 'And indeed the Scripture is the *lapis Lydius*, the *Touchstone*, the only Authentick Rule of *Manners*, *Faith*, and religious *Worship*; a Rule so *plain* and easie in all necessary points, that in order to the trial of our Religion we have no absolute need of any Book but Gods.'[42] Apart from Holy Scripture, Gregory recognised only the writings of the Church Fathers as having any authoritative power.[43] This canon of Christian belief was not up for debate; it was not to be subjected to a process of critical and open reflection. Rather, Gregory saw it as a closed cosmos of binding truths. It was therefore superfluous to introduce new considerations into the public discourse with the help of the press. 'No Man', he argued, 'whether learned or unlearned, can need any *new* Arguments from the Press to confirm his Judgment in Matters of Religion.'[44]

For Gregory, liberty of the press was synonymous with undermining the one true faith. He was convinced that introducing press freedom to any extent would open the floodgates to heresy and act as 'an in-let to Schisms, Heresies, and a great variety of Opinions and Practices in Matters of Religion'.[45] Gregory blithely ignored Tindal's plea for freedom of conscience and toleration; in his view, toleration towards other faiths was in line neither with divine law, nor with the practices of early Christianity.[46] And he strongly opposed Tindal's dictum that to restrain free public reasoning was an offence against the natural rights of man:

> To restrain this unchristian Liberty of the Tongue, Pen, and Press, is not as this Author doth boldly assert, *To invade the natural Rights of mankind, nor to destroy the common Tyes of humanity*. For if it be a Man's natural Right to persuade his Neighbour, either by his *Tongue* or his *Pen*, to entertain an Opinion really heretical, whether he thinks it so or not; 'tis also his natural Right to *draw* him into *Sin*.[47]

The logical conclusion of this chain of thought was strongly to support the restriction of free public debate. With reference to St Paul he wrote: 'See what St Paul saith concerning Hereticks, *Their mouth must be stopped.*'[48] Elsewhere, Gregory argued: 'When the Press tend to promote *Vice* and *Irreligion*, it ought to be *discountenanced* and restrained.'[49] To exercise censorship, to reject and suppress 'Heretical Papers', was to serve 'God and men'.[50]

But who did Gregory want to see entrusted with the role of censor? The answer to this question revealed a clergyman in thrall to High Church attitudes: ''tis very necessary, that all Writings offered to the Press about Matters of Religion, should carefully be *examined* by Conscientious and Judicious Divines.'[51] While Tindal, in his pamphlet, had expressed deep distrust of spiritual tutelage, for Gregory there was absolutely no doubt that the Anglican clergy was still the natural judge in matters of faith.[52] And it was to bring its authority to bear especially where the religious beliefs of the lower classes were exposed to danger.[53]

At almost the same time as Gregory's *Modest Plea*, an anonymous author published *A Letter to a Member of Parliament. Shewing the Necessity of Regulating the Press*. While Gregory had given the Anglican clergy a central role in the fight against heterodox literature, *A Letter* developed the idea that the state should be entrusted with this task. It began by looking at the basic arguments about the relationship between secular and spiritual power, and uncompromisingly suggested that the secular authority was also responsible for religious affairs.[54] The *Letter* argued that, originally, one person had undertaken the duties of 'prince' and 'priest' and concluded: 'The *Magistrate* is not only *Pater Patriae*, but *Pater Ecclesiae*.'[55] These two functions had diverged in the course of time, but the supremacy of the secular power had always been maintained. In the past, this had been true of both the Jewish and the Christian worlds, and it still applied: 'The Civil Magistrate' is 'still the *Supreme Guardian* and *Protector*, in the *oeconomy* of *Religion*, as well a *Civil Polity*. He's *Custos utriusque Tabulae*.' From this it followed that the civil magistrate was:

> not only entrusted to enforce the Observance of all *Social Vertues*, upon which the *Peace* and *Interest* of Government moves, as upon its *Axis*; but a *True* and *Orthodox Faith*, and *pure Worship*, and the *Honour* and *Glory* of that *Great* God, that has made him his *Viceregent* and *Representative*.[56]

The *Letter*, however, not only argued that the secular authorities were guardians of the true faith by divine commandment, but also stoutly defended the institution of a state church. The principle of unity in faith here merged into the concept of a national church. This was, so it was claimed, of apostolic origin, and, by the laws of natural as well as revealed religion, under the protection of the authorities put in place by God. Anything that offended the integrity of the Anglican faith or the Anglican Church was to be subjected to the sanctions of the secular regime.[57]

This brought the contemporary press into the picture. Where it deployed its destructive power to undermine the established religion and church, the intervention of the authorities was required:

> If therefore the *Liberty* of the *Press*, is highly destructive of the *Interests* of *Religion*, and particularly as 'tis cultivated in *National Churches* ... the *Magistrate*, who by Divine Appointment is constituted a *Guardian* and *Protector* in the cause of *Religion* is indispensibly bound to remove the mischief, by laying a powerful Restraint on the Press.[58]

There was no hestitation in specifying what sort of literature should feel the weight of official intervention. In a highly revealing passage, the author of the *Letter* listed a number of works that he held responsible for the contemporary process of destruction. These included Toland's *Christianity not Mysterious* (1696), Blount's *Oracles of Reason* (1693), Milton's *Eikonoklastes* (1649), Ludlow's *Memoirs* (1698) and, finally, *A Short History of Standing Armies* (1698) by Moyle, Toland and Trenchard.[59] High Church resentment was thus directed, predictably, at deistic tracts and writings in the Commonwealth tradition.

The specific aim behind this reasoning, as with Gregory, was the reintroduction of the licensing system. In order to give this plea for stricter regulation of the press more weight, it was claimed that printed material posed special dangers. The printed word, it was argued, possessed a different quality from the spoken word; it was a medium that lasted: 'The *Press* is a standing *Monument* and *Record*, that not only communicates the whole Poison, and leaves it to *rest* upon the *Mind* or *Judgment*; but conveys it to *Posterity*.'[60] It was also argued that the press dignified misconceptions: 'An Unrestrained *Press* gives a kind of *Imprimatur* to every thing that comes from it ... every thing that appears in publick, must pass for *Orthodox*.'[61]

Against the background of such sentiments, it is hardly surprising that the author of the *Letter* criticised Tindal and his call for press freedom. Tindal's argument that the principle of free communication was an essential prerequisite for the search for religious truth was condemned.[62] And Tindal's view that any restriction of press freedom was an offence against natural rights was rebutted with one of the classical arguments of political theory, the primacy of the interests of the state over those of the individual:

> It's an indisputable Truth, That the *Natural Rights* and *Duties* of *Private Persons*, are perpetually consonant to the *Rights* and *Interests* of *Publick Societies;* and the Exercise of the former, is for the most part to be regulated, and determined by the latter. Again, Whatever the Rights and Interests of Private Persons may be, the Magistrate is absolutely entrusted with the Preservation of the Publick Peace; and consequently may rightfully suppress every thing that is level'd against any Branch of the *Publick Establishment*; since such Attempts unsettle the Minds of a People, and engender intemperate Heats and Animosities, and consequently carry a direct Tendency to Disorder and Confusion.[63]

Tindal did not allow these attacks to go unanswered. In 1704 he published his second pamphlet on the subject of press freedom, *Reasons against Restraining the Press*. Tindal had undoubtedly taken note of the arguments of his Orthodox opponents, but they did not impress him in the least. In 1704 he restated, in abbreviated form, what he had already explained in 1698. Among other things, he articulated his profound hostility to authoritative religion; he repeated his dictum that to seek for religious truth with the aid of reason fulfilled the divine commandment; and expressed again the view that free communication was the prerequisite for the individual's quest for knowledge. In 1704, as in 1698, press freedom was presented as the natural vehicle for promoting independent thinking in matters of religion: 'The Press ought to be open to all. And when a Discourse is printed, Men by viewing and reviewing it, may form a better Judgment; than when 'tis only spoken.'[64]

For those who favoured stronger control of the press, Tindal's firm commitment to freedom of the press was an irritation. In 1712 Queen Anne urged Parliament to take action against the licentiousness of the press, and soon thereafter an anonymous text was published under the title *Arguments Relating to a Restraint upon the Press*.[65] For long stretches it was a detailed, although not very substantive, debate with Tindal's *Letter* of 1698. Among other things, the anonymous author objected to Tindal's view that 'the Liberty of the Press was a great furtherance of the Reformation' and argued instead that the printed word was part of the reason why the Reformation had degenerated into a breeding ground for heresies.[66] This destructive potential of the printed word, he argued, continued to be felt in the present: 'Bad Principles are the Cause of bad Lives, and all our bad Principles are owing to bad Books.' These 'bad Principles', manifested in 'bad Books', included almost all the evils of the world, such as 'Detraction,

Buffoonry, Slander, Strife, Lying, Heresy, Sedition, Rebellion, Treason, Deism, Atheism, Blasphemy and other such Sins'.[67] In the *Arguments*, the contemporary press was associated with the odium of treachery, subversion and crime.

Given this view of things, it was only consistent that the author of the *Arguments* called for the revival of the old 1662 Printing Act. In his plea for stricter control of the press, he appealed, among other things, to Jesus Christ. Referring to Matthew 12:30 and I John 3:8, he wrote: 'He that is not with me, saith Christ, is against me, and such is an Enemy to Christ and his Religion. Christ came to destroy the Works of the Devil.'[68] Such rigid biblicism corresponded to a narrow definition of the liberty of conscience as 'the free enjoyment of one's own private Opinion, and every Man because his Opinion is Orthodox to himself, hath a just Title to it, so long as he doth not thereby disturb the Peace of the Church and State'. This formulation was designed to undermine the close connection between the liberty of conscience and the liberty of the press, which had played such a central part in Tindal's argument and was a potentially explosive combination. By asking 'whether the licentiousness of the Press, doth not yet obstruct the enjoyment' of liberty of conscience, the author turned Tindal's arguments on their heads.[69]

III

The year 1724 saw the publication of Anthony Collins's *Discourse of the Grounds and Reasons of the Christian Religion*.[70] Collins's work was a critical debate with William Whiston's *Essay Towards Restoring the True Text of the Old Testament*.[71] The controversy between Collins and Whiston was part of the early eighteenth-century debate about whether the Old Testament prophecies were to be taken as literal or allegorical, and whether they had been fulfilled in Jesus as Messiah.[72] This touched on a central problem for the Christian understanding of faith. Whiston argued that the Old Testament prophecies were to be taken literally. He blamed forgeries of the Old Testament for the contradictions between the Old and New Testaments and, as a Newtonian, believed he could remove them by means of rational source and textual criticism. Collins, who in any case did not see Jesus as the Messiah, disagreed with Whiston on this matter, but staunchly defended his right to put extreme theological positions into the public domain. He argued this in a lengthy foreword to his *Discourse*, tellingly entitled 'An Apology for free debate and liberty of writing'. What moved Collins to write this more than fifty-page-long plea is not clear. The debate about re-establishing the licensing system was moribund at this time and Collins made no reference to the problem of pre-censorship. Nor did he discuss the Law of Libel or the Blasphemy Act. His text was more a general discussion of the freedom of public discourse.

Collins began his *Apology* with a passage in which he powerfully claimed thinking for oneself, independently of any authority, as a natural right and duty: 'In matters of opinion, it is every man's natural right and duty to think for himself, and to judge upon such evidence as he can procure to himself, after he has done his best endeavours to get information.'[73] From this natural law argument, Collins derived the right of free speech and free communication: 'As it is every man's natural right and duty to think, and judge for himself in matters of opinion; so he should be allow'd *freely* to *profess* his opinions, and to endeavour, when he judges proper, to *convince* others also of their truth.'[74] Collins's demands for freedom mainly targeted the scholarly world, especially the spheres of theology and philosophy, but in principle they were universalist. Like Tindal, Collins started from the assumption that man was a social being and that, in consequence, the search for truth could not take place in a state of social isolation, but only in a situation of communicative exchange.

As far as Collins was concerned, the history of Christianity was largely one of dogmatic narrow-mindedness, intellectual paternalism and repression.[75] By contrast, he looked back to antiquity as a model. Like other contemporaries who dealt with the problem of press freedom, Collins praised Greece and Rome for having established free, public discourse. He described the situation in ancient Greece as follows:

> After the days of Socrates, *Greece* for a long time abounded in philosophers, who were divided into all possible sentiments concerning the most important points of speculation, and disputed with each other and wrote books without number and without controul on behalf of their Schemes. And the variety and alteration among them whetted and improv'd the wits of *Greece*, insomuch that *Athens* by their means became the theatre of learning and politeness.[76]

References to Greece and Rome served a very specific purpose, namely, to demonstrate the pacifying effect of free public debate. This, at least, is how Collins interpreted the history of the two ancient polities.[77] In addition, he pointed to the Netherlands, which provided current evidence that open debate promoted internal social harmony. Collins deliberately opposed the traditional argument that diversity of opinion and controversy undermine social harmony. On the contrary, he regarded them as positive qualities:

In reality, the allowance of *free debate* is the method to obtain a more solid and lasting *peace* (*peace* flowing from temper and principle) than that mere *outward form* of *peace*, which is sometimes obtain'd by force and an inquisition. For if debates are *free*, that is, if no man gets or loses by maintaining particular opinions, the grand motives which make men disturb one another about opinions will cease; and they will sensibly fall into a *due temper of mind*.[78]

In another respect, the positive effect of free public discourse seemed obvious to Collins. Free public discourse on matters of religion, he thought, would strengthen faith, while authoritatively imposed religion would sow doubt and unbelief. Free debate, according to Collins, 'is the way to make man honest and sincere in the profession of religion (as imposition is only the way to make men knaves and hypocrites)'.[79] The background to this was Collins's assumption that a plurality of opinions was inherent to the world as a result of divine will: 'God himself, by forming men as he has done, and by placing them in their present circumstances, seems to have design'd, that they should not agree in opinion; or at least, seems not to have designe'd, that they should agree.'[80] To this extent, truthfulness in matters of faith could only be expected if everyone was free to discuss it. This discussion was to take place on the basis of reason and Holy Scripture. For Collins it was not important if 'mistaken opinions' came out of this process of reflection.[81] What he considered crucial was that the individual set out on the path towards an independent, rational knowledge of God. Such explanations might create the impression that in making his plea in favour of free speech and a free press, Collins only had the religious sphere in mind. This was not the case. His understanding of free public debate was wider, and in his view it was a general civilising power: 'The Adavantage of *free debate* to society is infinite. It is not only the way to true religion, and *true peace*, but the way to *knowledge* and *arts*, which are the foundations for politeness, order, happiness, and prosperity.'[82]

IV

If we review the texts by Tindal, Collins, Gregory and others, much in them seems like an echo of the debate on the freedom of the press that was conducted before 1695. But they do not only bear the stamp of the familiar, they also contain something new. This includes their references to the idiom of natural rights. In his cursory outline of theories of the press in the seventeenth and early eighteenth centuries, Leonard W. Levy remarks: 'Tindal may have been the first to elevate freedom of speech and press to the status of a natural right, a rhetorical achievement, to be sure, but a crucial step in the creation of a theory of intellectual liberty.'[83] Against Levy, it has been argued that in Tindal's *Letter*, 'Press freedom was a natural right only insofar as it formed the counterpart of the duty of communication' in religious matters. This may be true, but the fact remains that Tindal adopted a new tone in writing about the freedom of the press.

In any case, it is remarkable that not only Tindal but also Collins and others used the idiom of natural rights. In 1712 John Asgill, who had been excluded from the English and the Irish parliaments because of a 'blasphemous' pamphlet, wrote in his *Essay for the Press*: 'The Use and Intent of Printing, is (the same with that of Preaching) for communicating our Thoughts to others ... This Communication being the natural Right of Mankind.'[84] It is true that these sentences are not based on a subtle theory of natural right, but the growing prominence of natural right rhetoric gave the plea for press freedom a new quality. Finally, the fact that opponents of a 'liberal' press regime, such as Francis Gregory, clearly rejected the idea that the liberty of the press was a natural right and went to some lengths to do so, points to the novelty and increased importance of this idiom.

Notes

1 Georg Jellinek, *Die Erklärung der Menschen- und Bürgerrechte: Ein Beitrag zur modernen Verfassungsgeschichte* (Leipzig, 1895).
2 Ernst Troeltsch, 'Die Bedeutung des Protestantismus für die Entstehung der modernen Welt', *Historische Zeitschrift*, 97 (1906), p. 39.
3 Justin Champion, 'Some Forms of Religious Liberty: Political Thinking, Ecclesiology and Religious Freedom in Early Modern England', in Eliane Glaser (ed.), *Religious Tolerance in the Atlantic World: Early Modern and Contemporary Perspectives* (Basingstoke, 2014), pp. 42–3.
4 It forms part of a larger project that aims to reconstruct the discourse on the liberty of the press during the eighteenth century. See Eckhart Hellmuth, 'The Palladium of all other English Liberties: Reflections on the Liberty of the Press during the 1760s and 1770s', in Eckhart Hellmuth (ed.), *The Transformation of Political Culture: England and Germany in the Late Eighteenth Century* (Oxford, 1990), pp. 467–501; idem, 'After Fox's Libel Act: Or, How to Talk about the Liberty of the Press in the 1790s', in Ulrich Broich, H. T. Dickinson, Eckhart Hellmuth and Martin Schmidt (eds), *Reactions to Revolutions: The 1790s and their Aftermath* (Munster, 2007), pp. 137–75.
5 Jellinek, *Die Erklärung der Menschen* (4th edn, Munich, 1927) p. 61. This sentence is missing from the first edition of 1895.
6 Nigel Smith, '*Areopagitica*: voicing contexts, 1643–45', in David Loewenstein and James Grantham Turner (eds), *Politics, Poetics, and Hermeneutics in Milton's Prose* (Cambridge, 1990), pp. 103–18.

7 For the wider debate, see Geoffrey Kemp, 'Ideas of Liberty of the Press, 1640–1700' (unpublished PhD dissertation, University of Cambridge, 2001), pp. 222–62.
8 Raymund Astbury, 'The Renewal of the Licensing Act in 1693 and its Lapse in 1695', *The Library*, 5th ser., 33 (1978), pp. 296–322.
9 Gareth V. Bennett, 'Conflict in the Church', in Geoffrey Holmes (ed.), *Britain after the Glorious Revolution 1689–1714* (London, 1982), pp. 155–75; idem, *The Tory Crisis in Church and State, 1688–1730: The Career of Francis Atterbury* (Oxford, 1975); George Every, *The High Church Party 1688–1718* (London, 1956); Martin Greig, 'Heresy Hunt: Gilbert Burnet and the Convocation Controversy of 1701', *Historical Journal*, 37 (1994), pp. 569–92.
10 Justin A. Champion, *The Pillars of Priestcraft Shaken: The Church of England and its Enemies 1660–1730* (Cambridge, 1992); Joseph M. Levine, 'Deists and Anglicans: The Ancient Wisdom and the Idea of Progress', in Roger D. Lund (ed.), *The Margins of Orthodoxy: Heterodox Writing and Cultural Response, 1660–1750* (Cambridge, 1995), pp. 219–39.
11 Justin A. Champion, *Republican Learning: John Toland and the Crisis of Christian Culture, 1696–1722* (Manchester, 2003), pp. 69–89.
12 Francis Atterbury, *A Letter to a Convocation Man. Concerning the Rights, Powers, and Priviledges of that Body* (London, 1697), p. 6.
13 The Printing Act of 1662 had already put books on divinity, philosophy, science and art under the surveillance of the archbishop of Canterbury and the bishop of London, see Frederick S. Siebert, *Freedom of the Press in England 1476–1776* (Urbana, 1965), pp. 242–3.
14 On Tindal and recent work on English deism, see Stephen Lalor, *Matthew Tindal, Freethinker: An Eighteenth-Century Assault on Religion* (London, 2006); Wayne Hudson, *The English Deists: Studies in Early Enlightenment* (London, 2009), pp. 106–13; Jeffrey R. Wigelsworth, *Deism in Enlightenment England: Theology, politics, and Newtonian Public Science* (Manchester, 2009); James A. Herrick, *The Radical Rhetoric of the English Deists: The Discourse of Skepticism, 1680–1750* (Columbia, 1997); Wayne Hudson, Diego Lucci and Jeffrey R. Wigelsworth, 'Atheism and Deism Revived', in Wayne Hudson, Diego Lucci and Jeffrey R. Wigelsworth (eds), *Atheism and Deism Revalued: Heterodox Religious Identities in Britain, 1650–1800* (Farnham, 2014), pp. 1–12.
15 Dimitri Levitin, 'Matthew Tindal's *Rights of the Christian Curch* (1706) and the Church–State Relationship', *Historical Journal*, 54 (2011), pp. 717–40.
16 The text is discussed in detail by Ernest Sirluck, 'Areopagitica and a Forgotten Licencing Controversy', *Review of English Studies*, 11 (1966), pp. 260–74.
17 Jonathan I. Israel, *Radical Enlightenment: Philosophy and the Making of Modernity 1650–1750* (Oxford, 2001), p. 117.
18 Matthew Tindal, *A Letter to a Member of Parliament, shewing, that a Restraint on the Press is inconsistent with the Protestant Religion, and dangerous to the Liberties of the Nation* (London, 1698), p. 11.
19 Tindal, *A Letter*, pp. 9, 12.
20 Ibid., p. 22.
21 Ibid., p. 13.

22 Ibid., p. 4.
23 Ibid., p. 6.
24 Ibid., p. 9.
25 Ibid., pp. 4–5.
26 Ibid., p. 18.
27 Ibid., pp. 19–20.
28 Ibid., p. 7.
29 For examples, see Hellmuth, 'The Palladium of all other English Liberties', pp. 492–5.
30 Tindal, *A Letter*, p. 24.
31 Ibid., pp. 24–5.
32 Ibid., p. 27.
33 Ibid., pp. 26–8.
34 Ibid., p. 27.
35 *The Country Journal; or, The Craftsman, by Caleb D'Anvers*, 7 vols (London, 1731), II, p. 252.
36 Tindal, *A Letter*, p. 28.
37 Francis Gregory, *A Modest Plea For the Due Regulation of the Press, In Answer to several Reasons lately Printed against it* (London, 1698).
38 Newton E. Key, 'Gregory, Francis (1623–1707)', in H. C. G. Matthew and Brian Harrison (eds), *Oxford Dictionary of National Biography* (Oxford, 2004).
39 Gregory, *A Modest Plea*, p. 54.
40 Ibid., p. 5.
41 Ibid., p. 7.
42 Ibid., p. 13.
43 Ibid., p. 27.
44 Ibid., p. 28.
45 Ibid., p. 41.
46 Ibid., pp. 42, 51.
47 Ibid., p. 21.
48 Ibid.
49 Ibid., p. 8.
50 Ibid., p. 17.
51 Ibid., p. 10.
52 Ibid., p. 23.
53 Ibid., p. 12.
54 Anon., *A Letter to a Member of Parliament Shewing the Necessity of Regulating the Press* (Oxford, 1699), p. 6.
55 Ibid., pp. 5, 10.
56 Ibid., pp. 10–11.
57 Ibid., pp. 34–5, 38–9.
58 Ibid., pp. 38–9.
59 Ibid., pp. 36–7.
60 Ibid., pp. 40–1. Gregory had argued in a similar vein that the permanency of the printed word ensured that 'heretical' texts posed a more serious threat, see Gregory, *A Modest Plea*, p. 10.

61 Anon., *A Letter*, pp. 41–2.
62 Ibid., p. 54.
63 Ibid., p. 58.
64 Tindal, *Reasons*, p. 6.
65 Anon., *Arguments Relating to a Restraint upon the Press, Fully and Fairly handled in Letter to a Bencher from a Young Gentleman of the Temple* (London, 1712).
66 Ibid., pp. 11–12.
67 Ibid., pp. 43–4.
68 Ibid., p. 45.
69 Ibid., p. 35.
70 Anthony Collins, *Discourse of the Grounds and Reasons of the Christian Religion* (London, 1724). On Collins, see James O'Higgins, *Anthony Collins: The Man and his Works* (The Hague, 1970); Hudson, *English Deists*, pp. 98–106; David Berman, 'Anthony Collins and the Question of Atheism in the Early Part of the Eighteenth Century', *Proceedings of the Royal Irish Academy*, 75 (1975), pp. 85–102.
71 William Whiston, *An Essay Towards Restoring the True Text of the Old Testament* (London, 1722); Henning Graf Reventlow, *Bibelautorität und Geist der Moderne. Die Bedeutung des Bibelverständnisses für die geistesgeschichtliche und politische Entwicklung in England von der Reformation bis zur Aufklärung* (Göttingen, 1980), p. xxx.
72 For the controversy, see James E. Force, *William Whiston: Honest Newtonian* (Cambridge, 1985), pp. 77–89; O'Higgins, *Anthony Collins*, pp. 154–99.
73 Collins, *Discourse*, p. v.
74 Ibid., p. vi.
75 For examples, see ibid., pp. xx, xxix.
76 Ibid., p. xxv.
77 Ibid., pp. xxv–xxix.
78 Ibid., pp. xxii–xxiii.
79 Ibid., p. xxxvi.
80 Ibid., p. xxxix.
81 Ibid., p. liv.
82 Ibid., p. xxxvi.
83 Leonard W. Levy, *Emergence of a Free Press* (Oxford, 1985), p. 102.
84 John Asgill, *An Essay for the Press* (London, 1712), pp. 2–3.

CHAPTER 2

'Could the Scots Become True British?' The Prelude to the Scottish Peerage Bill, 1706–16*

Shin Matsuzono

Then let us all to the treatie, For they will do wonders there;
For Scotland is to be a bryd, And maried by the Earle of Stair.
Ther's Q[ueensber]ry, Seafield and Marr, And Morton comes in by the by
Thers Loudoun, Leven and Weems And Sutherland frequently dry
Ther's Roseberry, Glasgow and Duplin, Lord Archbald Campbell and Ross,
The President, Francie Montgomery Who ambles like any paced horse.
Ther's Johnston, Campbell and Stewart Whom the Court holds still on the hinch;
Ther's solid Pitmedden and Forglan Who designs to jump on the binch.
Ther's Ormiston and Tillicoutrie And Smollet for the toun of Dumbarton
Ther's Arniston and Carnwath, Put in by his uncle Lord Wharton
Ther's yong Grant and yong Pennicook Hugh Montgommery and David Dalrimple
And ther's one who will surely leen bulk Prestongrange who inded is not simple
Now the Lord bless the glimp one and thirtie If they prove not traitors in fact,
But see the bryd well drest and pretty, Or else the De'il take the pact.[1]

This anonymous ballad recites the names of the thirty-one Scottish commissioners for the Treaty of Union between England and Scotland. The commissioners met their English counterparts in June 1706 and, after heated discussions, they succeeded in making a framework for the Union. But did the so-called 'bryd' named 'Scotland' really live a happy married

---

* I am grateful to the dukes of Atholl and Roxburghe and Sir John Clerk of Penicuik, Bt for allowing me to consult the MS sources in their possession. I am thankful to the Huntington Library and the William Andrew Clark Memorial Library for awarding me short-term fellowships. The research for writing this paper has been supported by JSPS KAKENHI Grant Number 26370879.

life? Even before the ratification of the Union, Scotland's approach to the nuptials was fraught with numerous challenges, one of which was the Scottish peerage question. In 1719 the Whig ministry expected that a Peerage Bill would answer it, by turning the notorious system of representative peers into one based on heredity, but the government failed to pass the legislation. Even before this, however, there had been numerous controversies around the Scots peers in the House of Lords. This essay aims to reconstruct these controversies, which involved ongoing questions surrounding the Union negotiations of 1706–7 and provided a crucial and instructive prelude to the crisis around the Peerage Bills in 1718–19.

I

One important problem was how a newly minted constitution of Great Britain should be framed. Some Scots insisted on a merger on an absolutely equal footing with all peers, shire and burgh representatives in the Scottish Parliament able to participate in a British Parliament. Some intellectuals, such as Andrew Fletcher of Saltoun, were of the opinion that Scotland should establish a federal union with England, though English politicians, both Tories and Whigs, turned a deaf ear to these arguments. The earl of Nottingham, a Tory who had played an important role in an abortive union negotiation in 1702–3, 'foretold that the nobility of that nation would never agree to any union, till the parliament of England should first agree on the numbers and rank of such as they would admit into the parliament of Great Britain'.[2] For Nottingham, a merger on an equal footing was hardly worth bringing up. For the leading English politicians, the most important thing was what standard England should adopt in receiving Scots peers and commoners, and how many Scots delegates should be admitted to a new, British, Parliament.

In the parliamentary session of 1705–6 (a time when the Scottish court was convinced that the retaliatory 'Alien Act' enacted by the English Parliament would be repealed and when it saw some hope for a union), the earl of Roxburghe was apprehensive of 'the degradation to Scottish nobility' and believed that the election of peers would be inevitable if the Scots wished for a union.[3] In this session the Whig Junto lords had started to discuss the outline of the prospective union and focused on the principle to be used in fixing the number of Scots representatives in the British Parliament. Lord Somers, a Junto member, thought that the English Parliament should decide the number of the Scottish lords and MPs before entering into the negotiation of the Union treaty. He reached an agreement with bishop Nicolson of Carlisle on the following point: '[i]f Scotland were now admitted to a Community of Trade with England, paying their proportion of the public Taxes and having a like proportionable Number of their Lords and Commons at the passing of Money-Bills, 'twould be sufficient for the present: For that a farther Union (in Religion laws and Civil Government) must be the Work of time.'[4]

The English and Scots commissioners met for the first time on 16 April 1706.[5] However, it was not until the middle of June that they began to proceed to debate the number of Scottish peers and MPs that might sit at Westminster. It appears that most of the Scots commissioners recognised that only a small number of peers and commoners could represent their country and thought that these peers should be elected. George Lockhart of Carnwath, an anti-unionist Scots commissioner, was outraged because he was convinced that the Union would deprive '[Scotland's] nobility of their birthright by reducing their number in the House of Lords to a certain quota to be elected by the whole'.[6] The other commissioners, however, were interested only in the number of representative peers. In the negotiation between the English and Scots sides, the English commissioners decided first to propose the number of Scottish MPs. The Scots commissioners anticipated that the number of representative peers would be decided in proportion to the Scots commoners.[7]

On 7 June 1706, the commissioners expected that they would discuss the number of representative peers and commoners. The Scots naturally regarded this negotiation as important and they proposed free discussion instead of an exchange of papers between the sides. The English commissioners showed their disapproval of this. They were afraid that 'speeches from both sides would lead to quarrels reflecting the strong convictions, anger and impatience of both nations, and that these would disrupt negotiation and perhaps nullify attempts to bring about union'. In the face of the inflexible attitude of the English commissioners, the conference was halted, but soon both sides compromised. The English accepted free discussion, while the Scots side guaranteed that 'they would not be so inflexible as to frustrate the Queen's hopes'.[8]

At six in the evening of the following day, the earl of Pembroke, Tory Lord President of the Council, handed in a paper and suggested that the number of Scots representative MPs should be thirty-eight. This number disappointed and enraged the Scots commissioners, and the earl of Seafield, Lord Chancellor of Scotland, immediately argued against the proposal. The earl of Godolphin, Lord Treasurer of England, made a long speech, which was eloquently answered by the earl of Stair. Then Robert

Harley, the English Secretary of State for the Northern Department, made an 'effrontery' speech. Sir John Clerk of Penicuik, a moderate pro-union Scots commissioner, recorded that 'the Scots commissioners were surprised at the reading of this paper, because the number of Representatives in the House of Commons was much smaller than was expected ... upon our representation in parliament & tho[ugh] we cou'd not pretend to ask a very great number, yet we thought what was offered was too little, some were for proposing 60, but at length in case we should be affronted with a refusal, it would be better to ask only a great number'.[9] The Scots decided to avoid a break and seek further discussion of the matter, but Lord Leven, a Scots commissioner and courtier, was obliged to admit that the number of Scots representatives in both Houses was 'like to be very small'.[10]

John Clerk summarised the speeches on that day. The Scots side emphasised that the number of representatives should be based on population and 'dignity'. While there was acceptance that a man might have held two or three votes in the past, this was no longer considered permissible by Clerk. With the establishment of a completely new state, the franchise system should start from scratch and a new Parliament should be based on the principles of population and dignity. Some Scots commissioners had entertained the idea that the two Parliaments would emerge on an equal footing, but after listening to Lord Pembroke's proposals, they came to see the idea as unrealistic and discarded it. Clerk also made it clear how the English commissioners had formed their scheme for a new British Parliament. Starting from the rejection of any notion that the English and Scots members would be represented on an equal footing, they assumed that the Scottish Parliament should be absorbed into a British Parliament, within which the existing representation of the English Parliament would be completely maintained. The method to fix the number of Scots representatives in the British Parliament should be based not on population and dignity, but on the 'revenue'. Even though the English representation did not uniformly operate on this basis, the Scots were expected to accept the principle.

On 12 June 1706, the commissioners restarted the conference. Seafield first explained 'the reasons why we insisted on a greater number' and his speech was answered by several English delegates. Finally, Robert Harley 'made a very foolish speech wherein he told us that he did not doubt but we came there to give down some of 38 for that we certainly thought them too many'. During this debate Clerk felt 'more heat than reason' from the discussion.[11] Without reaching any conclusions, the conference was adjourned to 14 June.

Before the meeting was resumed, the Scots talked the question over and considered how they would reply to the English commissioners. The Scots divided over the number of representatives they would have in the House of Commons. Most of them thought that thirty-eight was too few. The Scots commissioners also feared that politically ambitious Scots would discard their Scottish nationality and stand as candidates for English constituencies, a haemorrhage that would devastate Scotland. The Scots side was also convinced that the English commissioners would adhere to the 'revenue principle' (basing representation, above all, on the land tax). If this principle should be adopted it would afford the Scots one fortieth of the English representation and so the Scots would return only twelve MPs. In light of this discussion the Scots changed their tactics. They gave their insistence on fixing representation to population (which would give the Scots one sixth or one seventh of the English total) and decided instead to assent to the terms offered by the English side if the English commissioners would accept a greater number than thirty-eight.

On the 15 June 1706, the English side 'proposed 45 members in proportion to 16 peers'.[12] The Scots were divided over the number of MPs suggested, but most of them seem to have been satisfied with a total of sixteen representative peers, since this figure would make a good balance for the number of the Scots representatives in the Commons. They feared, however, that many Scots peers who might be elected as representatives would not be able to bear the expense of London. Clerk thought that 'a greater number of peers would by carrying out large sums of money from Scotland to England ... [do] more hurt than the most severe tax'.[13] Nevertheless, the Scots accepted this suggestion of fixing the Scottish presence at sixteen representative peers and forty-five commoners.

Neither the Scots nor the English commissioners, who clung to the principle of the land tax, were entirely satisfied with this compromise. Godolphin and his followers placed a premium on the conclusion of the Union treaty and they seem to have accepted more members than the tax principle would have admitted. It is remarkable that Robert Harley, later 'the premier minister', was one of those elements that held out against the Scots commissioners. He thought that if the commissioners had stuck to the tax principle, even thirty-eight Scots MPs would have been too many and remarked that 'we have stretch'd our consciences to forty-five *and no more* for the House of Commons, and sixteen for the Lords'.[14] Nor was his view exceptional within the ministry. The duke of Newcastle, a wealthy moderate Whig and Lord Privy Seal, stated:

When they [the Scots commissioners] had got their land tax lowered as much as they could, they would not abate us one member for it. Nay I find artifice has had a very ill effect with them, though many of them said when they came first to town, they should ask a greater number to exonerate themselves (as they call it); yet did seem as if they would have been content with thirty-six of the Lower House.[15]

Having heard this proposal, George Lockhart spoke of 'my certain knowledge that the English did design from the beginning to give the Scots forty-five Commoners, and a proportionable number of peers', and he gave it as his opinion that:

had the Scots stood their ground I have good reason to affirm that the English would have allowed a much greater number of representatives and abatement of taxes, for the English saw too plainly the advantage that would accrue to England by an union of the two kingdoms upon this scheme and would never have stuck at any terms to obtain it. And indeed they cannot be blamed for making the best bargain they could for their own country, when they found the Scots so very complaisant, as to agree to everything that was demanded of them.[16]

Most of the Scots commissioners, however, did not agree. As noted above, the Scots commissioners had doubts that many peers would be able to stand the expense of London.

II

The financial situation of the Scottish peers, however, was not the only or the most important reason that the Scots commissioners amenably accepted a relatively small number of representative peers. Clerk gave another reason:

Most of them [the Scots commissioners] had promises made to them that the restrictions of their number to sit in parliament needed be no ob[ject]ion to them for the most of them wou'd be after the union created a new peers of Great Britain with the privilege of sitting in the house of Peers & that by degrees all the noble Families in Scotland wou'd be received into the full Enjoyment of the peerage of Great Britain. I know that such promises were made by the Queen and her chief Ministers.[17]

Clerk registered this English promise so vividly that he still had it fixed in his memory sixteen years later. In 1722 Clerk wrote that the

English ministry had promised that every Scots peer could take a seat in the British House of Lords if he were ennobled as a British peer, and that this promise had been made 'when I was a commissioner to the Treaty of Union ... Nor do I see what prejudice it [the promise] would [offer] to our present constitution tho[ugh] all the Peers of Scotland were assumed.'[18] He also wrote that '[t]he King and his successors' were empowered to 'bring as many of the Peers of Scotland into the House of Lords as shall merit that Honour'.[19] Promises of this kind were clearly heard by most of the leading Scots politicians, which raises questions about how sincerely they were made.

There were some favourable precedents for the Scots. In 1705 the duke of Argyll was ennobled as an English peer, the earl of Greenwich. The duke of Marlborough was a Scots peer as well, having been created the Scottish Lord Eyemouth of Churchill in 1672. Thus, Marlborough and Argyll, each having both an English and a Scottish title, could sit in both Parliaments before the Union. Similarly, an Irish peer could take a seat in the English (before 1707) or British (after 1707) House of Lords, once he was created an English or a British peer. A Scots nobleman could thus reasonably expect to become a British peer and sit in the House of Lords. In fact, the Scots duke of Queensberry was created the British duke of Dover in June 1708 and took his seat in the House of Lords accordingly. John Clerk's hope seemed to have been fulfilled.

However, this promotion was regarded with suspicion by some English peers, who feared that there would ultimately be no limit to the advance of Scots peers into the House of Lords.[20] Nevertheless, ministers continued to believe that they could secure a British title for a Scots peer and thus place him in the House of Lords as a hereditary peer. In August 1710, Robert Harley succeeded in overturning the Godolphin ministry and in the following year he was created the earl of Oxford and appointed as Lord Treasurer. Oxford secured a crushing victory in the 1710 general election and his allies enjoyed a clear majority in the House of Commons. In the Lords, however, the government's majority was more precarious, because the militant Whig Junto lords displayed strong leadership there and openly opposed Oxford and the Tories. Oxford thus had every reason to make some faithful Scots hereditary peers in addition to the sixteen representative peers, who had normally been controlled by the government patronage.

Oxford made his approach, naturally, to Scots Tories. With his advice, the Queen created the duke of Hamilton, who had been prominent in the anti-Union group and was a crypto-Jacobite, a British peer as the duke of Brandon on 11 September 1711. Most of the Whig peers and some temporary deserters among Tory peers, such as the earl of Dartmouth, resolutely opposed this creation and succeeded in denying Hamilton his seat in the Lords in December 1712.[21] This raised the question that had been broached during the Union negotiations in a very pointed manner. The Scots peers complained to the ministry of 'the insupportable hardship ... [which] Scotland thinks is put upon its peers, and ye delay of giving relief in that affair'.[22] The Scots apparently appealed to public opinion by publishing *A Representation of the Scotch Peers, 1711/12 on Duke Hamilton's Case* (1712), in which the Scots peers and MPs claimed that the apparent flexibility suggested in 1706 had disappeared: '[s]ixteen shall be the Number to sit', and the Queen 'was disabled to grant Patents of Honour to the Peers of Scotland'.[23]

For some time the Scots representative peers and commoners staged a boycott in Parliament. Their tactics were unsuccessful, however, since Oxford succeeded in making twelve new ministerial peers (the so-called Oxford's 'dozen') from the end of December 1711 to early January 1712. The Scots even dropped a hint of a possible proposal to dissolve the Union. The grievances of the Scots peers, however, continued to accumulate. In 1713 the Scots criticised the government policy of Scottish malt tax and once again raised the question of the numbers of Scots peers and commoners. In late May, Scots MPs gathered and severely criticised the government's Scottish policies. George Lockhart proposed 'it was necessary they should show their resentment of such usage and endeavour to get free of the Union and for the purpose that they should move for leave to begin in a bill to dissolve it & added that tho he did not think it could carry at this time yet it would leave on record their sense'. After Lockhart finished, 'All the Scots Members seemed very keen and therefore they wrote down their names' and hoped that the Scots peers would join them in meeting. This meeting was held, at which 'the Duke of Argyle said he heartily agreed to the measure and he thought a dissolution of the Union absolutely necessary'. He was supported by the earl of Mar and 'several more of the peers'.[24]

The Oxford ministry finally managed to dissuade the Scots peers and commoners from insisting on the dissolution of the Union. In the last years of Queen Anne's reign, however, there were repeated calls for the dissolution of the Union on the basis of its manifold disadvantages for the Scots. If many of these pamphlets were Jacobite productions, some Hanoverian Tories and even Whig Scots were also disenchanted with what they saw as unjust treatment by the government.

III

This feeling was maintained during the early days of the reign of George I. In the autumn of 1714, not only Scots Tories but also some Whigs attacked the new Hanoverian court fiercely and demanded a change in Scottish policies. The duke of Montrose, a *Squadrone* Whig and an intimate ally of such English peers as the earl of Sunderland and James Stanhope (created Viscount Stanhope in 1717 and promoted to an earldom in 1718), informed the earl of Sutherland that 'some of the Scots peers, whom I have lately had occasion to wait on, having thought it necessary for the Interest of the Peers in general, that there should be a meeting of such of them as are now in town'.[25] Various plans were drawn up and some peers again expressed a desire to sit in the House of Lords as hereditary peers and abolish the representative system:

> Though this current [Queen Anne's] parliament is not dissolved yet some last occurrences, which seem levelled at our privilege of peerage doe in an extraordinary manner, call for our precautions ... I must begin at the original of this project, which was entered into first when Duke Hamilton was refused his place in the house of peers ... the project then talk'd of, was to make so many of us and our heirs, constant hereditary sitting British peers, and to degrade the whole remaining peers of Scotland, from their privilege of electing sixteen.[26]

The general election and the Scots peers' election in January to February 1715 resulted in a crushing defeat of the English and Scots Tories. The Scots Tories were forced to extremes and demanded the dissolution of the Union, which inevitably alienated such Scots Whigs as the *Squadrone* and the duke of Argyll's interest generally called the 'Argathelians'.[27] Montrose was informed that 'addressing against the Union, is still carried on, and that particular persons are appoint'd in every shyre to propagate ... D[uke] of Atholl had best found in the west'.[28] Atholl claimed that he never participated in the project to criticise the government and the call for the dissolution of the Union, but the ministry refused to put his name on the Court list.[29] Nevertheless, many of the Scottish Tory peers were convinced by this turn of events to adhere to the representative system. As long as it was maintained, a Tory peer still had a slim hope of being elected one of the sixteen. He would have no chance if the ministry should decide that only hereditary Scots peers, who had been nominated by the Court, could sit in the House of Lords.[30]

The Scots Court peers were moving in a different direction and the ministry was considering a new system for the Scots peers. An anonymous letter probably addressed to the earl of Stair, a Scots courtier, addressed the political situation at the Court and Parliament just before the 1715 session opened. At first, the writer was apprehensive that the government had not proposed anything to redress those grievances which would further fuel Jacobitism and calls for the dissolution of the Union:

> the affair of our Peerage the Ministry have agreed that it must redress, but don't explain themselves ... some notice shoul'd have been taken ... the ministry here, thought the time improper, & defended themselves by saying there was no time to prepare ... I am sure this way of proceeding gives handles to the folks in Scotland who are for dissolving the union.[31]

The Jacobite rebellion, which started in September 1715, entirely stopped any attempts to change the representative system. However, in early April 1716, the duke of Argyll and the earl of Ilay seem to have considered that the repeal of the Triennial Act and the passage of the Septennial Act afforded a perfect opportunity to realise the reform of the Scots representative system.[32] Successive ministries had been too wary of changing the framework of the Treaty of Union, but, because peers' elections were held in conformity with the Triennial Act, its repeal created a space within which to revisit the question. Anonymous letters, possibly to the earl of Stair, in April 1716 spoke eloquently of the political circumstances. On 4 April, a correspondent stated:

> the great subject of conversation here, is repealing the Triennial Bill, and the enacting a septennial one in its place ... The Peers of Scotland who are of the House have thought this a proper time to meet, and deliberate concerning the obtaining a redress of their grievances ... At the first every bodie [sic] was of opinion that it was proper to make an application to the ministrie [sic], to have the incapacitie [sic], upon the Peers of Scotland taken off.[33]

Despite some disagreement between Ilay and Roxburghe, the Scots peers decided to negotiate *en bloc* with the English ministry.[34] At the ministry, Viscount Townshend dealt with them. He obviously understood the importance of this negotiation, and tried, in the first instance, to postpone the meeting.

Though the contents of the discussion between Scots peers and the English ministry is not very clear, it appears that the Scots asked about the possibility that the King would appoint a certain number of Scots peers as representative peers. These would not be 'elected' any more, but instead represent Scotland as 'hereditary' peers. A direct descendant would inherit this privilege after a peer died. In April 1716, a prototype of the Peerage Bill might have appeared. Nevertheless the negotiation resulted in failure. There are at least two possible reasons. First, the number of hereditary peers proposed was not enough for the Scots: 'if you'll read over the list of the peers of Scotland, you'll finde [sic] it will be hard to accommodat [sic] those who have very good pretentions, with that number'.[35] Second, the Scots had a very difficult problem on their hands. The English ministry still adhered to the principle on which the duke of Hamilton had not been admitted to the House of Lords as a hereditary peer. The English Court maintained that the number of the Scots peers should be fixed and those who could not be 'hereditary representatives' could not take seats in the House of Lords, even if they were created British peers:

> The taking off the Bar is a great point, which in my opinion will by no means be effectually done by the method propos'd in that scheme which leave it open to much greater and stronger objections than it was lyable [sic] to from the strained sense that was put upon the articles of union. After what has happen'd in the house of Peers, nothing but the most express words can ... fix that point.[36]

The duke of Hamilton's case still defined the limits of any possible solution to the Scots peerage question.

The Scots continued to discuss this problem with the Court, but the 'Whig Schism' in 1716–18, between the earl of Sunderland and Earl Stanhope on the one hand and Robert Walpole and Viscount Townshend on the other, made it impossible for the Scots to obtain an agreement.[37] The confrontation in Scotland between the *Squadrone* and the Argathelians made the situation worse. The problems surrounding the Scots peerage in the British Parliament from 1706 to 1716 provided a prelude to and framework for the Scottish dimension to the well-known Peerage Bill controversy in 1718–19. For the Scots peers, the road from the Union negotiations to the renewed controversy in 1718–19 was a long and bitterly disappointing one.[38]

Notes

1 Historical Manuscripts Commission [hereafter HMC], *Various MSS*, V, Sir John James Graham of Fintry MSS, pp. 272–3. This ballad was presumably made soon after the Union was concluded.
2 Geoffrey Holmes and Clyve Jones (eds), *The London Diaries of William Nicolson Bishop of Carlisle 1702–1718* (Oxford, 1985), p. 249.

3 Gilbert E. M. Kynynmound (ed.), *Correspondence of Duke of Roxburghe and George Baillie of Jerviswood 1702–1708* (Edinburgh, 1842), p. 138.
4 Holmes and Jones (eds), *Nicolson Diaries*, p. 358.
5 For the official proceedings of the commissioners for the Union in 1706, see *The Journal of the Proceedings of the Lds Commissioners of Both Nations, in the Treaty of Union* (London, 1706).
6 Daniel Szechi (ed.), *Letters of George Lockhart of Carnwath 1698–1732* (Edinburgh, 1989), p. 31.
7 The following proceedings of the commissioners of the Union are based on National Records of Scotland [hereafter NRS], GD 18/3132/2, John Clerk of Penicuik, 'MS journal of the proceedings of the Scots & English commissioners in the Treaty for an Union ... anno 1706'; Douglas Duncan (ed.), *History of the Union of Scotland and England by Sir John Clerk of Penicuik* (Edinburgh, 1993).
8 Douglas, *History*, p. 85.
9 NRS, GD 18/3132/2, John Clerk 'MS journal'.
10 Joseph M'Cormick, *State Papers and Letters addressed to William Carstares* (Edinburgh, 1774), Leven to Carstares, 11 June 1706, p. 754.
11 NRS, GD 18/3132/2, John Clerk, 'MS journal'.
12 Ibid.
13 Ibid.
14 HMC, *Portland MSS*, II, [Harley] to [duke of Newcastle], 15 June 1706, p. 193.
15 HMC, *Portland MSS*, IV, [Newcastle] to [Harley], 17 June 1706, p. 313.
16 Daniel Szechi (ed.), *'Scotland's Ruine' : Lockhart of Carnwath's Memoirs of the Union* (Aberdeen, 1995), p. 132.
17 Duncan, *History*, p. 196.
18 NRS, GD 18/3193, [Sir John Clerk of Penicuik] to [earl of Galloway], 2 April 1722.
19 Duncan, *History*, p. 196.
20 See, for example, H. L. Snyder (ed.), *Marlborough–Godolphin Correspondence*, 3 vols (Oxford, 1975), II, p. 991.
21 Gilbert Burnet, *Bishop Burnet's History of His Own Time*, 6 vols (Oxford, 1833), VI, pp. 89–90.
22 Blair Atholl, Atholl MS 42/I/(1)/17, 'Heads of something concerning Scotland to be represented to ye Ld High Treasurer' [1712].
23 *A Representation of the Scotch Peers* (n.p., 1712), p. 2.
24 The following description of the Scots' opposition against the ministry is based on BL, Add. MSS 70158, an anonymous letter dated 'London, 26 May 1713'. For the details of the malt tax crisis and Scottish opposition, see Geoffrey Holmes and Clyve Jones, 'Trade, Scots and the Parliamentary Crisis of 1713', *Parliamentary History*, 1 (1982), pp. 47–77.
25 National Library of Scotland [hereafter NLS], Dep. 313/532, Montrose to [Sutherland], 14 October 1714. For Scots Whigs' dissatisfaction with the English ministry, see Floors Castle, Roxburghe MS. Bundle 756, Roxburghe to [countess of Roxburghe], 9 December 1714.

26 NRS, GD 45/14/827, a copy letter to the peer, November 1714.
27 A Scotch-Man, *The History of the National Address for Dissolving the Union* (London, 1715).
28 NRS, GD 220/5/813/18, [Mungo Graham] to [Montrose], 29 March 1715.
29 K. T. John (ed.), *Chronicles of the Atholl and Tullbardine Families*, 5 vols (Edinburgh, 1908), II, pp. 242–3.
30 NRS, GD 45/1/199, 'The Humble Representation of the Peers of Scotland' [1715].
31 NRS, GD 135/145, 'To My Lord' [earl of Stair?], 18 April [1715].
32 NLS, MS 2985, fo. 94, John Forbes to [Duncan Forbes], 19 April 1716; NLS, MS 25281, fo. 6, [Sir James Dalrymple] to [Sir David Dalrymple], London, 3 April 1716. See also Spencer Cowper (ed.), *Diary of Mary Countess Cowper, 1714–1720* (London, 1864), pp. 102–3.
33 NRS, GD 135/145, 'To My Lord' [earl of Stair?], 4 April [1716]. The negotiation between the Scots peers and the English ministry is described by this letter unless otherwise stated. See also NRS, GD 220/5/819/43, [Montrose] to [Graham], 29 March 1716; Henry Huntington Library, LO 7634, earl of Stair to [earl of Loudoun], 22 April/3 May 1716.
34 Huntington Library, LO 7650, Stair to [Loudoun], 15/26 May 1716: 'our own little divisions have weakened our hands and rendered what was proposed for ye good of ye whole inefectuall [sic]'.
35 NRS, GD 135/145, anonymous letter to [earl of Stair?], 28 April 1716.
36 NRS, GD 135/145, 'To My Lord' [earl of Stair?], 28 April 1716.
37 For this, see W. A. Speck, 'The Whig Schism under George I', *Huntington Library Quarterly*, 40 (1976–7), pp. 171–9.
38 For studies on the Peerage Bill, see Clyve Jones, '"Venice Preserv'd; or A Plot Discovered": The Political and Social Context of the Peerage Bill of 1719', in Clyve Jones (ed.), *A Pillar of the Constitution: The House of Lords in British Politics, 1640–1784* (London, 1989), pp. 79–112; Clyve Jones, 'Of Male and Female Heirs; of English and Scottish Peerages: The Fine Tuning of the Peerage Bills of 1719', *Parliamentary History*, 29 (2010), pp. 308–30.

CHAPTER 3

Parliament and Church Reform: Off and On the Agenda*

Joanna Innes

As the graph in Figure 3.1 shows, attempts by Parliament to improve the Church of England's performance of its pastoral functions ceased following the Hanoverian accession, but resumed in the later eighteenth century, first tentatively, and then from 1800 in a more determined and focused way. During the intervening period – as Figures 3.2 and 3.3 demonstrate – Parliament passed increasing numbers of acts relating to individual parishes or churches and also many acts adjusting or revising rules relating to merely tolerated religious sects, but by contrast left the established church in charge of its own pastoral operations.[1] In the opening years of the eighteenth century, Convocation provided a forum for clerics to promote their own ideas about how to improve pastoral efficacy. The Hanoverian muting of Convocation discouraged such initiatives; it is not surprising that legislation then fell away.[2] Why and how interest and activity revived at the turn of the eighteenth and nineteenth centuries are issues that have not received much attention.[3] This essay seeks to illuminate these matters through a close study of the ways in which relevant legislative proposals came to Parliament and were dealt with there.

Some of the background circumstances which shaped interest in legislating have been well studied by historians, with particular emphasis on the effects of the French Revolution on the relation between Church and Dissent, and on the character of Dissent itself, as changing structures of authority and the chiliastic atmosphere of the later 1790s set the scene for the dramatic rise of evangelical itinerancy.[4] Responses to these developments were shaped by a slowly unfolding movement for religious renewal within the Church (which still deserves more study than it has received) and by discussions associated with Pitt and his cousin

---

* I would like to thank Mark Smith, Arthur Burns and Grayson Ditchfield for comments on an earlier version and the various colleagues and friends who have commented on this version.

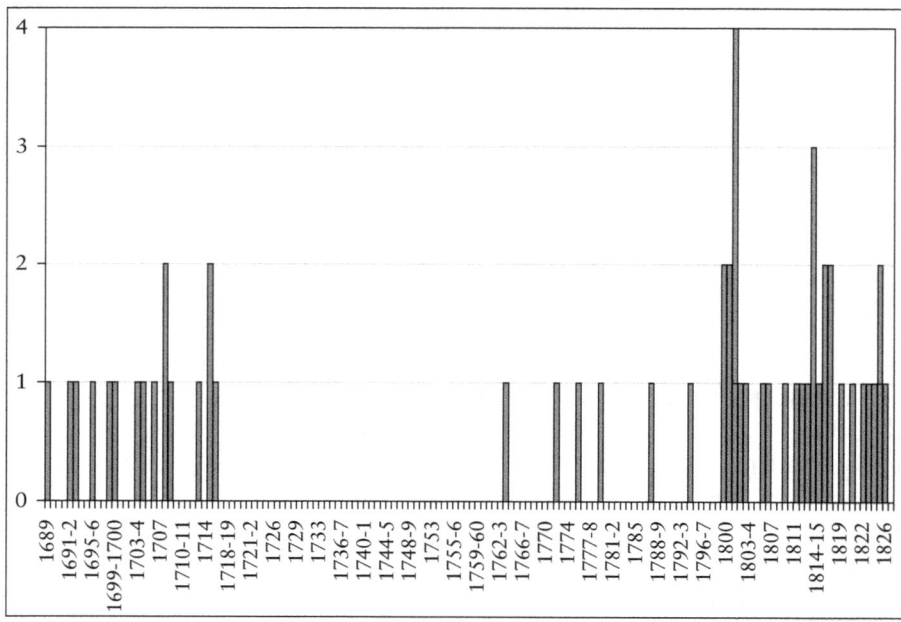

Figure 3.1 English general acts concerning parishes and parochial clergy, 1689–1830

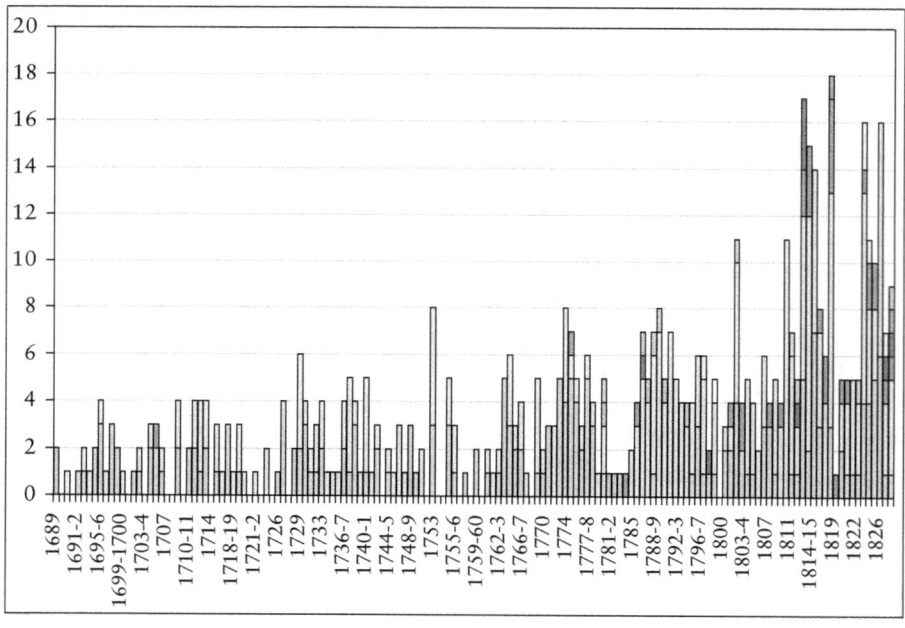

Figure 3.2 English local acts concerning church building, etc., 1689–1830

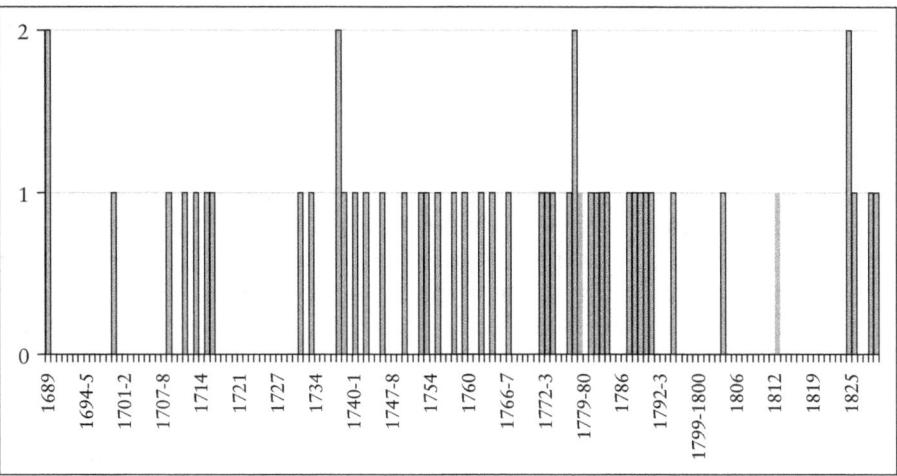

Figure 3.3 English general acts concerning non-Anglican sects, 1689–1830

Grenville's attempt to develop an 'Ecclesiastical Plan' – the lineaments of which only came clearly into view with the arrival of Grenville's papers at the British Library.[5] Pitt's fall in 1801 sent this project up in smoke, though not, as we shall see, without leaving some residue.

The immediate stimulus to action following Pitt's fall was provided by a worried William Dickinson, MP for Somerset. He came to Parliament in May 1801 urging that something be done to protect clerics in the West Country and elsewhere from informers running a prosecution campaign, targeting clerics who failed to fulfil the parochial residence requirements stipulated in a statute of Henry VIII. He said that some two hundred suits had been started (others said as many as eight hundred); informers were said to be writing to non-residents threatening to prosecute unless they were paid off.[6] The press noted uncertainty as to whether these informers were motivated by religion or pelf; according to the *Gentleman's Magazine* they comprised 'a Junto of Jacobins and Atheists' who were 'some time ago expelled from a cellar notorious for sedition in the vicinity of one of our inns of court'; they were said to have circularised 'all the principal Dissenters' asking for support.[7]

The prosecutions struck a chord: it was noted that 'the clamour throughout the country against non-residence had been very great', though the prosecution tactic itself was more ambivalently received. Judges happy to be asked to uphold standards when the first such cases came their way became critical of these 'cruel and vexatious actions'. Parliament agreed to pass temporary relief acts to halt prosecutions, and meanwhile to consider what might be the best way forward.[8] The following year, MPs would take a similar course in relation to old statutes regulating the woollen industry that were being used as a basis for arguably harassing prosecutions. In that case, they decided, after some years' soul-searching, simply to deregulate. It was not by contrast judged appropriate to deregulate the clergy. Debate about how they should be regulated, however, threw up all sorts of concerns, picking up the threads of discussions that had gone on behind the scenes during Pitt's ministry and inaugurating a parliamentary phase of discussion, which thereafter unfolded fairly continuously into the era of Victorian church reform. In what follows, I set out to relate circumstances promoting interest in reform to actions taken in Parliament. Parliamentary action was mediated not just by the views that members formed in changing times but also by structures of authority in government and Parliament, by who seized the initiative and how effectively they pursued their projects.

I

Reforming the Church of England was always bound to be a complicated matter, because of the complex ways in which church, state and society were imbricated.[9] The archbishops and bishops might be expected to have played a crucial role in bringing such matters to Parliament and indeed they did play a part, sometimes as the initiators of action, sometimes as interlocutors. They exercised general oversight over their dioceses through their visitations. As *ex officio* members of the House of Lords and as among the more regular attenders and active members of that body they had many opportunities to meet, as well as to initiate and respond to legislative proposals and to interact with ministers. In as much as they had been appointed by the monarch in consultation with ministers, they were often linked into political networks (though not always the networks of the current ministry).

However, they shared power over the Church with many others. They controlled only a share of clerical appointments. Since monastic patronage had largely passed into the hands of the laity during the English Reformation, it often fell to lay patrons to determine who should be nominated to serve a particular parish (though the credentials of the nominee had to be approved by the bishop). Archbishops and bishops had some opportunities to promote men they approved of – for example, to archdeaconries or cathedral prebends – but clerics who looked to lay patrons for advancement did not always readily accept bishops' claims to leadership. The leading ecclesiastical lawyer

Sir William Scott channelled elite lay views when he brought to his scrutiny of Church reform proposals the conviction that to tamper with the rights of patrons would be to assault property. Scott also approved of the wildly varying extents, populations and wealth of English parishes, which he saw as mirroring the subtle gradations of the social order: he did not think they should be reduced to 'Presbyterian equality'.[10] Others supported lay rights for other reasons: the rising evangelical party within the Church appreciated the chance to make the establishment a vehicle for variant forms of belief and practice. Some half of those ordained spent the bulk of their careers as curates – doing the duties of absent incumbents, or having sole charge of under-endowed parishes; such men might operate under still more layers of influence, or alternatively, be left largely to their own devices in communities too far from the great world to attract interest from the well-connected. In the early nineteenth century, they began to barrage members of Parliament with letters urging their own case.[11]

Bishops' room for manoeuvre in relation to ministers or within Parliament was also restricted. Ministerial support for any legislative proposal was desirable, while ministerial disapproval tended to be fatal – though there was always a middle ground, which ministers left open to men motivated to develop their own projects. It is improbable that any senior cleric would have brought an ambitious church-reform initiative to Parliament without first checking with ministers; such men indeed sometimes contented themselves with canvassing ministers, leaving it to them to take the lead. Ministers with the energy to formulate their own schemes felt entitled to do so, though they in turn were unlikely to bring anything into Parliament before they had sounded out episcopal (and perhaps other clerical) opinion – and would desist if unable to gain support. Ministers had no special right to introduce such proposals, except insofar as they involved public funding: any MP agitated by something that had come to his notice (perhaps something about which he had been canvassed by clerics of his acquaintance) might come to Parliament with his own more or less well-developed ideas about what needed to be done, as William Dickinson apparently did in relation to prosecutions for non-residence.

II

William Pitt was unusually legislatively-oriented for a prime minister of his day. Most of his predecessors had engaged with no more than a limited range of issues; they had thought they had their hands full with financing government, managing foreign policy and wars, keeping a weather eye on the state of the economy and maintaining their support base. Pitt had the same priorities but could be distracted by the hope of making any institution better, in part no doubt because he came to maturity and launched his dazzling political career in a decade, the 1780s, marked by an unusual efflorescence of reforming enthusiasm. Addington, who succeeded him, was a more cautious operator; Pitt in his brief second ministry was not the man he had been; Grenville's largely Whig ministry was full of would-be reformers, but they were in office too briefly to do much; Portland proved little more than a stop-gap; Perceval was more in Pitt's mould, but his career was cut short by assassination. The effect of all this was that a number of hares started under Pitt continued to run erratically for some time thereafter.[12] Church reform was among these.

Even given Pitt's distinctive governing temperament, his interest was most often engaged when church issues intersected with others more clearly his responsibility: financial issues, or major political questions of the day.[13] He began to consider, and had the Treasury look into, alternatives to tithes as a way of financing the Church in the early 1790s, when a county MP whose opinion he respected, John Rolle, put it to him that the issue was being agitated at county meetings, and was exacerbating already inflamed relations between Church and Dissent. Dissenters had had high hopes of Pitt's reforming proclivities; many had voted for him on that ground at the 1784 election, which had secured his hold on power. But when towards the end of the decade they decided to petition for the repeal of the Test and Corporation Acts, Pitt found himself under pressure from the bishops, vocal clerics and sections of public opinion not to concede. As Dissenters' repeated applications failed, tensions rose – interacting with the taking of sides over the early phases of the French Revolution. There were fierce polemics in print, and some towns were riven by factional animosities, sometimes tipping over into riot.[14] Some supporters of the Church began to argue that it would be prudent for it to put its house in order. Pitt saw tithe reform as a possible contribution to that effort. Often a source of conflict between cultivators and tithe owners (not all of whom were clerics), tithes had also been argued to obstruct improvement, because they limited cultivators' gains from new investment. It was not easy to devise an alternative, however, and as France radicalised and France and Britain went to war in 1793, Pitt set the project aside.

When he turned back to church matters in the late 1790s, it was initially from a fiscal standpoint. Characteristically, he took a bold line with problems of war finance. He sought to tap national income more even-handedly through his income tax, while offering those with obligations under the old land tax (which was made perpetual) the chance to buy them out by purchasing government stock (bringing money into the funds).[15] Debates in Parliament over income tax saw some muttering about Church and other corporate wealth escaping the tax (though individual clergy were liable if their incomes crossed the threshold).[16] Both Church and municipal corporations were drawn into the land-tax redemption scheme. In consultation with the bishops, Pitt set up a special advisory board to help them manage the sale of some lands to free others (releasing land from the undying hold of the Church could be seen as a good in itself). He then began to consider whether some similar redemption scheme might not offer a basis for a new attempt to replace tithes.

By this point – 1799 – he was deeply engaged with the task of effecting a union with Ireland. But issues around Church and religion were also central to the Irish puzzle. Pitt began to envision parallel reform schemes for the two kingdoms, including tithe reform, new modes of financing English and Irish Churches (which the act of union rhetorically united), and further adjustments to religiously linked rights (including possibly a purely political – loyalty – 'test' for MPs).[17] When the King's refusal to sanction the lifting of the ban on admission of Catholics to high office drove Pitt to resign, early in 1801, his former tutor George Pretyman, now bishop of Lincoln, a sorry comforter, told him that in any case the bishops would all have opposed the last, and – he was confident – would have carried the Lords with them in a religious matter.[18]

Pitt was interested in the larger role of the Church in society: he probably agreed with the group which he assembled to plan the reform of the poor laws in 1796 that a resident clergy could do much to improve care of the poor.[19] But there were many other demands on his time, and he lacked deep interest in Church affairs. It was otherwise with his cousin, and Foreign Secretary, William Wyndham Grenville.[20] More pious than Pitt, Grenville also dabbled in Church politics: he had a little stable of protégés among the bishops; in 1810 he would secure election as Chancellor of the University of Oxford – a position only likely to be won by a serious friend to the Church. Bishop Pretyman's correspondence suggests that he was much less close to Grenville than to his former pupil Pitt (though he told his wife that Grenville was always 'very friendly') yet, suggestively, it was to Grenville that Pretyman turned when he sought someone in high places who would take Church concerns to heart.[21]

The file of Grenville's letters which focuses on 'Church Reform' begins in the early 1790s, with a proposal from one of the Church's leading intellectuals, William Paley. At a time when Church–Dissenting tensions had turned the minds of a number of contemporaries to ways in which the Church might be helped better to serve its purposes, Paley responded to the ancient challenge of finding ways to make sure that the country was effectively blanketed with active clergy. Part of the problem was the many livings too poorly endowed to support a full-time cleric; the trustees of Queen Anne's Bounty had been ploughing money into that problem for almost a century, with some success. Additionally, university-educated clerics just did not find it attractive to live in remote districts, especially if they had marriageable daughters, or were ageing and wanted medical care. Or they might have duties elsewhere, as cathedral prebends, fellows of Oxford or Cambridge colleges, or schoolteachers. Paley suggested that non-resident clergy should be taxed, and the proceeds directed towards further improving the value of poor livings.[22] Interestingly, Grenville sent the proposal for comments to bishops Barrington and Porteus, who had been to the fore during the 1780s in a range of social and moral reform projects. Barrington thought the plan would be popular among the laity, but also noted that it might open the way to repealing the provision for informers to sue non-resident clergy under the statute of Henry VIII, which he said was open to abuse.[23]

In the late 1790s, the challenge of providing a more effective parochial ministry gained in urgency; in this context, bishop Pretyman stirred Grenville to action, and Pitt's engagement with Church matters widened in scope. In the course of the 1790s the challenge from Dissent shifted from the high public sphere of parliamentary combat, pamphlet war and factional conflict in counties and large towns to focus instead on rural parishes, as leadership passed from the hands of an older Dissenting elite towards the grass roots. Methodists split from the Church, sections of old Dissent turned evangelical, and preachers, including students at Dissenting academies, fanned out across rural England, organising prayer meetings, sometimes in the form of Sunday schools. They found fertile soil in parishes shaken by recent dearth and sometimes by industrial change, for example the collapse of handspinning. Emotionally the scene was further set by the chiliastic atmosphere associated with the French invasion of Italy and dethronement of the Pope (who was held prisoner by the French from 1797 until his death in 1800). Adding insult to injury, the emissaries of 'new dissent' claimed to respect the Church where it was effective; they said they operated only in places where it was clearly failing.[24] There were Anglican evangelicals – including William Wilberforce – who were happy about these developments, but for many clergy this was as bad if not worse than the efflorescence of Paineite radicalism around 1792. The *Anti-Jacobin* lent some support to this view, starting a new line of polemic against puritanical fanaticism. Some magistrates took the threat seriously too: one publicly advertised his willingness to employ existing laws against field-preaching.[25] Yet from a clerical standpoint not enough gentlemen really took the cause to heart. Many did not see this as a socio-political crisis, more a wake-up call for a Church riddled with lax practices.

Acting in response to a visitation charge from bishop Pretyman, and having gained his permission, clergy in part of the diocese of Lincoln enquired into the problem during the late summer and autumn of 1799.[26] They pooled estimates of the proportion of parish populations attending church (less than a third, they thought) and taking communion (less than a sixth). They did not think competition came from 'real' Dissent; instead it was provided by Methodism and by 'a wandering tribe of fanatical teachers'. They identified (without trying to quantify their size) several groups of non-attenders distinct from 'real' Dissent: Methodists who attended the Church but also Methodist meetings; Methodists who attended their own meetings only (a number set to grow, they hinted, now communion was offered at such meetings), and finally those who patronised the fanatical teachers. They thought that clergy in the district had been stirred to unwonted diligence by new challenges, but that more could be done. Clerics should be highly conscious of the example they set by their own conduct; they should consider laying on extra Bible-study meetings in church, and pay more attention to teaching the infant poor. Magistrates could help by acting against competing entertainments, but Parliament could help too by amending the Toleration Act, not to challenge old Dissent, but rather to stop new-style itinerants acquiring licences as Dissenters; they suggested that such licences might be issued only to those who could show that their services were needed by a settled congregation. Bishop Pretyman sent the report to Grenville, hoping that he might urge its recommendation on Pitt.[27]

As the historian W. R. Ward nicely put it, Grenville's response was 'Josephinist'. That is, he did not accept the suggested division of labour, in which the state would constrain Dissent and leave the Church to address its internal problems. Instead – like Joseph II of Austria – he set about deploying state power to improve pastoral functioning (though it has to be said that by Joseph's root-and-branch standards, Grenville was a mere tinkerer).[28] Grenville and his brother, the marquess of Buckingham (whose estates fell within Pretyman's sprawling diocese), had already represented to him how poorly served were many parishes in that neighbourhood: the nearness of Oxford meant that many were in the hands of absentee Oxford fellows, and among local residents, several were evangelical.[29] Grenville thought that the state could assist in reducing non-residence, if only by increasing the disciplinary powers of bishops. He began to work on heads of an 'Ecclesiastical Plan', which would occupy him throughout the following year. Pretyman found himself reduced to a merely consultative role; others consulted included Paley, Samuel Horsley (bishop of Rochester), and the leading civil lawyer Sir William Scott. By April 1800, the consultative circle had broadened to include the archbishop of Canterbury and through him the bishops at large.[30]

Exposed to so much creative and critical comment, the 'plan' went through many mutations. At its broadest extent, it specified the duties of the clergy; expanded the power of bishops to enforce these duties (inter alia by reviving the office of rural dean); vested in trustees for each diocese the power to join or subdivide parishes, so as to make them viable in terms of the income they yielded and the scale of work implied; and identified new funding to improve curates' stipends, in the form of monies arising from the Church's land-tax redemption payments (under Pitt's new scheme).[31] New constraints on the issue of Dissenters' preaching licences may have been in view at one point; later versions of the plan envisioned restrictions on the licensing of meeting houses. Though it is not apparent from surviving written versions, Grenville later told the House of Lords that the plan he had in view would have extended to Ireland.[32]

Even before the ministry fell, the plan – both in its narrower sense, and in terms of the still grander visions the cousins were developing – was falling apart. Proposals to tighten control over Dissenters were dropped, as it became clear what a storm this would provoke; the launching of the torrent of prosecutions for non-residence could be taken as a warning shot.[33] Those consulted differed about who could be trusted with enhanced powers: some worried that the proposed trustees would impinge on the power of bishops; others that the bishops would lack appetite for disciplining the clergy. And what was implied about the rights of lay patrons? As to associated outliers of the plan, Pitt dropped his tithe redemption scheme when the bishops balked.[34] Finally, George III delivered the coup de grace when he refused to countenance the admission of Catholics to high office. Concerned that if he pressed the case he might upset the King's mental balance, but also almost beside himself with exhaustion, Pitt judged it best to resign.

III

Many in Pitt's circle thought that his successor, the former speaker Henry Addington, would not be up to the job, and bemoaned Pitt's injunction to support him; Grenville found one reason for discontent in his failure to pick up the baton on church reform.[35] Though the issue was admitted to need addressing, Addington largely left it to others to shape a response. Of course this was not necessarily a bad thing: Grenville and Pitt's bolder approach had arguably run into the sand because they had assumed that, amateurs though they were, they could hack out solutions.

Addington had hardly taken office when William Dickinson's representations directed the attention of the Commons to the non-residence prosecutions. Dickinson's under-informed floundering does not suggest that he was front-man for any serious actor, and he agreed to withdraw the motion, but conversations evidently went on behind the scenes. A month later he was back, proposing now that the House sit as a committee to consider the Henrician non-residence statute.[36] In the absence of any lead from the government, discussion was unfocused. It was agreed that it was important that the clergy did their jobs, but also that sixteenth-century specifications of what this entailed were not suited to the modern age and that modes of enforcing residence might need to be rethought. Addington was content to let the House play for time by passing a temporary relief act, though it was also agreed that work needed to be done towards a solution.

By Addington's later account, at this point 'the wishes of the House turned, he believed universally' towards Sir William Scott, who as well as being among the most eminent civil lawyers was also an MP for Oxford University, and thus the closest thing there was in the Commons to an official representative of the Church.[37] Scott had already revealed his conservative instincts in his comments on the previous ministry's plans. He not only had a lawyer's caution about messing with anything which was not clearly broken, but was also personally disinclined to disturb the complex balance of different kinds of power and freedom within the Church – though he did express regret that the Reformation had not left the Church better provided for, and thought that deficiency needed further attention. Addington may have set Scott up to play this role; if so, he cannot have expected more than a patching-up job from him (though he did affirm that at some future date his government would find means to augment the incomes of the poorer clergy).[38] Scott professed to find his task unwelcome, and it does seem to have made him the target of a flood of correspondence from every other clergyman in England.[39]

Yet from his point of view it cannot have been all bad news to find himself licensed for the moment to shape policy.

Scott's first attempt to discharge his task – by means of a bill that he brought in towards the end of the 1802 session – failed to secure agreement, though with mainly minor amendments it was passed in 1803.[40] Predictably, his bill was less disciplinarian than Grenville's. Indeed, Scott adapted to the pressures of modern times as he understood them by extending the grounds on which clerics could automatically claim the right not to reside, by authorising them to absent themselves for rest and recuperation for up to three months of each year and by specifying a variety of further grounds on which bishops might at their discretion authorise non-residence. By these means he sought better to protect the clergy from harassment by informers – though the implication was that conformity to these modernised regulations was expected: no longer could they be dismissed as simply out of date. Scott's bill provided for two parallel enforcement systems, one as before via private informers, the other through bishops, whose powers – previously exercised purely under ecclesiastical law – were now specified by statute and clarified. The main respect in which his bill was amended within Parliament was by the addition of reporting requirements: bishops were to record permissions and monitor performance, and forward all this data to the Privy Council.

Though Scott maintained a focus on the specific issue he had been asked to address – amendment to parts of the Henrician statute – debate on his proposals ranged widely, with such little respect for the conventions formally governing debate that speakers in both Houses were moved to call participants to order.[41] Members of both Houses were full of observations and ideas about the state of the Church generally, canvassing (to the frustration of the members of the former ministry) many matters that their plan had aimed to address. The need to attend to the Church in Ireland, now formally united with that of England, was often stressed.[42] It was repeatedly argued that things could not really be put right unless the Church was given more money, and also that in some districts more places of worship were needed. Attention was drawn to the inadequacies of parsonage houses, and to the hardships of poor curates. Francis Burton, MP for the City of Oxford, responded to a widely held view that Scott's bill did not go far enough by introducing – and in short order obtaining assent to – two further, relatively modestly conceived bills, facilitating legacies and gifts for the building of parsonages and churches and to augment poor livings.[43] It is a sign of changing times that the main effect of these acts was to alleviate restraints imposed by mortmain legislation: the 1736 Mortmain Act had given classic expression to Whig reluctance to let the Church accrue landed property. Scott himself brought in a further bill to ensure that curates supplying the place of non-resident clergy were properly remunerated, and that any displaced as a result of clergy newly taking up residence would be relieved, though neither element was agreed at this time, and further attempts to address the curates' pay issue were thwarted for several years following.[44] The fact that debate ranged so widely partly reflects the fact that these issues had been canvassed in conversation and print for the previous decade and more; also their importance to many thousands of clergy: probably most MPs will have had their ears bent by clerics. Canvassing of these issues in the course of ministerial consultations during the 1790s probably had an effect too. Important also must have been the rather casual and unplanned way in which the issue finally came to Parliament. MPs seem to have felt that they had been presented with not just a bill to debate, but also a problem to solve.

What became clear, in relation to the issues on which Scott had focused, was that there was limited enthusiasm for the Grenvillian approach of strengthening the power of the bishops.[45] The radical MP Sir Francis Burdett put the case especially starkly when he termed the proposal 'a bill for enslaving the clergy'. Echoing his concerns from a different angle were Church evangelicals, men such as Sir John Simeon, older brother of the Cambridge evangelical Charles Simeon, and Spencer Perceval, who had just begun his rise through the *cursus honorum*, securing appointment first as Solicitor and then as Attorney General. Wilberforce is not reported as having spoken, but we know from his diary that he thought Perceval was making the right points.[46] Church evangelicals defended the right of laymen to a voice in Church affairs – in that context even defending the activities of informers. Scott's proposal was sensitive to these concerns; it both constrained bishops' judgement by specific rules, and maintained a role for informers.

Though speakers found much to disagree about, consensus that it would be good to strengthen the Church's parochial ministry is striking. The Test Act had long served to ensure that Parliament remained a body of Churchmen, yet its members had not sought to enhance the Church's effectiveness during many preceding decades.

IV

The stimulus to the re-emergence of church reform on the parliamentary agenda was a crisis, or sequence of crises, in relations between Church and Dissent. This sparked calls for reform, and also overturned the classic case against attempting reform – that it stirred up unnecessary trouble – for trouble had already arrived. As Grenville expressed it to Pitt: '*quieta non movere* no longer applies. These things are all stirred up by the restless spirit of the times, and our duty is to give them a right direction.'[47] During this decade, Church–Dissent relations changed significantly. From the start they had some novel elements (particularly in terms of the public-campaigning approach adopted by both sides), yet only towards the end of the decade did the battle move out into the parishes, in tandem with changes in power structures within Dissent. Some traditional Dissenters may have had their own reservations about undisciplined upstarts. Yet, even had Churchmen been so inclined, they probably could not have made common cause with them: Old Dissent was always likely to rally on principle to the cause of religious freedom.[48]

Church leaders responded to these crises defensively – by considering ways of directly constraining dissent – but also constructively, by considering how to equip the Church to function better. Politically the constructive response was much more viable. The ground for it had been prepared by a long tradition of effort on the part of senior clerics to augment the resources of the poorest parishes, and to see that all parishes were appropriately served, if not by incumbents then by curates. It had been further prepared in recent years by the social and moral reform movement of the 1780s, which had inspired many clergy to establish Sunday schools and sometimes to support other new initiatives (for example, friendly societies and spinning schools). That movement had also inspired some exceptional bishops, such as Barrington and Porteus, to experiment with new approaches to the promotion of religion and morals. Finally, formulation of a constructive response was aided by the ambitions of certain bishops, notably Pretyman, who had his eye on an archbishopric, and was probably spurred by that to try to prove himself a man of action.[49]

Though they were shaped in various ways by the reverberations of the French Revolution, tensions between Church and Dissent chiefly affected the Church insofar as they concerned religion. Perhaps their most significant effect was to unleash religious energy: they encouraged efforts by some Churchmen to make common cause with Dissenters and to develop the evangelical work of the Church, and by others to renovate Church institutions and practices. There was a spectrum of possible approaches, which should not be distinguished too sharply: early decades of the new century saw many rows about whom Churchmen should and should not collaborate with and what they should and should not do, but alliances were complex and battle-fronts mobile.[50]

It was not inevitable that the challenges presented to the Church at this period would bring reform of its structures on to Parliament's agenda. I have suggested that that development was importantly shaped by the Pitt ministry's 'Josephinist' response. Abortive though that proved to be, the process of devising a ministerial plan created new expectations. When the issue came on to Parliament's agenda in more particular form by another route, debate was coloured by those prior discussions and aspirations. The view began to crystallise both that wide-ranging action was needed and that ministers must take the lead. Spencer Perceval, who while law officer tried to carry the curates' cause forwards for several years, was the next prime minister seriously to gird himself to undertake the larger challenge. He did in 1809 obtain a parliamentary grant for the Church; he was poised to do more when he was shot.[51] Debate in preceding years had sharpened some differences of view; Perceval would have put his own spin on things, possibly not to most bishops' taste.[52] History determined that we cannot know whether or in what form he might have prevailed. What we know is what was done later, in a not totally different but continually developing context, under the hands of Liverpool and Peel.[53]

Notes

1 These graphs draw on work by Julian Hoppit in connection with our Leverhulme-funded project on Failed Legislation (see Hoppit (ed.), *Failed Legislation: Extracted from the Commons and Lords Journals 1660–1800* (London, 1997)) and on work with Andrew Hann jointly funded by the British Academy and Oxford University, 2000. No categorisation of legislation is definitive and these graphs draw on 'primary codes' used in that work: for parishes and parochial clergy, categories 400–2; for non-Anglican, 410–19. All 40 codes are used in the chart of local acts.
2 Stephen Taylor, 'Bishop Gibson's Proposals for Church Reform', in Taylor (ed.), *From Cranmer to Davidson: a Church of England Miscellany* (Bury St Edmunds, 1999), pp. 171–86.
3 The story gets lost in the crack between two useful if brief accounts: Grayson Ditchfield, 'Ecclesiastical Legislation during the Ministry of the Younger Pitt, 1783–1801', *Parliamentary History*, 19 (2000), pp. 64–80; S. J. Brown, *The National Churches of England, Ireland, and Scotland, 1801–46* (Oxford, 2001), pp. 62–74.
4 W. R. Ward, *Religion and Society in England, 1790–1850* (London, 1972), ch. 2 ; Deryck W. Lovegrove, *Established Church, Sectarian People: Itinerancy and the Transformation of English Dissent, 1780–1830* (Cambridge, 1988).

5 Geoffrey Best, *Temporal Pillars: Queen Anne's Bounty, the Church Commissioners and the Church of England*; Joanna Innes, 'Politics and Morals: The Reformation of Manners Movement in later Eighteenth-Century England', in Innes, *Inferior Politics. Social Problems and Social Policy in Eighteenth-Century Britain* (Oxford, 2009), pp. 179–226. For research using these newly deposited papers, see Peter Jupp, *Lord Grenville 1759–1834* (Oxford, 1985); Ditchfield, 'Ecclesiastical Legislation'.

6 *Parliamentary Register* [hereafter *PR*], 11 May 1800. The campaign can be traced in the press and in the following law reports: 8 Esp. 80; 2 Bos. and Pull. 282, 395; Forrest 117.

7 *Gentleman's Magazine*, 89 (January 1801).

8 *PR*, 9 June 1801; *Morning Chronicle*, 11 November 1800; 41 Geo. III c. 102; 42 Geo III c. 30 and c. 86; 43 Geo. III c. 34.

9 Useful surveys include Peter Virgin, *The Church in an Age of Negligence: Ecclesiastical Structure and Problems of Church Reform 1700–1840* (Cambridge, 1989); William T. Gibson, *The Church of England 1688–1832: Unity and Accord* (London, 2001); Jeremy Gregory and Jeffrey S. Chamberlain (eds), *The National Church in Local Perspective: the Church of England and the Regions, 1660–1800* (Woodbridge, 2003).

10 British Library [hereafter BL], Dropmore Papers, Add. MS 59307, f. 53ff. also in Historical Manuscript Commission, *The Manuscripts of J. B. Fortescue, Preserved at Dropmore*, 10 vols (London, 1892–1927) [hereafter HMC Fortescue], 87; *PR*, 7 April 1802.

11 BL, Dropmore Papers, Add. MS 59307, fos 190, 195, 197. See also remarks by Sir William Scott in *PR*, 6 April 1803.

12 This view of Pitt is set out in Joanna Innes, 'Forms of "government growth"', in David Feldman and Jon Lawrence (eds), *Structures and Transformations in Modern British History: Essays for Gareth Stedman Jones* (Cambridge, 2011), pp. 74–99.

13 Ditchfield, 'Ecclesiastical Legislation', pp. 72–4; Eric Evans, *The Contentious Tithe: The Tithe Problem and English Agriculture 1750–1850* (London, 1976), pp. 79–80.

14 Ward, *Religion and Society*, pp. 22–5.

15 Also F. C. Mather, *High Church Prophet. Bishop Samuel Horsley (1733–1806) and the Caroline Tradition in the Later Georgian Church* (Oxford, 1992), pp. 145–8.

16 For example, Tierney in *PR*, 17 December 1799.

17 Jupp, *Grenville*, pp. 272–80; D. H. Akenson, *The Church of Ireland: Ecclesiastical Reform and Revolution 1800–85* (New Haven, 1971), pp. 99–100.

18 Ipswich Record Office, HA 119/T108/45/1, Pretyman to his wife, 25 February 1801.

19 See for example the very early draft for a new poor bill in Kent History and Library Centre [hereafter KHLC], Stanhope of Chevening MSS, U1590/S5/O10/6.

20 Jupp, *Grenville*, pp. 305, 356.

21 G. M. Ditchfield, 'Sir George Pretyman-Tomline: Ecclesiastical Politician and Theological Polemicist', in William Gibson and Robert G. Ingram (eds), *Religious Identities in Britain 1660–1832* (Aldershot, 2005), pp. 277–98; Ipswich Record Office, HA 119/T108/45/1, Pretyman to his wife, dated in pencil 'about 1803', in fact 1800.
22 BL, Dropmore Papers, Add. MS 59307, fos 1–28. A version of Paley's scheme is also preserved in Pitt's papers, among papers relating to the later 1790s: National Archives, PRO 30/8/310, f. 135ff.
23 BL, Dropmore Papers, Add. MS 59307, fos 29–33.
24 Ward, *Religion and Society*, pp. 27–51; Lovegrove, *Established Church*.
25 F. K. Brown, *Fathers of the Victorians: the Age of Wilberforce* (Cambridge, 1961), pp. 156–9, 168–70, 220, 232; Carolyn Steedman, *An Everyday Life of the English Working Class: Work, Self and Sociability in the Early Nineteenth Century* (Cambridge, 2013), pp. 162–4.
26 Kent History and Library Centre, U1590/S5/C34, Pretyman to Pitt, 7 June 1799; *Report from the Clergy of a District in the Diocese of Lincoln, convened for the purpose of considering the State of Religion in the Several Parishes in the said District* (London, 1800).
27 BL, Dropmore Papers, Add. MS 59003, f. 13.
28 Ward, *Religion and Society*, p. 52.
29 BL, Dropmore Papers, Add. MS 59003, f. 31, Buckingham to Pretyman, 23 April [1799?]; KHLC, U1590/S5/C34, Pretyman to Pitt, 20 October 1799.
30 Jupp, *Grenville*, pp. 272–7. BL, Add. MS 59307; 59001, fos 38, 105–35; 59003, fos 13–36; HMC Forstescue, VI, 5–16, 20, 84, 86–8, 135–7, 152–3, 160, 181, 192, 197, 265. KHLC, U1590/S5/C38, bishop of London to Pretyman, [December 1800] emphasises Pitt's commitment to particular features of the plan.
31 *PR*, 22 June 1803.
32 *PR*, 2 June 1802.
33 The Whig MP and magistrate Michael Angelo Taylor complicated things by announcing his intention of bringing in a bill of his own on the subject, putting those hostile to restrictions on guard (a possible copy of this, along with a variant, can be found in Grenville's papers). When Wilberforce went to see Pitt on the subject he found him keen on some restraining measure, prejudiced (as Wilberforce thought) by Pretyman; *Times*, 4 February 1800; Bernard Manning, *Protestant Dissenting Deputies* (Cambridge, 1952), p. 134; BL, Dropmore Papers, Add MS 59307, fos 38, 47 (misdated 1794); R. I. and S. Wilberforce, *The Life of William Wilberforce*, 5 vols (London, 1838), II, pp. 360–5.
34 Evans, *Contentious Tithe*, p. 80.
35 *PR*, 2 and 22 June 1803.
36 *PR*, 9, 15, 19, 22 June 1801.
37 *PR*, 31 May 1802. R. A. Melikan, 'Scott, William, Baron Stowell (1745–1836)', in H. C. G. Matthew and Brian Harrison (eds), *Oxford Dictionary of National Biography* (Oxford, 2004). Scott had already

helped with a 1796 bill to set minimum salaries for curates (responding to rocketing prices in 1795–6) agreed in consultation among the bishops, and initiated in the Lords by the archbishop of Canterbury, in the Commons by the prime minister: 36 Geo. III c. 83; Lambeth Palace, Porteus Notebooks, MS 2100, f. 101; *Lords Journal*, 22 March 1796; *Commons Journal*, 21 April and 9 May 1796.

38 *PR*, 31 May 1802. As George Rose reported this to Pitt, Addington 'assured the House very distinctly ... that he should very soon propose a considerable augmentation to the incomes of the clergy who stand in need of it': National Archives, PRO 30/8/173, f. 190.

39 *PR*, 6 and 7 April 1802.

40 [1801–2] *Bill to amend and render more effect an act, made in the twenty-first year of the reign of Henry VIII*; 43 Geo III c. 84.

41 *PR*, 7 April, 31 May, 2 June 1802 and 30, 31 March, 1, 6 April, 3, 5, 10, 11, 26 May, 7, 16, 22 June, 6 July 1803.

42 The Irish civil lawyer Duigenan may have played some role in drafting bills; proposals relating to the Church in Ireland were brought into Parliament by men active in Irish administration at the end of the 1803 session and, according to Brynn, an Irish bill to enforce residence was also urged by Irish church leaders, though the first motion for one was made by Duigenan only in 1805: Akenson, *Church of Ireland*, pp. 117, 124; Edward Brynn, 'Some repercussions of the Act of Union on the Church of Ireland', *Church History*, 40 (1971), p. 291.

43 *PR*, 11 May, 4, 6, 15 July 1803. 43 Geo. III, c. 107 and c. 108.

44 [1802–3] *A Bill for Encouraging the Residence of Stipendiary Curates on their Cures*; *PR*, 15 July, 4, 5 August 1803. Compensation for displaced curates, recommended by King 25 July 1803, was agreed at the start of the following session: 44 Geo. III c. 2.

45 *PR*, 31 May 1802 and 26 May 1803.

46 Wilberforce, *Life*, III, 49, 102.

47 HMC Fortescue, VI, 6. Among other similar remarks, see Sheridan in *PR*, 22 June 1801.

48 Lovegrove, *Established Church*, p. 136 for Addington's claim that his 1811 attempt (as Viscount Sidmouth) to attempt restraining legislation had been endorsed by 'respectable' Dissenters.

49 Ipswich Record Office, HA 119/T108/45/1, Pretyman's letters to his wife December 1804 to January 1805 are full of his ultimately disappointed hopes on this score.

50 See Brown, *Fathers of the Victorians*; Elizabeth A. Varley, *Last of the Prince Bishops: William Van Mildert and the High Church Movement of the early Nineteenth Century* (Cambridge, 1992). I have profited from conversations with Mark Smith on these themes.

51 Grenville might well have done more had his ministry lasted: Jupp, *Grenville*, pp. 364, 400; Akenson, *Church of Ireland*, pp. 101, 122–3.

52 BL, Dropmore Papers, Add. MS 59003, f. 100ff., Pretyman to Grenville, August 1809, when both were at odds with post-Pittite administrations. Pretyman argued against giving Perceval's ally Harrowby a copy of the plan, arguing that he and Perceval would call it Mr Pitt's plan, and use it to justify their own.
53 Brown surveys the legislation in his *National Churches*; Frances Knight, *The Nineteenth-Century Church and English Society* (Cambridge, 1995) provides a good local study (of the diocese of Lincoln).

CHAPTER 4

Liberty, Property and the Post-Culloden Acts of Parliament in the *Gàidhealtachd**

Matthew P. Dziennik

In the aftermath of the Jacobite rebellion of 1745–6, Parliament passed a series of measures designed to end forever the Jacobite threat to the Hanoverian state. The accepted association of the Gaelic-speaking Scottish Highlands with Jacobitism made the *Gàidhealtachd* the explicit target of these measures. Not satisfied with the apocalyptic violence that accompanied the pacification of the region, the Hanoverian regime believed that only by purging the Gael from the culture map of Great Britain would there be any end to the Stuart challenge. A tradition of local autonomy, the supposedly 'savage' nature of the Gael, and the 'slavish servitudes' of the people toward the clan elites were supposed to have created the conditions for the rebellion and were to be removed root and branch. Changes were to be made to Highland landholding, cultural traditions, religious persuasions and language. As 'Justus' reported in the *Scots Magazine* in 1746, 'The name of *Highlanders* would, by this means, in another century scarcely exist'.[1]

Historians have long been convinced of the importance of the post-Culloden acts in undermining the political and cultural autonomy of the *Gàidhealtachd*. Since the emergence of the cultural turn in historical studies and J. G. A. Pocock's crucial 1975 plea for a new subject, we have become increasingly aware of the cultural dimensions of 'four nations' British history. The post-Culloden acts are situated not only as political measures, but also as reflections of the ethnic hostility of the English-speaking world. In many studies, either implicitly or explicitly, the acts served as the agent of change in the Gaelic world and had considerable successes in oppressing the culture of Gaelic Scotland. Recent contributions to the history of the Highlands by literary scholars have further added to our understanding of the colonisation of the *Gàidhealtachd* and the devaluing of Gaelic culture which accompanied it.[2]

---

* I would like to thank the earl of Seafield for the permission to cite from restricted items belonging to his collections.

A crucial point, however, has been neglected. How were these measures received and evaluated *within* the region? To what extent was cultural colonisation transferred from the pages of Anglophone parliamentary proceedings and political pamphlets into the Highlands and Islands? By considering the difficulty of translating political thought into political action, this essay re-evaluates the impact of the post-Culloden acts of Parliament. It does not suggest that ethnic conceit was not part of the formulation of British policy; nor does it dismiss the horrific suffering of the region as inconsequential. Rather, the essay suggests that the acts drew sharp ideological distinctions across ethnic lines and that both in thought and, especially, in action the acts did not constitute an ethnic assault to the extent that is often assumed. Ultimately, the essay seeks to recentre the Highland experience in narratives of the post-Culloden acts and to assert the agency of regional elites as they took sides in the unresolved issues of British politics.

In eschewing a narrative which posits a dichotomous relationship between a hegemonic metropole and the colonised Gaelic 'other', the essay draws on H. T. Dickinson's work on the political ideologies of eighteenth-century Britain. While rarely focused on northern Scotland, Dickinson's scholarship nevertheless outlines the importance of considering political ideology as a significant determinant of political culture. In *Liberty and Property* (1977), Dickinson noted that ideological debate had to confront 'political and social reality'; while in *The Politics of the People* (1994), he emphasised the role of ordinary people in shaping their political world. Both themes are key points of departure for this essay, which forwards a preliminary investigation of how Gaels negotiated the application of state authority.[3] It focuses on the most explicit 'cultural' act of the 1740s – the Act of Proscription (1746) – in order tentatively to suggest further scope for the reconsideration of metropolitan authority in the eighteenth-century Scottish Highlands.

I

The Act of Proscription (19 Geo. II c. 39) was the second of four major parliamentary acts – with the Attainder Act, the Vesting Act and the Heritable Jurisdictions (Scotland) Act – passed in conjunction with the suppression of the Jacobite rising. The Act was largely a restatement of the Disarming Acts of 1716 and 1725 (1 Geo. I c. 54 and 11 Geo. I c. 26), which had some success in denying the clans access to arms. While the impact of the earlier legislation should not be overstated – it tended to disarm dutiful loyalists far more frequently than their Jacobite neighbours and analysis of various Highland estates suggests that the military capacities of the average

Highland tenant had been in severe decline even before the passage of these acts – the government in 1746 was convinced that further disarmament was essential. The 1746 measure was intended to disarm entirely Scotland north of the Forth and levied exorbitant penalties on the possession of all 'warlike weapons', including fines of £15 sterling, six months in prison, indentured servitude in the colonies for seven years or forced impressment into regiments bound for America.[4]

It was a newly inserted clause, however, that symbolised a more rigorous approach to the *Gàidhealtachd*. The Act made it an offence to wear 'Highland clothes (that is to say) the Plaid, Philabeg, or little Kilt, Trowse, Shoulder-belts, or any part of what peculiarly belongs to the Highland Garb; and that no tartan or party-coloured plaid of stuff shall be used for Great Coats or upper coats'. In an age when human taxonomy was best understood as a product of climate, soil, language and culture, Highland dress was seen as key evidence of the Highlanders' lack of civility. The link between Highland clothing and 'savagery' was, to most commentators, so self-evident as not to require careful examination and provided an argument of first resort for Whig writers in the period.[5]

The cultural ramifications of the Act were deeply significant. Gaelic writers had long identified individual prowess and collective confidence with the *breacan-an-fhèilidh* or belted plaid. As the *Gàidhealtachd* was ever more integrated into national and European politics in the seventeenth century, Highland dress became a potent means of demonstrating Gaelic superiority in an increasingly complex world. Tartan became, in the words of Hugh Cheape, 'idealised' and provided a 'stock phrase in conventional praise poetry'. By contrast, English fashions became symbolic of effeminacy, weakness and cultural declension. Iain Luim, the great Keppoch bard, attacked Lord MacDonald of Aros for his attention to English clothing: 'B'fheàrr leam còt' is breacan ort Na pasbhin chur air cleòc [I would prefer you in a coat and plaid than in a cloak which fastens]'. By the eighteenth century, dress was an established part of the Gaelic panegyric code and heroic figures were regularly praised through the medium of clothing. As a song for Rob Roy MacGregor put it: "S math thig breacan mun cuairt is claidhe dhuit [You look good wearing plaid and sword]'. Clothing was central to the political and cultural autonomy of the region.[6]

The condemnation the Act received in the *Gàidhealtachd* was comprehensive. Jacobite propagandists, including Alasdair Mac Mhaighstir Alasdair and Lachlann Mac a' Phearsain a' Shrath-Mhathaisidh, were quick to criticise the measure. But it was the vituperation expressed against the Act by Whig Gaels which suggests how devastating the ban was deemed to be. Mairearad Chaimbeul, the wife of a Presbyterian minister and certainly no Jacobite, declared:

Thàinig achd ro chruaidh oirnn	Too hard an act has been imposed
A-nuas á Sasainn.	On us from England.
Maoidheadh air ar n-éideadh –	Threatening the clothes we wear –
Chan eil e tlachdmhor.[7]	It isn't pleasant.

Donnchadh Bàn Mac an t-Saoir, who had fought against the Jacobites, captured a more venomous attitude in 'Òran don Bhriogais [Ode to Trousers]', warning that if Charles returned, there would be no loyal Whigs in the Highlands and that 'Gheibhte Breacain Chàrnaid, "S bhiodh àird air na gunnachan [Scarlet tartans would be got, and the guns would be taken up]'. Duncan Forbes of Culloden, the Lord President of the Court of Session and a major intermediary between a vengeful regime and Scotland, did not find the Act to his 'taste'. As well as defending the practicalities of the garb for the environment of northern Scotland, Forbes stated that since most Highlanders had remained loyal, to punish all Gaels 'in so severe a manner, seems to be unreasonable'. Opposition to the Act of Proscription in the *Gàidhealtachd*, from both Whig and Jacobite, was near universal.[8]

II

That the Act struck at the heart of Gaelic confidence is not in question; it is difficult to argue with the assertion that the Act of Proscription was a seminal event in the history of the Highlands. But was it the profound and symbolic statement of Anglo-supremacy it was later made out to be? It is important to consider both the context in which the Act was formulated and, more significantly, how and by whom the Act was applied in the Highlands. In each case, close analysis does raise some interesting questions as to the coherence of ethnic hostility in Hanoverian politics.

The notion that a unified metropolitan elite worked unremittingly towards the destruction of Highland culture does not reflect the complexities of eighteenth-century British politics. The Act exposed severe divisions in the Whig groups which controlled the Westminster Parliament. The duke of Newcastle, the principal Secretary of State and a key ally of the duke of Cumberland, took the initiative in pursuing repressive legislation for Scotland. But dissenting voices could be heard. There was considerable opposition to the type of savagery exhibited by Cumberland's army in the aftermath of Culloden – the duke's famous sobriquet 'Butcher Cumberland' originated in London – and many Whigs were troubled by what the government's Scottish policies might mean for Walpole's legacy of political and constitutional stability. The prime minister, Henry Pelham (Newcastle's younger brother), was a moderate who acknowledged the need to manage rather than rule Scotland. Pelham stated that he wished to find 'the fairest means we are masters of' for ending the Jacobite threat. In the years from 1746 to 1748, much of Pelham's energies, as well as those of his Scottish ally, the duke of Argyll, were devoted to moderating parliamentary legislation so that no 'irreparable damage' was done to the Union.[9]

Beneath the vagaries of personality and interest, ideology played a crucial role. Whig ideology centred on the idiom of rights and the dignity of the rule of law. While hardly objective in their application of such 'rights', the assumption that all free-born Britons were entitled to certain liberties profoundly constrained political action in Hanoverian Britain. Newcastle, hardly the most sympathetic figure of the government, told the duke of Richmond that 'we must consider that they [the Highlanders] are within our island and have the benefit of our laws'.[10] The most disturbing element of the aftermath of the rebellion, from a Whig perspective, was the role of the military in its suppression. The idea of the military having authority over civil officials, even in the context of the *Gàidhealtachd*, was deeply disturbing to Whig sensibilities. The Act of 1725 had been widely criticised on the grounds that it had appointed military officers to civil appointments in order to collect arms. The government's only defence at that time had been that this move had been 'justified by necessity' and that, since six of the ten officers were Highlanders and possessed estates in the region, this did not constitute a slide towards Jacobean-era tyranny. In 1746, removing legal and coercive authority from the hands of the military and placing it in the hands of civil officers was deemed an absolute necessity; indeed, the post-Culloden acts were the product of this fixation. The military, and Cumberland in particular, who claimed that 'the greatest part of this kingdom [Scotland] are either openly or privately aiding the rebels', was astonished at the lacklustre degree to which they were supported by civil officials. Cumberland's successor, Humphrey Bland, joined with his master in railing against the constitutional constraints imposed on the military's freedom of action in the Highlands.[11]

In an effort to adhere to the rule of law – and pass legislation through a potentially unsympathetic Parliament – the Pelham government took a moderate line in designing the acts. The system could not operate without a degree of consensus. Even Newcastle understood that the government had to 'get some of the considerable Scotch nobility to join with us; to prevent its being call'd a national measure, & a national affront, & Injury'. Constitutionalism and the parliamentary system, however flawed, constrained the application of policies advanced by figures such as Chesterfield, the Lord Lieutenant of Ireland, who argued that the rebels were 'not enemies, but criminals, we cannot be at war with [th]em ... I would starve the loyal with the disloyal ... the Loyalist Highlander shall not have an oatcake'. The only scholar to analyse the development of the post-Culloden acts in detail concluded that figures such as Chesterfield were marginalised in the interests of compromise. According to B. Frank Jewell's study, the acts were produced in a climate of 'political moderation' as English Whigs favoured stability over the application of harsh measures that would upset the delicate balance of post-Union Britain. While Jewell's study is legalistic and institutional in nature, his discovery that the Pelham ministry favoured 'traditional' means of dealing with Jacobitism, over radical and regressive policies, is highly significant. In the end, arch-Whigs were as disappointed with the legislation as their Scottish counterparts. One opponent proclaimed that the acts were 'so full of Provisos and exceptions that ... [they] will be quibbl'd away to nothing by Scotch Lawyers and Scotch Lords'.[12]

This moderation took two major forms. First, the authors of the Act were acutely aware that political ideology had to confront social realities. They formulated its provisions with this in mind. There already existed a history of parliamentary resistance to outlawing Highland dress and the objections which had prevented such a measure from being enacted in 1716 and 1725 remained significant. Proscription, it was argued, would alienate loyalists within the region and make them both unwilling and unable to defend the government in future. As legal niceties demanded that proof of wrongdoing had to be furnished in order to convict a man of a crime, the House of Lords had argued in 1725 that any indiscriminate ban would be illegal. It would also, it was said, disproportionately hurt the poorest in Scotland. This was not an insignificant consideration given the surprising degree to which Jacobitism was understood as an expression of poverty and economic exclusion. Discussion in the Lords also concluded that a ban would give local magistrates too much discretionary power. While many of these concerns were ignored in the summer heat of 1746, not even the authors of the Act – the earl of Hardwicke, the Lord Chancellor, and Sir Dudley Ryder, the Attorney General – conceived of it as a blanket ban. The original bill demanded that only heritors – proprietors who contributed towards public burdens – be proscribed from wearing the dress. This would have left the vast majority of the Highland population free to wear the *breacan-an-fhèilidh*. It was only when Cumberland

and the Scottish Lord Advocate, Robert Craigie, objected that the ban became general. But the government avoided a greater evil by ignoring the demand that 'The Lowland habit to be used [henceforth in the Highlands] ought to be described in the Act of Parliament'.[13]

Second, the Act carried numerous exceptions and clauses that reflected ministerial understandings of the Act's innate weakness. Concerns over the Act's application and its effects on those who could not afford to change their garb led to continued delays in its implementation. The Act passed in 1746 did not fully come into force until 1 August 1749. The most significant exemption after this date related to the landed gentry. The Act of 1746 made no exemptions to the statutes but subsequent legislation granted exemptions to certain groups. Legal officers, peers, their sons, members of Parliament, qualified voters and, eventually, all significant landowners were permitted to ignore the proscription on carrying arms. The legislation permitted all landowners holding land valued at over £400 Scots to keep three firearms, three swords and three pairs of pistols, as well as permitting such arms to be used by the landowner's 'Family, and Servants'.[14]

These qualifications were carried over into the clause against dress. The Act did not – as countless modern commentators assert – ban the wearing of tartan but only those articles of tartan which made up the Highland dress. Tartan could not be used for plaids and coats but nothing in the legislation banned all Highland garments *per se*.[15] The sheriff-substitute for Killin in Perthshire, Duncan Campbell of Glenure, was ordered to publish the Act in Gaelic on church doors. Crucially, however, he was ordered to 'take all the opportunities you can of letting it be known that tartan may still be worne in cloaks westcoats, breeches or trews, but that if they use loose plaids they may be of tartan but either all of one colour, or strip'd with other colours than those formerly used'. This advice – inaccurate according to the letter of the law since it suggested plaids were not prohibited – suggests that few magistrates fully understood the Act's provisions and that its application was anything but uniform. Printed versions of the Act available in Scotland similarly made it clear that the legislation only prohibited 'Certain Items' of Highland dress. The means by which numbers of Highlanders avoided prosecution by adapting their dress – including reputedly stitching up the centre of the *fèileadh beag* or kilt to create a pair of shorts – suggests that, even where it was enforced, the Act did not encompass an outright ban on Highland garb. Indeed, landed elites – as well as soldiers – were explicitly exempt from the prohibition against Highland dress. The exemption of elites demonstrates the considerable degree to which the Act was formulated on class as well as ethnic lines.[16]

III

Exceptions were only one part of the problematic enforcement of the Act. There is no question that military rule had been a disaster for Whig and Jacobite Gael alike. The re-establishment of civil authority, however, made local civil magistrates – as they had been before the rebellion – responsible for the implementation of Hanoverian policy. And herein resides the great misconception of the post-rebellion Highlands: the government derived its power not from repressive laws or military rule but from local elites who, while protective of their autonomy, were extremely ambitious for government patronage and saw no problem in using state power to cement local power. Pelham admitted as much to the King in 1752 when, pressured by Cumberland and the duke of Bedford to act more vigorously against Scotland, he produced a wide-ranging report on the administration of the North. According to Pelham, the appointment of offices was the best means of 'promoting the interest of their [the government's] friends' but that, since knowledge of Highland localities was often limited, 'Gentlemen are frequently obliged to make them [appointments] at the instance of low people, who are guided chiefly by private considerations of relation, friendship, and neighbourhood'. Pelham's report, intended to placate vengeful Hanoverians, actually demonstrated how little government oversight there was in the management of the post-Culloden Highlands.[17]

In some areas, the Act was ignored because Jacobites still controlled local administrative structures. Hardwicke told his Scottish ally, the earl of Findlater, that 'It has been always my opinion that it were much better not to make any laws of that kind, than, when they are made, to suffer them to be overruled by a factious popular Dissent or to be defeated by the neglect of enforcing them.'[18] Hardwicke's fears were fully realised. Some clerks and other legal officers were described as 'notorious Jacobite[s]' and continued to administer their districts through the ignorance or even collusion of the landed aristocracy. Findlater believed, albeit with the bias of a fierce anti-Jacobite, that the region's 'poor Whigs ... dare scarce show their faces or live at home such is the audaciousness and violence of their Jacobite neighbours'.[19]

Even discounting the possibility of Jacobite sympathies – which depended very much on local politics – civil justice was an uncooperative instrument of government power. Local sheriffs and the deputies, while loyal Whigs, might have possessed a degree of sympathy for both the dress and for those most exposed to prosecution. Local magistrates made it clear to their constituents that the Act did not ban all items of traditional clothing but only those most associated with the martial traditions of the Gael. They also attempted, where possible, to advise rural people on how to avoid prosecution. People were encouraged to 'make them [their old plaids] into the shape of a cloak and so wear them in that way, which tho' button'd or tied about the neck, if long enough, may be taken up at one side and throwne over the other shoulder by which it will answere most of the purposes of the loose plaid'.[20]

A crucial reason for this 'loose' interpretation of the Act was that most Highland magistrates did not construe the law in the way intended by arch-Whigs. For Anglophone army officers such as Major John Roydon Hughes, 'the true intent and meaning of the law is to oblige the Highlanders to conform in the dress with His majesty's other subjects'. Hughes viewed any deviation from this aim as evidence of disaffection. In contrast, local magistrates, including Campbell of Glenure in Killin, believed that encouraging full observance of the law was as far as their ideological imperatives extended. In a draft letter defending those who continued to wear tartan, Glenure stated, 'I'm fond of being able to assure you that no part of the Highlands seem more forward to comply with the acts tutching the Highland cloths ... but as they [the people] believed the short coat of one colour and wide trewsers of tartan did not come within the description of the act they made no scruple either to wear them'. It is likely that Glenure resented the intrusion of a military officer into his jurisdiction as well as Hughes' threat to inform Newcastle of failures to enforce the Act to its fullest extent.[21]

Complaints about the lackadaisical attitudes of magistrates towards enforcing the law grew as the Jacobite threat withered in the 1750s. In 1753 complaints were made at Moniack near Beauly that servants were being protected from prosecution, presumably by employers who did not wish to lose trusted labourers to what was considered to be an out of touch decree from London. Local elites similarly worked with their tenants to ensure that the army could not illegally use the Act to force young men into the army. One *fear-taca*, a senior tenant farmer on the duke of Gordon's estates, informed the duke's factor that he was advising his sub-tenants to lay aside 'everything particular to the [H]ighland garb' when recruiting parties were close. The use of the Act by the military was, by this point, well known and William Grant assured the factor that he was using all of his influence to 'prevent ... their using any illegal means with any of the Duke's people'. In a deeply revealing comment on Highland attitudes to the law written in 1778, one north-eastern Highland observer thought 'it cannot be considered obsolete ... I believe any person complaining of any such contravention or offense [of the Act] would be heard not very favourably'.[22]

This is not to say that civil magistrates were willing to defend the people in their jurisdictions on the basis of cultural sympathies alone. Indeed, sympathy for the traditions of the region were probably the least important element in determining how local elites interacted with Hanoverian law. The aforementioned resistance to seeing servants or tenants prosecuted under the provisions of the Act suggests that, while obedient to the laws, few elites were willing to allow the courts to adversely affect the management of their households and estates. While greater analysis of the court records relating to the Act of Proscription is certainly needed – though many records from Highland jurisdictions have not survived – many of those prosecuted seem to have come from the lowest sections of Highland society. This reflected the inability of the poor to replace their clothing. It also meant, however, that those most prosecuted under the Act came from the very sections of society who could be most easily spared from an estate. Evidence in the letters of legal officers relating to 'common beggars' prosecuted under the Act even suggests the possibility that the law was manipulated to rid estates of undesirable individuals.[23]

We should not be surprised by this. Some Highland estates had taken measures against the *breacan-an-fhèilidh* well before 1746. In the parishes of the duke of Gordon's estates bordering Aberdeenshire, tenants had previously been offered ploughs in exchange for the surrender of weapons and plaids. In the parish of Rhynie, half of those surrendering weapons also gave up their plaids. These exchanges contained a greater ambiguity than the parliamentary Act – some of the surrendered tartan appears to have been redistributed among the tenantry – but its objective was clear. Estate improvement was being increasingly measured by productive and active tenants, and the garbed husbandman who worked away from the crop-growing fields was seen as less and less useful in this new world.[24]

Tellingly, when Highland elites realised that they could profit from recruiting men for the army, there was a corresponding shift in their attitude towards the Act of Proscription. Glenure, who had been so resistant to the inappropriate use of the Act in the 1740s, developed a reputation for its illegal use in the 1750s when members of Clan Campbell became active recruiters during the Seven Years' War. The clause allowing magistrates to direct violators into the military seems to have been abused with abandon. Since most army commissions in the Highlands were secured by recruiting a sufficient number of men for new regiments, there was pressure on magistrates to assist family members with military ambitions. In 1762 Glenure was censured by the local Justice of the Peace, Archibald Campbell, for using the Act of Proscription to conduct illegal recruiting. Archibald warned that it was unacceptable for Glenure to 'make use of the Law to cover Irregularities'.[25] The Act of Proscription had come full circle: it had evolved from a law designed to break the power of Highland elites to become a legal pillar of their unbroken authority in the *Gàidhealtachd*.

Glenure's apparent and dramatic shift of attitude suggests that the power of the post-Culloden laws was not to be found in their cultural restrictions – and less still in their London-orientated legal framework. The potency of the Act of Proscription was found in its local interpretation. Just as Highland magistrates had resisted the army and Hanoverian law in the 1740s, they were equally willing to collude with their peers and patrons to manipulate the law in their favour two decades later. The common denominator in both cases was the authority of local elites and *their* role in the reconstruction of the post-Culloden Highlands.

IV

Recognition of this point suggests a more thoughtful consideration of the post-Culloden acts is essential. There is no escaping – nor forgetting – the savagery of government agents in the post-rebellion *Gàidhealtachd*. Nor is it possible to interpret the Act of Proscription without acknowledging the cultural imperialism that underlay Hanoverian Britain. What this essay suggests, however, is that such an interpretation provides only one lens through which to understand authority in the Highlands and Islands. There are others. The Act of Proscription was formulated in a fractious political environment. The Act was a forceful assertion of the supremacy of civil law and constitutionalism, at least as it was understood. Despite the acknowledged limitations of the Scottish civil administration, the Act was intended to displace the military as the instrument of control in a region many considered to be alien and disaffected. It evidenced Whig political thought and reflected the ideological conflicts of the age as much as it signalled an unerring commitment to Anglo-cultural hegemony.

This raises important concerns about our interpretation of the post-Culloden acts. The Act did not impose an English legal system on the region but, rather, underpinned and entrenched the dominance of local elites in the administration of the Highlands. The Act was only, in part, 'assimilation through repression'. The British legal system was less 'imposed' than it was received and adapted to the imperatives of Highland elites.[26] In consequence, changes within the region need to be understood as the product of internal realignments among Whig elites rather than developments imposed by external sources. If traditional Highland clothes diminished in the eighteenth century – which they certainly did – it was not because of the power of the Act but, rather, because the Act was deemed useful to elite objectives within the region. While many attributed the decline in the *breacan-an-fhèilidh* to the Act, it is likely that this was simply convenient shorthand for the wider societal changes that were as much internal as external to the *Gàidhealtachd*. The desire of the landed gentry to expand trade and emulate their Lowland neighbours – as many commentators noted – must be centred as the key motive behind this change.[27]

External forces cannot, of course, be excluded from discussions of the Highlands. But we should be wary of overemphasising parts of the region's history for narrative effect. It is revealing that the most controversial parts of the Act at the time, those concerning legislation against non-juring meeting houses and the oaths taken by Episcopalian ministers, receive no attention whatsoever. The penalties for attending a non-juring meeting house were harsher than they were under the dress clause. The Georgian world was one of religious, ideological and hierarchical oppressions and to privilege its ethnic component at the expense of these alternative hierarchies will offer only the most partial understanding of the period. At the very least, the idea of a culturally homogenous military-backed state operating on a socially united and enfeebled *Gàidhealtachd* needs to be laid to rest.

This is why political ideology continues to deserve our attentions. Harry Dickinson's scholarship on the interaction between political ideology and social reality remains as crucial now as it was when it first challenged the findings of Namierite historiography. There was, of course, an Anglo-British bias to these ideologies and the universalism of English rights disguised a particularism in the application of those rights. But, in acknowledging the supremacy of Whig ideology in Hanoverian Britain, new means might be found of reinterpreting what have typically been simplified as cultural oppressions alone. More importantly, the universalism of political ideology allows us to divide the Highlands along more sophisticated ideological and social lines; to integrate the history of the Highlands in, rather than segregate it from, the wider frameworks of eighteenth-century Britain.

Notes

1 The National Archives [hereafter TNA], SP 54/34, fos 5–20, Albemarle to duke of Newcastle, 7 October 1746; National Records of Scotland [hereafter NRS], GD 112/47/1, fos 5–9, Memorandums on the Highlands submitted to the duke of Argyll, [1746]; [Anon.], *Remarks on the People and Government of Scotland, Particularly the Highlanders* (Edinburgh, 1747), pp. 7–10; *The Scots Magazine*, 8 (1746), p. 475.
2 J. G. A. Pocock, 'British History: A Plea for a New Subject', *Journal of Modern History*, 47 (1975), pp. 601–21; Bob Harris, 'Jacobitism', in Anthony Cooke et al. (eds), *Modern Scottish History, 1707 to the Present: The Transformation of Scotland, 1707–1850* (East Linton, 1999), p. 40; C. George Caffentzis, 'Civilizing the Highlands: Hume, Money and the Annexing Act', *Historical Reflections/Réflexions Historiques*, 31 (2005), pp. 169–94; Geoffrey Plank, *Rebellion and Savagery: The Jacobite Rebellion of 1745 and the British Empire* (Philadelphia, 2005); Martin Shaw, 'Britain and Genocide: Historical and Contemporary Parameters of National Responsibility', *Review of International Studies*, 37 (2011), pp. 242–5. For literary contributions, see Janet Sorenson, *The Grammar of Empire in Eighteenth-Century British Writing* (Cambridge, 2000); Kenneth McNeil, *Scotland, Britain, Empire: Writing the Highlands, 1760–1860* (Columbus, OH, 2007); Juliet Shields, *Sentimental Literature and Anglo-Scottish Identity, 1745–1820* (Cambridge, 2010); Silke Stroh, *Uneasy Subjects: Postcolonialism and Scottish Gaelic Poetry* (Amsterdam, 2011).
3 H. T. Dickinson, *Liberty and Property: Political Ideology in Eighteenth-Century Britain* (London, 1977), p. 1; H. T. Dickinson, *The Politics of the People in Eighteenth-Century Britain* (London, 1994).
4 British Library [hereafter BL], Add. MS 33,049, f. 268, List of arms and warlike weapons delivered up in 1725, n.d.; TNA, SP 36/104, f. 201, Memorial of the State of the North and Highlands of Scotland, [1747]; Andrew Mackillop, *More Fruitful than the Soil: Army, Empire, and the Scottish Highlands, 1715–1815* (East Linton, 2000), p. 7; Christopher Duffy, *The '45: Bonnie Prince Charlie and the Untold Story of the Jacobite Rising* (London, 2003), pp. 115, 175.
5 Andrew Simmons (ed.), *Burt's Letters from the North of Scotland* (Edinburgh, 1998), p. 234; TNA, SP 54/38, fos 351–2, Some Hints Relating to Amending the Laws of Scotland, [1747]; BL, Add. MS 35,890, fos 158–60, Some Thoughts Concerning the State of the Highlands, [1747].
6 Hugh Cheape, *Tartan* (Edinburgh, 2006), pp. 14–15, 19; Annie M. Mackenzie (ed.), *Òrain Iain Luim: Songs of John Macdonald, Bard of Keppoch* (Edinburgh, 1964), pp. 124–7; Ronald Black (ed.), *An Lasair: Anthology of Eighteenth Century Scottish Gaelic Verse* (Edinburgh, 2001), p. 146.
7 Black (ed.), *An Lasair*, p. 186.
8 Angus Macleod (ed.), *Songs of Duncan Ban Macintyre* (Edinburgh, 1978), p. 15.

POST-CULLODEN IN THE *GÀIDHEALTACHD* 71

9 Horace Walpole, *The Letters of Horace Walpole*, 3 vols (Philadelphia, 1842), I, p. 493; NRS, GD 248/565/83, f. 46, Pelham to Lord Deskford, 14 May 1752; Byron Frank Jewell, 'The Legislation Relating to Scotland after the Forty-Five' (unpublished PhD dissertation, University of North Carolina, 1975), pp. 41–52.

10 Dickinson, *Politics of the People*, pp. 5, 174–89; Jewell, 'The Legislation Relating to Scotland', p. 63.

11 BL, Add. MS 33,049, fos 253–64, Memorial touching the bill now depending for Disarming the Highlands, n.d.; fos 270–2, Bill for renewing Highland Bill, n.d.; BL, Add. MS 32,706, fos 233–4, Cumberland to Newcastle, 28 February 1746; NRS, GD 248/565/83, f. 49, Bland to Findlater, 1 September 1748.

12 BL, Add. MS 32,706, fos 259–62, Newcastle to Cumberland, 6 March 1746; fos 286–9, Chesterfield to Newcastle, 17 March 1746; Jewell, 'The Legislation Relating to Scotland', pp. 1–3, 125; BL, Add. MS 33,049, f. 267, Annotation to legislation, n.d.

13 [Anon.], *An Enquiry into the Causes of the Late Rebellion and the Proper Methods for preventing the like misfortunes for the Future* (London, 1746), pp. 24–30. For the role of poverty, see *Manuscripts of the Earl of Egmont: Diary of the First Earl of Egmont* (London, 1923), III, p. 46; [Anon.], *An Appeal to the Common Sense of Scotsmen, Especially those of the Landed Interest* (Edinburgh, 1747), p. 2; Jewell, 'The Legislation Relating to Scotland', p. 124; BL, Add. MS 33,049, f. 230, papers on Heritable Jurisdictions and Disarming, n.d.

14 BL, Add. MS 33,049, f. 230.

15 Matthew Wickman, *The Ruins of Experience: Scotland's 'Romantick' Highlands and the Birth of the Modern Witness* (Philadelphia, 2007), p. 73; Colin Calloway, *White People, Indians, and Highlanders: Tribal Peoples and Colonial Encounters in Scotland and America* (Oxford, 2008), pp. 92, 242; John Darwin, 'Empire and Ethnicity', *Nations and Nationalism*, 16 (2010), p. 384.

16 NRS, GD 170/1213, f. 5, James Erskine to Duncan Campbell, 22 November 1748; NRS, GD 36/454, f. 1, *An Act to amend ... as it Relates to the more effectual disarming the Highlands in Scotland* (London, 1748); David Stewart, *Sketches of the Character, Manners, and Present State of the Highlanders of Scotland*, 2 vols (Edinburgh, 1822), I, p. 119.

17 BL, Add. MS 33,050, fos 184–5, Pelham's Report on figures employed by Treasury, 1752.

18 NRS, GD 248/572/8, f. 1, Hardwicke to Findlater, 25 August 1747.

19 NRS, GD 248/565/83, f. 24, Earl of Hopetoun to Findlater, 2 May 1748; NRS, GD 248/173/2, f. 69, Lachlan Grant to Ludovic Grant, 16 April 1748; NRS, GD 248/572/8, f. 23, Findlater to Hardwicke, 19 September 1747.

20 NRS, GD 170/1213, f. 5, James Erskine to Duncan Campbell, 22 November 1748.

21 NRS, GD 170/1249, f. 1, John Roydon Hughes to Duncan Campbell, 1 September 1749; NRS, GD 170/423, fos 2–5, Duncan Campbell to James Erskine, September 1749; see also NRS, GD 170/1213, f. 16 (2), draft letter to unknown recipient, n.d.
22 NRS, GD 137/3355, Hugh Frazer to David Scrimgeour, 2 March 1753; NRS, GD 44/47/2/1, f. 6, William Grant to Alex Milne, 2 February 1778; NRS, GD 44/43/195, f. 33, Alexander Gordon to James Ross, 9 January 1778.
23 NRS, GD 170/1213, f. 27, James Erskine to Duncan Campbell, 16 February 1751.
24 The date for these exchanges is unknown but the nature of the manuscript suggests a date in the first three decades of the eighteenth century, see NRS, GD 44/51/167/4, List of plaids, tartan, serge, hose, swords and guns given in by tenants, n.d.
25 NRS, GD 170/1076, f. 2, Archibald Campbell to Duncan Campbell, 17 February 1762.
26 Allan I. Macinnes, *Clanship, Commerce, and the House of Stuart* (East Linton, 1996), p. 205; T. M. Devine, *Clanship to Crofters' War: The Social Transformation of the Scottish Highlands* (Manchester, 1994), p. 106.
27 Alexander Campbell, *A Journey from Edinburgh through parts of North Britain* (London, 1802), p. 175.

CHAPTER 5

Political Toasting in the Age of Revolutions: Britain, America and France, 1765–1800

Rémy Duthille

H. T. Dickinson's work has done much to demonstrate the vibrancy of 'out-of-doors' opinion in eighteenth-century Britain. Drinking and toasting were integral to the expression of popular politics. Electoral campaigns involved an enormous amount of 'treating' and voters fully expected candidates to ply them with wine and punch.[1] By the 1790s, the bibulous nature of British politics had become a rich source of inspiration for caricaturists, who loved to satirise the epicureanism of a Wilkes or a Fox and to depict the seedy underworld of Jacobin taverns.[2] Contemporaries and historians have used toast lists as precious, if rough, indexes of popular opinion and, during the 1790s, as evidence of sympathy for the French Revolution and transnational republicanism.

Though perceived as a peculiarly English custom by foreign travellers, toasting was usual in the American colonies and the young republic, and was adopted later in France. Following James Epstein's ground-breaking study of early nineteenth-century radical dining and toasting, historians have paid considerable attention to political drinking in Ireland and early-republican America.[3] This essay will build on this rich historiography and try to broaden the perspective, expanding it beyond the British Atlantic to examine political toasting in revolutionary France as well and ranging across the 'age of revolutions' from the Stamp Act of 1765 to around 1800. Though periodisation is difficult given the variety of local situations and dynamics, the end date is a turning point that witnessed some stabilisation after the ideological conflicts of the 1790s, while the consolidation of Napoleonic rule in France transformed the parameters of public expression.

Such an approach need not be predicated on a wholesale acceptance of the concept of an 'Atlantic revolution'. Rather it starts from the recognition that toasting involved crossing the seas and oceans in multiple, inter-related ways. First the very material basis of drinking was dependent on international exchanges: port, claret and other wines, and all the ingredients of punch were commodities traded across the Atlantic; so too were the drinking vessels and the materials necessary to craft them. Toasting was an act of self-definition and an affirmation of allegiance, loyalty or sympathy and, as such, was part of the repertoire of political expression, from Jacobitism and partisan strife in the early eighteenth century to revolutionary patriotism in Ireland and in the American colonies, and finally sympathy for the French Revolution. While loyal toasting was expected on all kinds of civic occasions, transnational toasting – understood here as ritualised drinking in the honour of a person or group located in another country, or of a universal or transnational idea – had a disruptive, seditious potential and was therefore taken very seriously by the authorities in Britain and the American colonies, as it could challenge the Hanoverian socio-political order and the very boundaries of the national community and the Empire.

I

Toasting can be understood as a 'rite of institution', as Pierre Bourdieu defined it, insofar as its effect was 'that of separating those who have undergone it [...] from those who will not undergo it in any sense, and thereby instituting a lasting difference between those to whom the rite pertains and those to whom it does not pertain'.[4] In that sense, toasting consecrates the exclusion of women and others from the political sphere. Recent historiography has often insisted on the limits of a public sphere that excluded various categories of people along gender, class and racial lines.[5] What is striking, however, is the expansion of popular politics well beyond the 'élites' (however the term might be construed). Many of the toasts published in the press were drunk by recently politicised men, be it the commercial middling sort of Dublin during the American Revolution or the English 'Jacobin' societies in the 1790s. The oral nature of toasting, and its pithy and repetitive form, helped to get messages across to the illiterate or the barely literate.

For those who did take part, toasting played an integrative function, cementing a group around shared values and aims through a process of emotional bonding.[6] As Peter Thompson noted, learning to drink 'was crucial to the process by which a gentleman adopted the forms of gentility and demonstrated his gentility to his peers and to society at large'.[7] Plebeians too had their own code of masculine honour, however 'unrespectable' it seemed to gentlemen. Everyone, however, accepted a man's basic right to refuse to drink a toast he disapproved of – which involved a constant risk of tension, scandal or brawls if someone gave the wrong toast, especially in the heated, bibulous atmosphere of taverns, or during public occasions such as political dinners. Young men had to learn to avoid antagonising the company with *faux-pas*,[8] but more experienced men could choose to give a contentious toast to disrupt a meeting. Frictions could be avoided by such simple means as socio-political segregation (like-minded men drank together and excluded their opponents) or rules passed by clubs or societies, some of them forbidding toasting altogether or banning political and religious topics.[9] Formal dinners were prepared well in advance, with organising committees meeting and negotiating the list of toasts, taking care to avoid offensive wording and agreeing on orders of precedence. However, violence and judicial proceedings multiplied in politically volatile contexts when men had to take sides and sedition, or fears thereof, was rife (as in Britain in the 1790s).

A short article published in the *Boston Post-Boy* on 13 February 1769 will provide the basis for a discussion of the issues raised by transnational toasting. It is dated 'London, November 10' and follows a paragraph on the subscription raised by several ladies 'of the first fashion and fortune in England' to support General Paoli, who was then fighting against France for the independence of Corsica:

> *Spoken Extempore by a young Gentleman (who was drinking Yorkshire Ale) on hearing the following Toast* Success to the two Cans *(meaning the* Americans *and* Corsicans*) given by a Gentleman who was drinking French Brandy Punch.*
> There is no Doubt they're brave and bold,
> Success their Names proclaim;
> Ameri-cans their Freedom hold,
> And Corsi-cans the same.
> In slavish Liquor, Sir, to quaff,
> Such noble Toasts I'm loth;
> In honest Yorkshire I'll toss off
> A merry Can to both.

The pun on the two cans conflates Paoli's fight for Corsican freedom against French aggression with the American colonists' resistance to British coercive policies. This linkage between libertarian causes is commonplace in patriotic discourse; equally significant is the blend of politics and entertainment: it was in the 1760s that John Wilkes managed to make politics more pleasurable and appealing to the middling and lower orders than it had ever been before.[10] The very form of the toast (essentially a tribute to a *person*, and, increasingly, a cause) and its adaptability made it a potent means of political communication, especially as the names of charismatic figures such as John Wilkes and General Paoli could be harnessed and combined with those of local worthies and heroes to defend various causes and served as bywords for the struggle for liberty in England, the Empire and beyond.[11]

The politicised choice of beverage reflects national self-perceptions and stereotypes. The article exploits the classic contrast between the Yorkshire ale of the stout, liberty-loving Englishman and the 'slavish' French wine. The opposition is to be taken more as a symbolic libertarian trope than as a realistic depiction of actual drinking practices. The relation between beverage choice and political affiliation in Britain and elsewhere was complex, as partisan issues intersected with economic, social and diplomatic factors. In late-Stuart England there was admittedly a well-marked divide between Whig, or even republican, ale and Tory, or Jacobite, claret. However, colonial and commercial expansion increased the availability of other beverages like madeira, rum and punch, which all had their political and social connotations. Toasts and beverages were part of a semiotic system of drinking which also encompassed vessels and various utensils.[12]

Also foregrounded in the article is the performance of toasting. The scene is set in an unspecified locale, probably a tavern, a place that has become associated with the idea of 'public opinion'. Toasting was one of the means by which strangers could mix and a fellowship of sorts was created among a diverse clientele.[13] This is a homo-social world, where 'gentlemen' interact and answer each other's toast. Women were toasts rather than toasters – a popular sentiment at the time was 'Miss Corsica'.[14] The article captures an instant of improvisation, an effusion of generous sentiment in an 'extempore' performance by a presumably dashing young man. And yet the poem sounds like a rebuke and a challenge to the other drinker, signalling that taverns were also competitive arenas where men vied for attention and were apt to fall to quarrelling or brawling.

The article purportedly transforms an oral performance into a print item that can be disseminated, and further commented on, imitated or parodied. The episode narrated actually seems too good to be true and might never have taken place. Such newspaper articles, and lists of toasts and accounts of dinners, more generally should be considered as idealised, rather than realistic, rhetorical and political constructions.[15] In the article under discussion, the toast expands into a short poem, in a process of literary elaboration that is found elsewhere, most famously in a poem attributed to Robert Burns, 'A Toast: Lines on the Commemoration of Rodney's Victory'.[16]

The 'can' toast and many others were published in London newspapers and then in the press along the Atlantic seaboard, from Canada to Georgia. The colonists were also informed of toasting-related incidents showing Lord Bute's, and later Lord North's, unpopularity.[17] A famous sentiment was coined by Thomas Paine at an 'elegant Supper' in London attended by John Adams in September 1774: 'May the Collision of British Flint and American Steel, produce that Spark of Liberty which shall illumine the latest Posterity'.[18] Toasts presented as popular in London or in certain partisan circles would be imitated elsewhere. Generally speaking, toasts were imported from England and then adopted, or adapted for voicing local grievances and expectations in the provinces, in the British Isles and in the American colonies.[19]

II

In the middle of the eighteenth century, the patriots both in America and in Ireland started to craft their own toasts in an inventive process showing an emerging sense of national identity. The dispute around the 1753 Money Bill prompted the emergence of Irish patriot clubs and an effervescence of political toasting.[20] In the next decade the Irish and, more famously, the Americans borrowed from the British supporters of John Wilkes the popular number 45 and added their own symbolic numbers to voice their opposition to Britain's attempts at regulation and taxation. From 1766 to around 1770 the Patriots of South Carolina drank to the numbers 45, 92 and 26, corresponding respectively to the notorious issue of John Wilkes's *North Briton*, and to the number of patriotic representatives in Massachusetts and in their own state.[21] Not only did the American insurgents draw on British oppositional rhetoric, but they also quickly transferred the rites in the honour of George III to the cult of George Washington; as early as 4 July 1779 they had converted monarchical rites to celebrate American independence.[22]

David Waldstreicher has shown the crucial role of civic celebrations and convivial gatherings in the forging of a new, republican identity during the American Revolution and in the early years of the republic. The role of the press was crucial: patriot groups often submitted their toast lists and dinner accounts directly to newspaper owners to give them the widest publicity possible, ensuring that toasts functioned as political statements aimed at a much larger audience than those present at the dinner. Waldstreicher drew on Benedict Anderson's analysis of the press's role in nation-building to argue that the simultaneity of toasting throughout the nascent United States created a sense of belonging and thus helped to build the 'imagined community' of American citizens.[23]

Martyn Powell followed a similar line of argument in his work on Ireland, showing how toasting, while drawing on English and American symbolism, displayed an increasing sense of Irishness after the 1760s.[24]

The 'imagined communities' thus created, however, did not conform to national boundaries. The ritual of toasting was not equally acceptable to all Americans, and dinner parties also revealed differences and divisions. The Quakers, in particular, had strict anti-toasting laws and did not take part in rituals of tavern fellowship, which could lead to tensions with men of other denominations.[25] The rise of partisan toasting in Britain, in Ireland and in America also signalled fissures within the national community, especially during the American War and in the 1790s as a result of sharp ideological conflicts.[26] Conversely, patriotism went hand-in-hand with a cosmopolitan commitment to universal liberty, and toasts drunk by 'patriots' juxtaposed national references and support to freedom-fighters elsewhere.[27]

Though the practice of toasting originated in England, toast lists were certainly more abundant in the American and Irish papers than in the British press during the 1770s and 1780s. Part of the explanation for this was the rise of revolutionary and patriot groups using meetings and festivals to proclaim their new loyalties and disseminate their aims and ideas. Toasts started to appear more frequently in the British papers in the 1790s, when radical and loyalist societies struggled for control of public space and published accounts of their dinners.

III

The French Revolution is also the moment when toasting emerged as part of the political repertoire in France. Some pro-American toasting did take place there during the American War, but the practice was not widely adopted. When John Adams – commissioned by Congress to secure a treaty of alliance with France – landed in Bordeaux in 1778, his French hosts treated him to a grand dinner. Adams recalled 'a List of Toasts in our fashion which was an entire novelty at Bourdeaux. They gave Mr Bondfield a Copy which he translated for me into English. The Toasts were announced by thirteen Guns in honor of the thirteen States.' There followed alternating toasts to American and French dignitaries and institutions, to 'Eternal Concord between the two Nations now Friends and Allies' and 'the French and American Ladies'.[28] In Marseille a *club des treize* was founded in 1778; its thirteen members met to sing thirteen-stanza songs and drink thirteen toasts to the thirteen American colonies. Whatever the depth of the club's political commitment, it must have remained in local memory, as English traveller

Anne Plumptre heard of it or read about it when she visited Marseille some twenty-five years later.[29]

It was in the early stages of the Revolution that political toasting and elaborate lists started to appear in France. Under the Directory (1795–9) it became part of the new syntax of the *fêtes révolutionnaires*. As the American insurgents had done before, the French adapted a British practice to their own ends. Since toasting was a rite of institution and a marker of loyalty, it is hardly surprising it should feature in civic festivals, which played a key role in transferring the focus of sovereignty from the monarchy to new, republican institutions. With the rapid expansion of revolutionary clubs, the French realised the value of toast lists published in the press.

Indeed, it was in such a form that the earliest manifestations of British sympathy for the French Revolution were expressed. On 4 November 1789, the London Revolution Society ostensibly celebrated the Glorious Revolution of 1688 and praised the French Revolution as the dawn of a new era of peace and liberty. The toasts juxtaposed homages to France and traditional Whig references to English liberties. The London Revolution Society sent a letter to the National Assembly, starting a correspondence that was to involve over fifty Jacobin clubs. On 14 July 1790, over six hundred people gathered at the Crown and Anchor to celebrate the Festival of the Federation. On the anniversary of the Glorious Revolution on 5 November 1790, Richard Price gave 'The Parliament of England, and may it soon become a National Assembly!' – a controversial toast that was interpreted as a wish for a French-style revolution in Britain.

The activities of the Revolution Society and other like-minded clubs soon became known in France through reports in the press and correspondence with clubs across the country.[30] French clubs started to publish toast lists, at a time when Britain was still considered as a model of political liberty and English public opinion seemed to be favourable to the Revolution. In August 1790, the Jacobin club of Nantes had invited British tradesmen and seamen present in the city to an Anglo-French festival, which featured eleven toasts to the Revolution Society, the peoples of France and England and peace between the two countries, universal liberty and the downfall of tyranny, and (in the last position) Louis XVI and George III – a clear sign that allegiance had shifted from the king to the nation. A rash of festivals to 'the four free nations' (France, Britain, the United States and Poland) involved political toasting in December 1791 and January 1792.[31]

When accounts of the Revolution Society dinners were published in the French press, they were interpreted by some in France as the expression of English public opinion, and the involvement of the National Assembly and the increasingly influential Jacobin clubs threatened to turn a *transnational* phenomenon (involving like-minded individuals in different countries) into an *international* process (involving interstate relations and diplomacy). Transnational marks of sympathy for independence fights, once condoned by the authorities of another state, turned into international signals. Edmund Burke's early detection of this possible drift was one of the motivations for writing his *Reflections on the Revolution in France*. He advised his French correspondent to look for 'the spirit of our constitution [...] in our histories, in our records, in our acts of parliament, and journals of parliament, and not in the sermons of the Old Jewry and the after-dinner toasts of the Revolution Society'.[32] To Burke, the club had usurped the sovereignty that belonged to the King-in-Parliament alone, and its friendly commerce with the French revolutionaries threatened to propagate revolution in Britain.

The authorities took toasting seriously, especially when practised by the new plebeian societies forming from 1792 in many parts of Britain. As the Home Office correspondence papers testify, Henry and Robert Dundas received from several parts of Scotland accounts mentioning toasts, which served as evidence for the state of loyalty, disaffection or sedition in a community. To give just one example, the Dalkeith tenant farmers were reported to drink loyal toasts to the King, cabinet ministers and Scottish noblemen, and satirical toasts punning with the names of leading Whigs and radicals: 'May we have no *Fox* in our Folds or *Greys* among our Corn', 'May we never have reason to reflect with *Pain* on our Constitution', 'May our Patriotism neither depend on *Price* or *Priestly* [sic] influence.'[33] The leaders of popular societies were thought to be using singing and toasting to instil French principles in convivial moments when ignorant men were least able to resist temptation.[34] Toasts were used as evidence during the trials of radical leaders, and in Scotland three men were condemned for celebrating the French victories, and drinking 'success to the French Revolution', 'George the third and last king' and 'liberty and equality to all the world'.[35] One of the strategies that loyalist societies such as Reeves' loyalist association employed to unmask traitors consisted in asking a suspect to drink a loyal toast. Not only words but facial expressions were scrutinised.[36] A well-documented example is that of Charles Pigott and William Hodgson, who were overheard in a coffee-house insulting George III, and who refused to drink the royal family's health – an attitude which led to their prosecution and eventual condemnation.[37] In many parts of Britain, local justices put pressure on tavern-keepers, and those who hosted 'seditious' meetings could lose their licence.[38]

In the fledgling United States, expressions of pro-French sentiment and transnational toasting proved contentious too and fed party polemics. Links were established with supporters of the French Revolution in the United States. French residents set up Jacobin societies in Philadelphia and Charleston and organised their own *fêtes* in those two cities and elsewhere; they sent their proceedings and toast lists to affiliated Jacobin clubs in France.[39] As the French Revolution took a more violent course, tensions hardened in the United States between the Federalists in power – who feared the excesses of uncontrolled democracy and sought an alliance with Britain – and the Republicans – who, like Jefferson, remained favourable to France. Festivals followed by extensive press reports on toasting became critical sites for the articulation of popular democratic ideals, crystallising Federalist anxieties and triggering adverse reactions.[40]

Republican cosmopolitan ideals were expressed through the organisation of French-American festivals, accounts of which were widely publicised in America but also in France. The *Gazette Nationale* gave the list of toasts drunk in America to commemorate the victories of the French Republic and covered the 14 July celebrations in 1792 and 1794.[41] As the French Directory lurched between democratic and monarchical tendencies, the republican paper *Le Bien Informé* published Jeffersonian toasts to argue that there was still hope that the Federalists would not turn the United States into a monarchy.[42]

As conviviality revived in Paris after the fall of Robespierre, toasting served diplomatic purposes at state dinners. The US ambassador to France, James Monroe, used the 4 July 1795 celebration to reaffirm friendship with the French Republic. Toasts served as public statements of international policy and, in the volatile context of the 1790s, entailed the risk of diplomatic incident and negative reactions at home.[43] Accounts of civic festivals and toasts drunk in the newly invaded territories started to appear in the French press. They functioned as pledges of allegiance to the Republic and as manifestations of popular opinion yearning for 'liberation' by the French army. The establishment of local popular societies was encouraged in cities invaded by the French in the Low Countries and the Netherlands, Rhineland, Italy and around the Mediterranean. The *Gazette Nationale* was increasingly filled with accounts of dinners at which local populations in the Sister Republics celebrated their union to the French Revolution, and toasted universal peace (equated with French expansion) and the downfall of Britain. The ruin of perfidious Albion became a favourite.[44]

Officials and military officers also staged their own patriotic *fêtes*. Toast lists routinely started with the French people and the Republic, and then moved down the military and civilian hierarchies, with, again, wishes for the downfall of Britain.⁴⁵ Particularly brilliant was the lavish entertainment given by the Directory to Napoleon Bonaparte on his triumphal return from Italy. The press in both France and Britain published accounts of the *fête*. The twelve toasts that were given to the tune of patriotic songs read as a manifesto of French republican values and warlike ambitions. Britain, again, was not forgotten: 'The Liberty of the Seas. May the Republican Armies soon emancipate the Ocean from the yoke of that Oppressive Government which has so long insulted and degraded the Universe.'⁴⁶

IV

Whether in private company, taverns, clubs or formal dinners, toasting followed the rules of face-to-face interaction and was a way for men to hold their ground, defend their honour and reputation, and sometimes denigrate others. At a time when loyalties were radically reconfigured, it is no wonder that toasts should have been highly divisive. Toasts acquired more prominence when groups published them to proclaim their new loyalties. In America, France and Britain, toasting served to bond individuals to new loyalties, celebrate dead and living leaders and heroes, advertise aims and threaten opponents. When France declared war on Britain in 1793 and supported the radicals in Scotland and especially Ireland, expressions of transnational republicanism became enmeshed in international relations. The Scottish patriot Thomas Muir was welcomed as a hero on arriving in Bordeaux in November 1797 after his escape from Botany Bay and a year-long series of tribulations. His answer to the toasts drunk at the French Ministry of Police expressed both his Scottish identity, and his solidarity and identification with the United Irishmen and other peoples struggling for their freedom:

> I read with the greatest sensibility in the Journal *L'Ami des Loix*, the Toasts given at your Civic Feast. I am a United Irishman; I am a Scotchman: I can answer in the name of the two Nations. The tears of affection and sympathy will flow when they shall be informed of the wishes of your Heart. You drank to the Victims of English Despotism, and may the blood they have shed, speedily ripen in their Country the seeds of Liberty and Equality. The blood has been shed, I myself have seen it. Alone I called for justice on the Assassins, and that was one of the causes of my proscription.
> You drank 'To the United Irishmen;' and 'The Highlanders of Scotland,' who wait only for the French to break their chains.

I assure you, in the name of the Irish and Scotch, that we will break our chains on the heads of our Tyrants. An effort remains to be made by the *Grande Nation*. It is not with the People of England it fights. It is only with a hundred scoundrels. Let them fall, and the Peace of the Universe is established.[47]

This solemn exchange is a far cry from the light-hearted article on the 'can toast'. Muir responds 'in the name of the Irish and Scotch', not as a single individual, to toasts raised at a government reception. Published as it was in the French and then the British press, his statement read as a challenge to England. It is evidence of diplomatic and propagandistic appropriation for power politics of expressions of transnational republicanism.

Notes

1 H. T. Dickinson, *The Politics of the People in Eighteenth-Century Britain* (Basingstoke, 1994), p. 44.
2 H. T. Dickinson, *Caricatures and the Constitution: 1760–1832* (Cambridge, 1986), pp. 189, 247.
3 James Epstein, 'Radical Dining, Toasting and Symbolic Expression in Early Nineteenth-Century Lancashire: Rituals of Solidarity', *Albion*, 20 (1988), pp. 271–91. On America, see P. S. Foner (ed.), *The Democratic-Republican Societies, 1790–1800: A Documentary Sourcebook of Constitutions, Declarations, Addresses, Resolutions, and Toasts* (Westport, CT, 1976); David Waldstreicher, *In the Midst of Perpetual Fetes: The Making of American Nationalism, 1776–1820* (Chapel Hill, NC, 1997); Simon P. Newman, *Parades and the Politics of the Street: Festive Culture in the Early American Republic* (Philadelphia, PA, 1997); Peter Thompson, *Rum Punch & Revolution: Tavern-Going & Public Life in Eighteenth Century Philadelphia* (Philadelphia, 1999). On Ireland, see Martyn J. Powell, 'Political Toasting in Eighteenth-Century Ireland', *History*, 91 (2006), pp. 508–29; James Kelly and Martyn J. Powell (eds), *Clubs and Societies in Eighteenth-Century Ireland* (Dublin, 2010).
4 Pierre Bourdieu, *Language and Symbolic Power*, ed. by John B. Thompson, trans. by Gino Raymond and Matthew Adamson (Cambridge, MA, 1991), p. 117. See also David Hancock, *Oceans of Wine: Madeira and the Emergence of American Trade and Taste* (New Haven, 2009), p. 559.
5 For a recent overview, see Brian Cowan, 'Public Spaces, Knowledge, and Sociability', in Frank Trentmann (ed.), *The Oxford Handbook of the History of Consumption* (Oxford, 2012), pp. 251–66.
6 Padhraig Higgins, 'Bonfires, Illuminations, and Joy: Celebratory Street Politics and Uses of "the Nation" during the Volunteer Movement', *Éire-Ireland*, 42 (2007), p. 174.

7 Peter Thompson, '"The Friendly Glass": Drink and Gentility in Colonial Philadelphia', *Pennsylvania Magazine of History and Biography* (1989), p. 550.
8 Lewis Namier, *The Structure of Politics at the Accession of George III* (2nd edn, London, 1957), p. 38.
9 See, for example, Nicholas Rogers, 'Clubs and Politics in Eighteenth-Century London: The Centenary Club of Cheapside', *The London Journal*, 11 (1985), pp. 51–8. On the management of toasting in clubs, see Valérie Capdeville, *L'âge d'or des clubs londoniens: 1730–1784* (Paris, 2008), pp. 139–43.
10 John Brewer, *Party Ideology and Popular Politics at the Accession of George III* (Cambridge, 1981), p. 191; H. T. Dickinson, *Liberty and Property: Political Ideology in Eighteenth-Century Britain* (London, 1977), pp. 205–20.
11 For examples, see *Nova Scotia Gazette*, 8 September 1768; Martyn J. Powell, 'The Society of Free Citizens and Other Popular Political Clubs, 1749–89', in Powell and Kelly (eds), *Clubs and Societies in Eighteenth-Century Ireland*, p. 246.
12 Karen Harvey, 'Ritual Encounters: Punch Parties and Masculinity in the Eighteenth Century', *Past & Present*, 214 (2012), pp. 165–203.
13 Thompson, *Rum Punch & Revolution*, p. 77.
14 Frank Brady and Frederick A. Pottle (eds), *Boswell in Search of a Wife, 1766–1769* (New York, 1956), p. 129.
15 Waldstreicher, *In the Midst of Perpetual Fetes*, pp. 32–3.
16 *Poems Ascribed to Robert Burns, the Ayrshire Bard, not Contained in any Edition of his Works hitherto Published* (Glasgow, 1801), p. 61.
17 For examples, see *Boston Post-Boy*, 16 January 1775; *Massachusetts Gazette: and the Boston Weekly News-Letter*, 7 December 1769; *Connecticut Gazette*, 21 March 1775.
18 Massachusetts Historical Society, Adams Family Papers: An Electronic Archive, John Adams Diary [hereafter Adams Diary], 15 August–3 September 1774, http://www.masshist.org/digitaladams/ [accessed 2 February 2015].
19 Powell, 'Political Toasting in Eighteenth-Century Ireland', p. 512.
20 Bob Harris, 'The Patriot Clubs of the 1750s', in Kelly and Powell (eds), *Clubs and Societies*, pp. 224–43.
21 Pauline Maier, 'John Wilkes and American Disillusionment with Britain', *The William and Mary Quarterly*, 20 (1963), p. 373; Jack P. Greene, *Negotiated Authorities: Essays in Colonial Political and Constitutional History* (Charlottesville, 1994), p. 403.
22 Newman, *Parades and the Politics of the Street*, pp. 34–7.
23 Waldstreicher, *In the Midst of Perpetual Fetes*, pp. 33–4.
24 For example, see Powell, 'The Society of Free Citizens and Other Popular Political Clubs, 1749–89', p. 261.
25 Thompson, *Rum Punch & Revolution*, p. 98; Jane E. Calvert, *Quaker Constitutionalism and the Political Thought of John Dickinson* (Cambridge, 2009), pp. 155–9, 227.

26 Waldstreicher, *In the Midst of Perpetual Fetes*, pp. 129–30; Pierre Gervais, '"Agriculture, and Commerce as its Handmaid": l'économie politique et les toasts publics en 1793', *Transatlantica* (2002) http://transatlantica.revues.org/463 [accessed 2 February 2015].
27 Anne-Marie Thiesse, *La création des identités nationales: Europe XVIIIe–XXe siècle* (Paris, 1999); Philipp Ziesche, *Cosmopolitan Patriots: Americans in Paris in the Age of Revolution* (Charlottesville, 2010).
28 Adams Diary, 2 April 1778, http://www.masshist.org/digitaladams/ [accessed 2 February 2015].
29 *Journal Politique, ou Gazette des Gazettes* (March 1778), p. 44; Anne Plumptre, *A Narrative of a Three Years' Residence in France, Principally in the Southern Departments, from the Year 1802 to 1805*, 2 vols (London, 1810), II, p. 152; Maurice Agulhon, *Pénitents et francs-maçons de l'ancienne Provence* (Paris, 1968), p. 219.
30 Rémy Duthille, 'Célébrer 1688 après 1789: le discours de la Revolution Society et sa réception en France et en Angleterre', in Alicia C. Montoya, Peggy Davis and Tristan Coignard (eds), *Lumières et histoire. Enlightenment and History* (Paris, 2010), pp. 245–62.
31 *Fête anglo-française, donnée par la Société des Amis de la Constitution de Nantes le 23 août 1790* (Nantes, 1790). On Anglo-French festivals, see Michael L. Kennedy, *The Jacobin Clubs in the French Revolution: The First Years* (Princeton, 1982), pp. 234–40.
32 Edmund Burke, *Reflections on the Revolution in France*, ed. by J. G. A. Pocock (Indianapolis, [1790] 1987), p. 27.
33 National Records of Scotland, RH 2/4/68, fos 64–5, William Scott to R. Dundas, 4 January 1793.
34 *First Report from the Committee of Secrecy... Ordered to Be Printed 17th May 1794* (London, 1794), pp. 26–7.
35 Bob Harris, *The Scottish People and the French Revolution* (London, 2008), pp. 78, 104.
36 Mark Philp, *Reforming Ideas in Britain: Politics and Language in the Shadow of the French Revolution, 1789–1815* (Cambridge, 2013), p. 82.
37 James Epstein, '"Equality and No King": Sociability and Sedition: The Case of John Frost', in Clara Tuite and Gillian Russell (eds), *Romantic Sociability: Social Networks and Literary Culture in Britain, 1770–1840* (Cambridge, 2002), pp. 43–61.
38 H. T. Dickinson, 'Popular Conservatism and Militant Loyalism 1789–1815', in H. T. Dickinson (ed.), *Britain and the French Revolution, 1789–1815* (Basingstoke, 1989), p. 118.
39 Michael L. Kennedy, 'La Société française des amis de la liberté et de l'égalité de Philadelphie (1793–1794)', *Annales historiques de la Révolution française*, 48 (1976), pp. 614–36; Lawrence Aje, 'L'évolution de la perception de la France et des français en Caroline du Sud à l'heure des Révolutions française et de Saint-Domingue, 1789–1804', *RSÉAA*, 69 (2012), pp. 85–116.

40 In addition to works by Foner, Waldstreicher and Thompson cited above, see Seth Cotlar, *Tom Paine's America: The Rise and Fall of Transatlantic Radicalism in the Early Republic* (Charlottesville, 2011), pp. 49–114.
41 *Gazette Nationale ou le Moniteur Universel*, 17 July 1792, 11 May 1793, 10 vendémiaire an III [1 October 1794]; Simon P. Newman, 'La Révolution française vue de loin: la célébration de Valmy à Boston, en janvier 1793', *Revue d'histoire moderne et contemporaine*, 58 (2011), pp. 80–99.
42 Marc Bélissa, 'La République américaine vue par les républicains français sous le Directoire', in Pierre Serna (ed.), *Républiques soeurs: le Directoire et la Révolution atlantique* (Rennes, 2009), p. 113. On Federalist criticism of French-American festivals, see Waldstreicher, *In the Midst of Perpetual Fetes*, pp. 136–7.
43 Ziesche, *Cosmopolitan Patriots*, p. 96.
44 For examples, see *Gazette Nationale*, 12 pluviôse and 4 messidor an VI [31 January and 22 June 1798], 19 messidor an VII [7 July 1799].
45 For example, see *Toasts, ou santés républicaines pour la fête du 9 ventôse-an V, célébrée en l'honneur de la prise de Mantoue* (n.p., n.d. [1797]).
46 *Oracle and Public Advertiser*, 21 December 1797.
47 *True Briton*, 8 January 1798, translated from *Gazette Nationale*, 15 nivôse an VI [4 January 1798].

Part II

Beyond Liberty and Property

CHAPTER 6

Edmund Burke, Dissent and Church and State

Martin Fitzpatrick

This essay examines Edmund Burke's attitude towards Protestant Dissenters, notably the more radical or rational Dissenters who were prominent in the late eighteenth century, as a way of understanding his changing attitude towards Church and state.[1] The Dissenters who attracted Burke's attention were those who were interested in extending the terms of toleration both for ministers and for their laity. Initially Burke supported their aspirations, but from about 1780 things began to change. It would, however, take another ten years before his opposition to Dissenters became open and virulent.

I

In the 1770s a group of Latitudinarian clergymen, led by Rev. Theophilus Lindsey, petitioned Parliament for relaxation of the requirement that clergy should subscribe to the Thirty-Nine Articles. The debate in the House of Commons on the Feathers Tavern Petition, as it was known, revealed that the government was against such a change but would not oppose a relaxation of the existing requirement that Dissenting ministers, tutors or schoolmasters subscribe to the doctrinal articles of the Thirty-Nine Articles. The Dissenters proceeded to petition for such change. There were, however, divisions within the petitioning camp, with some Dissenters being prepared to accept an alternative subscription requirement and others believing that the state had no right to demand any religious test at all. Burke favoured change, believing that a profession of faith should replace the existing requirement to subscribe to the Thirty-Nine Articles. At this time, Dissenters regarded him as an advocate of toleration.[2] Even Theophilus Lindsey, who was critical of Burke's opposition to the Feathers Tavern Petition, wrote of Burke speaking in favour of 'the most unbounded toleration to Dissenters'.[3] In the early 1770s, one might have thought that was indeed Burke's stance. In a speech on the Protestant Dissenters Relief Bill on 7 March 1773, which he made soon after he had visited France, he spoke in favour of toleration even for Deists. One may see this in part as a reaction to the atheism which he had found prevalent among the *philosophes*. After stating his strong preference for revealed religion and even more so for the Church of England, which he wanted to see so powerful that it could 'crush the giant powers of rebellious darkness', he conceded that 'episcopacy may fail and religion exist'. And so, in order to counter the evil of atheism, the widest toleration should be promoted:

> Let it be but a religion, natural or revealed, take what you can get; cherish, blow up that spark. One day it may be a holy flame. By this proceeding you form an alliance offensive and defensive, against those great ministers of darkness in the world, who are endeavouring to shake all the works of God established in order and beauty.[4]

Earlier in his speech Burke had argued that 'toleration is good for all or it is good for none'. As became clearer later in the speech, however, he was talking about *religious* toleration, which could not apply to atheists. Nor could it apply to those who dissented 'from a party ground of dissension, in order to raise a faction in the state'.[5] At the time there is no sign that Burke had any of the petitioners in mind. When he spoke again on the issue in 1779, when relief was granted, there were straws in the wind to suggest that Burke was changing his mind. He was beginning to worry about heterodoxy, but not enough to upset Lindsey, who was nevertheless mentioned in Burke's speech as one of the heterodox.[6] Unfortunately, accounts of Burke's role on Dissenters' relief at this time are secondhand and his contribution to the debates on the issue are poorly covered.[7] According to Lindsey, Burke played a key role in substituting the existing subscription requirement to the Thirty-Nine Articles with a declaration of faith based on the Holy Scriptures.[8] A petition from Lord North, in his capacity as Chancellor of the University of Oxford, presented a formulation aimed to ensure that those who subscribed to it were theologically orthodox. It appears that Burke 'pleaded strenuously for its insertion'.[9] It ran:

> I A.B. do solemnly declare in the presence of Almighty God, that I am a Christian and a Protestant, and as such that I believe that the Scriptures of the Old and New Testament, as commonly received among Protestant Churches, do contain the whole revealed will of God: and that I do receive the same as the rule of my Doctrine and Practice.

The Dissenters and their supporters managed to water down the declaration through the omission of the word 'whole', but they failed in their aspiration to be tolerated without a declaration of faith.[10]

Burke's position in the 1770s was thus in rhetorical terms highly favourable to the widest toleration for Dissenters; but the issue which exercised them, subscription to the Thirty-Nine Articles, involved only a relatively minor concession to the Dissenters. In the debate in 1779, he had argued that the Dissenters 'did not deny the right of the civil Magistrate to enjoin Principles and Opinions', and this was undoubtedly his own position.[11] Over this period, too, Burke had defended the Church establishment against any change. He spoke of 'a strict establishment narrowly watched'. By that he meant his determination to defend the establishment exactly as it stood. By 'strict' he did not mean theologically strict. His own position on the Articles of the Church was decidedly Latitudinarian, although different from that of the Feathers Tavern petitioners. Their suggestion that a simple subscription to Scripture should replace that to the Thirty-Nine Articles was ridiculed by Burke: 'subscription to the Scripture is the most astonishing idea I ever heard, and will amount to nothing at all.'[12] It was a somewhat amusing admission in view of his later role in insisting that the Dissenting subscription to the Thirty-Nine articles should be replaced by a tight formulary of adherence to Holy Scripture. Burke's predominant concern, however, was the peace of the Church, which allowed 'latitude of private opinion' so long as its teachers inculcated from the pulpit 'the religion of the state'.[13]

II

Burke's view of Dissent in the 1770s was not uncritical. His clearest exposition of Dissenting attachment to liberty of conscience came in his speech on conciliation with the colonies. Speaking of Protestantism in the northern colonies, he described their tradition: they were Protestants 'of that kind which is most adverse to all implicit submission of mind and opinion'. Such 'dissenting interests have sprung up in direct opposition to all the ordinary powers of the world'.[14] His purpose was to explain the range of reasons for the tensions with the colonies. It was not to endorse those traditions. One suspects that had he viewed Dissent at home in the same light he would have been a serious, not to say, a passionate critic. He did indeed distance himself from the views of Richard Price, whom he implicitly condemned for his abstract analysis of liberty in his *Observations on Civil liberty* (1776): 'Civil Freedom ... is not, as many have endeavoured to persuade you, a thing that lies hid in the depth of abstruse science. It is a blessing and a benefit, not an abstract speculation ...'[15] For Burke, free government was 'a matter of moral prudence and natural feeling'.[16]

Burke was also critical of Dissenters for wanting freedom from subscription though they willingly abjured popery.[17] Yet despite the rabid anti-Catholicism of the Gordon Riots, which was a highly traumatic event for him, he did not tar all Dissenters with the anti-Catholic brush, not least because he would have been aware that they were not all against toleration for the Catholics.[18] Sir George Savile, a fellow Rockinghamite, had introduced the bill for Catholic Relief in 1778. Like Burke, he was threatened by Lord George Gordon's mob.[19] Savile was a prominent supporter of the Unitarian Chapel in Essex Street, London, which Lindsey had founded in 1774 after leaving the Church of England, and Lindsey felt his chapel and house as well as his supporters were threatened by the rioters.[20] Soon after the riots, when considering whether to stand for election at his Bristol constituency, Burke acknowledged the importance of winning the Dissenting vote, but he also understood that Dissent was not monolithic. Among the Dissenters he viewed the Presbyterians as his supporters.[21] A few years later Burke visited Joseph Priestley at his laboratory in Birmingham and reported to his friends that he regarded Priestley 'as the most happy of men and most to be envied'.[22] Lindsey commented that Burke would perhaps not have been so impressed had he considered Priestley's Sunday work.[23] That is the point; Burke did not at this time show any interest in Priestley's religious views or activities, nor was he exercised by the latter's previous connection with Shelburne, whom he detested.[24]

For Burke, Dissenters were political allies, and despite the involvement of leading Dissenters in parliamentary reform, he did not fall out with them until they fell out with him over the Fox–North Coalition, which they regarded as an anathema. In the 1784 election, Dissenters voted for Pitt the Younger and not for the Foxite Whigs. Burke deeply resented their conduct, which he regarded as a betrayal. In 1787 the Dissenters began to campaign for the repeal of the Test and Corporation Acts. They had the nerve to canvass Whig support, notably that of Fox, who proved surprisingly willing to help. He had spoken in favour of universal toleration in 1779 and he continued to adhere to such views without reference to party affiliation. That was not Burke's position, but he kept his powder dry, aware of the value of winning over Dissenting support. As late as 1789, he had yet to declare his hostility to the political and theological radicalism of Priestley.

On 9 September 1789, Burke wrote to Fox to ask for a favour, and a surprising and slightly embarrassing one at that. A Mr Blair, a new neighbour of Burke's, had written to Fox on behalf of Joseph Priestley asking that he 'apply to the Prince of Wales for his leave to dedicate' to him a forthcoming scientific work. Fox had failed to reply to the request, and Burke wrote to chivy him up, suggesting that it would be useful to the party to have Priestley on their side. Pointing to the political value of obtaining the consent of the Prince of Wales, he described Priestley as:

> A very considerable Leader among a Set of Men powerful enough in many things but most of all in Elections: and I am quite sure that the good or ill humour of these men will be sensibly felt at the General Election.[25]

Burke's estimate of the strength of the Dissenters and certainly of the significance of Priestley as a leader – which he repeated in a subsequent letter to Captain John Willett Payne – may be exaggerated, but it explains why he would become so worried by what he perceived to be their republicanism and hostility to the Church establishment.[26]

When Fox was slow to convey the Prince of Wales's acceptance of Priestley's dedication, Burke was asked to transmit the news to Blair and Priestley. He refused on the grounds that it would be an 'officious intrusion into a Business not committed to me'.[27] He suggested, nonetheless, that a message should be conveyed from the Prince 'saying something civil on the part of his Rl Highness about Dr Priestley's Talents and merits'. This was Burke the diplomat, hoping that acceptance of the dedication would encourage Dissenters to return to the support of the Whigs in the forthcoming general election. His true feelings about them were revealed when in concluding his discussion of the matter in his letter to Fox, he observed, 'even if they cannot be wholly reclaimed, it would be something to neutralize the acid of that sharp and eager description of men'.[28]

Burke may have continued to be wary of expressing open hostility to the Dissenters had not other events at home and abroad brought to the fore some of his core religious and political concerns. He had prevaricated over supporting the Dissenters' campaign for the repeal of the Test and Corporation Acts in 1787 and 1789 by absenting himself from the debates, despite being canvassed by former Dissenting contacts in Bristol. All this changed during the course of 1789, with the fall of the Bastille in France and the subsequent revolutionary events.

The catalyst for Burke's dramatic emergence as leader of those who feared that revolution abroad might become a distemper at home was Richard Price's *Discourse on Love of Our Country*. Price saw the revolutionary events in France as part of a movement of enlightened constitutionalism, which had begun in Britain a century earlier, in 1688–9. The movement had gathered strength with the revolution in America and had now crossed the channel to France. Like the British experience, the events in America and France were 'glorious'. Price's *Discourse* was preached on the centenary of the Glorious Revolution on 4 November 1789 before members of the Revolution Society of London, composed mainly of Dissenters. It was published on 5 December and quickly sold out. Further editions followed, including an American edition and two French translations. Interest in the sermon was tailing off when Burke attacked it in his *Reflections*. This itself renewed interest in Price's sermon and another three editions were printed, all of which contained a new preface in which Price replied briefly to Burke.[29]

III

One way of looking at Price's *Discourse* is to see it as releasing all of Burke's pent-up feelings about Dissent. Burke's political instincts in the 1780s may have kept those feelings in check, but also he does not seem to have been very interested in the Dissenters' theology and its implications. This is not to say that he was unaware of the development of heterodoxy. In the debate on Dissenters' relief from subscription in 1779, he had referred to Lindsey and suggested that a Socinian could not be a Christian. Nevertheless, he was not interested in theological controversy – which had been a concern in his 'younger and more robust days' – and would only become interested when he saw it as threatening to the established order of things. The *Discourse* of Price, who regarded himself as a Unitarian, was crucial in this process because it encapsulated pretty well every aspect of that threat: the call for reform of the Church of England and of parliamentary representation; the enunciation of the principles of the Glorious Revolution as an assertion of liberty of conscience as 'a sacred right', of the right to resist 'power abused' and of the sovereignty of the people; and a euphoric celebration of the revolution in France and a warning to 'all ye oppressors of the world' that they would be unable to resist the movement of 'increasing light and liberality'.[30]

It is, therefore, a surprise to discover that when Burke wrote about his initial encounter with the *Discourse* in a letter of 1792, to William Wedell, his partner MP for Malton, he claimed that it was Price's attack on Fox's character that first upset him.[31] Given Fox's powerful support for universal toleration, finely expressed in his speech supporting the repeal of the Test and Corporation Acts in May 1789, it had been particularly impolitic of Price to attack his reputation in his *Discourse*, but the puritan in him was stronger than the politician. Price toned down the published version of the *Discourse*, and professed to be sorry if his words gave 'any just occasion' for offence. It was obvious enough, however, to know to whom Price was referring when he wrote:

> Oh! that I could see in men who oppose tyranny in the state, a disdain of the tyranny of low passions in themselves; or at least, such a sense of shame and regard to public order and decency as would induce them to *hide* their irregularities, and to avoid insulting the virtuous part of the community by an open exhibition of vice![32]

In 1784 Price had seen Fox flaunting his new mistress, Elizabeth Armistead, formerly the mistress of the Prince of Wales, in high society at Brighton. Price witnessed his 'immoral and indecent conduct' and reported it to the Earl of Shelburne.[33] Many felt that Fox had put his political career on the line, and Burke and others complained of his irresponsibility.[34]

What Price wrote in the published version of the *Discourse* was sufficient for Burke subsequently to claim that this was the aspect of the discourse which first gave offence. Burke was, however, already predisposed to take such a view. He read the *Discourse* after he had dined 'in a large and mixed company' which included some Dissenters. In the course of conversation he was informed that Dissenters spoke of Fox 'in a manner that one would not speak of some better sort of highwayman'.[35] Naturally Burke defended Fox. On returning from the dinner, he read Price's *Discourse* for the first time and it was in that context that he claimed that its leading feature was an attack on Fox. As a statement of his first reaction to reading the *Discourse* it is less than convincing; it was only towards the close of his address that Price's words could be construed as attacking Fox.[36]

Within a month of his robust defence of Fox, Burke was startled by his friend's enthusiasm for the French Revolution in the debate on the army estimates (9 February 1790). By the time he wrote the letter to Wedell he had split with Fox and the Whigs. The letter was initially intended as a public response to Wedell's thanks for his *Appeal from the New Whigs to the Old* and its core was a defence of his own conduct regarding the Whigs and Fox. Although Burke's account of his disenchantment with Dissent should not be entirely discounted, the letters he wrote *before* he published *Reflections* are better evidence of the nature of that disenchantment. Indeed, in his long letter to Wedell, Burke wrote that as soon as he read the *Discourse* he began to take notes 'intended for publication'; these were undoubtedly about disagreements with Dissent more serious than their uneasy relationship with Fox.[37]

When Burke sent his preliminary notes for *Reflections* to his friend Philip Francis, the latter's less than enthusiastic response led to this fierce riposte:

> But I intend no controversy with Dr Price or Lord Shelburne or any other of their set. I mean to set in a full View the danger of their wicked principles and their black hearts; I intend to state the true principles of the constitution in Church and state – upon Grounds opposite to theirs ... I mean to do my best to expose them to the hatred, ridicule, and contempt of the whole world; as I shall always expose such, calumniators, hypocrites sowers of sedition, and approvers of murder and all its Triumphs.[38]

Francis had made the mistake of criticising Burke's sentimental portrayal of Marie Antoinette. This was arguably the leading feature of his early response to the *Discourse* and encapsulated all he felt about the dangers posed by Price and the Dissenters. Their lack of reverence for monarchy epitomised their lack of reverence for the existing order of things. Price could rejoice in the King and Queen being mobbed, forcibly removed from Versailles and taken to Paris.[39] In *Reflections* he portrayed Price as a regicide like Hugh Peters, a leading Independent divine whose sermons justified the execution of Charles I. Against the background of events in France, Burke in the space of a year had become a fervent critic of Dissenters.

His criticism had become open in his speech against the repeal of the Test and Corporation Acts on 2 March 1790. Here his focus was upon rational Dissenters, whose works were evidence of their radical views, and crucially their desire and expectation that the Church establishment would collapse. The desire arose from the belief, common among Dissenters, that Church and state should be separated; the expectation from a combination of belief in the inexorable progress of truth and a millenarian view that the established churches would soon collapse, beginning with the papacy. In essence, Burke was catching up on works published in the first half of the 1780s, which now led him to regard rational Dissenters as subversives. At the top of his list was Priestley, who, in his usual forthright way, had suggested that rational Dissenters were:

> laying gunpowder, grain by grain under the old building of error and superstition which a single spark may hereafter inflame, so as to produce an instantaneous explosion, in consequence of this the work of ages, may be overturned in a moment and so effectually as the same foundation can never be built upon again.[40]

Burke quoted this from Priestley's recently published *Letters to Rev. Edward Burn*, but in fact it had been in the public domain since 1785 and had been harmful to the Dissenters' campaign for repeal of the Test and Corporation Acts.[41] Priestley tried to insist that it was a metaphor and that the grains of gunpowder were arguments; but repeating his argument did not help the Dissenting cause. Burke speculated that the danger the leading Dissenters posed to the Church was more serious than that posed to 'the church of France ... a year or two ago'.[42] Yet he did not vote against repeal of the Acts. He suggested that had the motion for repeal been brought ten years earlier he would have voted for it and claimed that he had long lived 'with several Dissenters in the greatest intimacy and happiness', and generally held Dissenters in 'great esteem'. He would prefer the House not to come to a decision over repeal but to provide the Dissenters with the opportunity of refuting his allegations. He ended by warning against the danger of acting 'under a blind idea' that MPs were supporting the established Church, but inadvertently exposing it to the sort of danger posed by Lord George Gordon's mob.[43] The House rejected the motion for repeal.

In this debate on the repeal of the Test and Corporation Acts, Burke took an attitude towards Church–state relations that differed from the prevalent Whig one, which saw the Church as an ally of the state in fortifying the moral order. Taking the sacrament in the established Church was therefore a qualification for, and a badge of, full citizenship. Burke was uneasy with the use of the sacrament in this way: 'the sacramental rite was too solemn an act for prostitution'.[44] He had an alternative test, one which reversed its priorities. The aim of the sacramental test was to ensure that those who served the state should be loyal to it, and taking the sacrament in the established Church provided such a guarantee. Here the Church was supporting the state. Burke's test, on the other hand, was designed to ensure that those who served the state would be loyal to and protect the Church. Here the state was supporting the Church. His test included a profession that one would not attempt to subvert the constitution of the Church of England. As Burke became ever more hostile to Dissent in the early 1790s, he would spell out a view of Church–state relations which not only reversed the priorities of the alliance between Church and state, but abolished the distinction between the two.[45]

After their failure in 1790, the Dissenters abandoned their campaign for the repeal of the Test and Corporation Acts; but in 1792 the rational Dissenters, who had recently formed a Unitarian Society, petitioned for toleration. In between, Burke had published in November 1790 his *Reflections* and, in August 1791, after his public breach with Charles James Fox, the *Appeal from the New Whigs to the Old*. In *Reflections* he argued that the 'majority of the people of England' believed the Church was not only essential to the state but that it was also inseparable from it. It formed 'the foundation of their whole constitution'.[46] A year later, in his *Appeal*, he would argue that his credentials as a Whig were unimpeachable. In authenticating his position, he drew on the Whig arguments put forward in the trial of the High Churchman Henry Sacheverell in 1710. Burke also located himself within the Whig tradition of tolerating Dissenters and instanced his support for clerical relief. Indeed, in the 1770s Burke could indeed be seen as within the Whig tradition regarding the relationship between Church and state as an alliance of convenience. J. C. D. Clark suggests that in *Reflections* Burke strengthened that notion by suggesting the contract between Church and state was indissoluble.[47] This can be seen as more than a gloss on the Whiggish notion of an alliance rather a departure from it. In the 1770s, in the debate on the Feathers Tavern Petition, as Clark notes, Burke had recommended the Lockeian notion of the Church as a voluntary society.[48] In the 1790s, he moved so far from such ideas that it is no longer possible to view him as a Whig in Church–state matters.

In 1792 Unitarians petitioned Parliament for relief from their disabilities.[49] This was the last attempt by Dissenters in the 1790s to widen the parameters of toleration. The debate was indicative of how Burke's ideas on Church–state relations were affected by his attitude towards Dissent. Early in the debate he argued against Fox that the issue was not toleration but the safety of the state. He reiterated his view that Church and state were inseparable: 'By a Christian Commonwealth there was established no alliance, as has often been erroneously stated between church and state'. Church and state were 'integral parts of the same whole'.[50] As the Unitarians were a threat to the Church they were a threat to the state: it was, as with their French counterparts, their 'avowed intent' to 'subvert and overturn every establishment, political and religious, of every kind, and a wish to extend that destruction to all nations'.[51] As Burke warmed to his task he became distinctly overheated. With a reference to Price's *Discourse*, he declared, 'Let not both Houses of Parliament be led in triumph along with him [the King], and have law dictated to them by the constitutional, the revolution, and Unitarian Societies.' He then described such societies as 'insect reptiles', which should not be allowed to grow beyond their natural size.[52] Fortunately for Burke's state of health that did not happen. Although the petition was quite well supported, it was decisively defeated by 142 votes to 63. This was the least Burke wanted; he was convinced that the Unitarians were engaged in treason. He was conversant with the details of the trial of Dr Sacheverell, and one wonders whether he read the sermon for which he was impeached: 'The Perils of False Brethren, both in Church and State'. This passage could very easily have been slotted into Burke's speech without anyone noticing the difference in sentiment or tone:

> Our constitution both in Church and State, has been so admirably contriv'd, with that wisdom, weight, and sagacity, and the temper and genius of each, so exactly suited and modell'd to the mutual support, and assistance of one another, that 'tis hard to say whether the Doctrines of the Church of England contribute more to authorize, and to enforce our civil laws, or our laws to maintain and defend the doctrines of our Church. The natures of both are so nicely correspondent, and so happily intermixt, that 'tis almost impossible to offer a violation to the one without breaking in upon the body of the other. So that in all those cases before-mention'd, whosoever to innovate, alter or misrepresent any point in the articles of the faith of our church, ought to be arraign'd as a traytor to our State; heterodoxy in the doctrines of the one, naturally producing, and almost necessarily inferring rebellion and high-treason in the other ...[53]

At both ends of the century, Tories and High Churchmen regarded Dissent as a serious danger. In theology, Burke may have remained a Latitudinarian, but as regards the Church and state his views had become indistinguishable from Tory notions.[54] At the same time, they contributed to the refurbishment of such ideas which would come to be expressed in Samuel Coleridge's notion of clerisy. Fortunately for Unitarians, the fault Coleridge found in them was not their danger to the Church–state, but rather the lack of mystery in their religion. That, at least, could be tolerated.[55]

Notes

1 This is a companion essay to one co-authored with Anthony Page, 'Burke and Rational Dissent', in Peter Jones and Martin Fitzpatrick (eds), *The Reception of Edmund Burke in Europe* (Bloomsbury, London, forthcoming).
2 See, for example, North Riding Record Office, Correspondence of Rev. John Disney, MSS ZFW 7/2/159/6, Disney to Rev. C. Wyvill, 9 July 1803.
3 G. M. Ditchfield (ed.), *The Letters of Theophilus Lindsey (1723–1808)*, 2 vols (Woodbridge, 2007–12), I, pp. 184–7, Lindsey to William Turner of Wakefield, 5 May 1774.
4 *The Speeches of the Right Honourable Edmund Burke in the House of Commons and Westminster Hall* [hereafter *Burke's Speeches*], 4 vols (London, 1816), I, pp. 162–3.

5 Ibid., I, p. 157.
6 Ditchfield (ed.), *Letters*, I, p. 290, Lindsey to William Tayleur, 27 March 1779.
7 Ibid., I, p. 290, n. 10.
8 Ibid., I, p. 292, Lindsey to William Tayleur, 21 April 1779.
9 [David Williams], *For the St James's Chronicle, Two Letters on Universal Toleration to Edmund Burke Esq.*, 26 April 1779; John Stephens, 'The London Ministers and Subscription, 1772–1779', *Enlightenment and Dissent*, 1 (1982), p. 67.
10 *Sketch of the History and Proceedings of the Deputies appointed to Protect the Civil Rights of the Protestant Dissenters* (London, 1813), p. 214. See also G. M. Ditchfield, 'The Subscription Issue in British Parliamentary Politics 1772–1779', *Parliamentary History*, 7 (1988), pp. 45–80.
11 Williams, *Two Letters*, 23 April 1779.
12 *Burke's Speeches*, I, p. 112.
13 Ibid., I, p. 97.
14 Ibid., I, p. 289.
15 *A Letter to the Sheriffs of Bristol on the Affairs of America* (1777), in Isaac Kramnick (ed.), *The Portable Edmund Burke* (London, 1999), p. 288.
16 Ibid. See also John Faulkner, 'Burke's First Encounter with Richard Price: The Chathamites and North America', in Ian Crowe (ed.), *An Imaginative Whig: Reassessing the Life and Thought of Edmund Burke* (Columbia, MO, 2005), p. 109.
17 Ditchfield (ed.), *Letters*, I, p. 292, Lindsey to William Tayleur, 21 April 1779.
18 A well-respected friend of Lindsey suggested that 'if the Riots had continued three days longer Burke would have gone out of his senses'. Ditchfield (ed.), *Letters*, II, p. 75, Lindsey to William Frend, 2 November 1790.
19 John Cannon, 'Savile, Sir George (1726–1784)', in H. C. G. Matthew and Brian Harrison (eds), *Oxford Dictionary of National Biography* (Oxford, 2004); Robert Kent Donovan, *No Popery and Radicalism. Opposition to Roman Catholic Relief in Scotland 1778–1782* (New York and London, 1987), p. 118.
20 Ditchfield (ed.), *Letters*, I, p. 317, Lindsey to William Tayleur, 10 June 1780, and appendix at I, p. 567.
21 See, for example, Thomas W. Copeland (ed.), *The Correspondence of Edmund Burke*, 10 vols (Cambridge, 1958–78), IV, pp. 266–75.
22 Ditchfield (ed.), *Letters*, I, pp. 386–7, Lindsey to William Turner of Wakefield, 1 September 1783.
23 Ibid. Priestley at that time was working on his highly contentious *An History of the Corruptions of Christianity* (London, 1782), in which he questioned the doctrines of original sin and the atonement.
24 In the 1790s, Priestley found it hard to understand why Burke regarded him as an 'enemy to the constitution' on account of his critical views on the established Church, which had been in print before he got to know him:

'in the more than twenty years of my acquaintance with him', he 'never ... intimated the least disapprobation'; see J. T. Rutt (ed.), *The Theological and Miscellaneous Works of Joseph Priestley*, 26 vols (London, 1817–31), XV, p. 497, 'Fast Sermon', 19 April 1793.
25 Copeland (ed.), *Correspondence*, VI, pp. 14–15, Burke to Charles James Fox, 9 September 1789. The work in question was *Experiments and Observations on Different Kinds of Air* (Birmingham, 1790).
26 Copeland (ed.), *Correspondence*, VI, pp. 22–4, Burke to Captain John Willett Payne, 24 September 1789.
27 Ibid., V, pp. 26–8, Captain John Willett Payne to Burke, 28 September 1789, and reply, 1 October 1789.
28 Ibid., VI, p. 15, Burke to Fox, 9 September 1789. Fox's powerful speech in favour of the repeal of the Test and Corporation Acts in the Commons in May 1789 helped to restore his reputation among the Dissenters; see Thomas W. Davis, *Committees for Repeal of the Test and Corporation Acts: Minutes 1786–90 and 1827–8* (London, 1978), pp. 34–7.
29 D. O. Thomas, John Stephens and P. A. L. Jones (eds), *A Bibliography of the Works of Richard Price* (Aldershot, 1993), pp. 149–61.
30 Richard Price, *A Discourse on the Love of our Country, Delivered on Nov. 4, 1789* (4th edn, London, 1790), pp. 16–17, 34–5, 50–1.
31 Copeland (ed.), *Correspondence*, VII, p. 57, Burke to William Wedell, 31 January 1792.
32 Price, *Discourse*, pp. 42–3.
33 W. B. Peach and D. O. Thomas (eds), *The Correspondence of Richard Price* (Durham, NC and Cardiff, 1983–94), II, pp. 249-51, Price to the Earl of Shelburne, 27 November 1784; L. G. Mitchell, *Charles James Fox* (Oxford, 1992), pp. 73, 178–82.
34 Mitchell, *Fox*, p. 73.
35 John Disney recalled that he had delivered 'some expressions of great asperity against Mr F', see North Riding Record Office, Correspondence of Rev. John Disney, MSS ZFW 7/2/159/6, Disney to Christopher Wyvill, 9 July 1803. We do have an account of what they might have been, from a pamphlet published in January 1790, which claimed: 'In the delivery of his sermon, he [Price] was so pointed in his description of a *Gambler* – a *Spendthrift* – and an *infidel* that the audience immediately recognized the portrait of – Mr. Fox?', see [P. Withers], *Theodosius: Or a Solemn Admonition to Protestant Dissenters on the Proposed Repeal of the Test and Corporation Acts* (London, 1790), p. 19.
36 Price, *Discourse*, p. 43.
37 Copeland (ed.), *Correspondence*, VII, p. 57, Burke to William Wedell, 31 January 1792.
38 Ibid., VI, pp. 91–2, Burke to Francis, 20 February 1790.
39 Here, I give Burke the benefit of the doubt that he had not wilfully misinterpreted the evidence against Price. See D. O. Thomas, 'Edmund Burke and the Reverend Dissenting Gentleman', *Notes and Queries*, 29 (1982), pp. 202–4.

40 J. Priestley, *Reflections on the Present State of Free Enquiry in this Country* (Birmingham, 1785), pp. 40–1.
41 William Cobbett (ed.), *Parliamentary History*, 41 vols (London, 1803–20), XXIX, p. 438.
42 *Burke's Speeches*, III, p. 480.
43 Ibid., III, p. 483.
44 Ibid., III, p. 481.
45 In his speech on the Unitarian petition, Burke argued that the care of religion should be the principal care of the Christian magistrate; *Burke's Speeches*, IV, p. 57.
46 J. C. D. Clark (ed.), *Reflections on the Revolution in France: A Critical Edition* (Stanford, [1790] 2001), pp. 263–4.
47 Ibid., p. 263, n. 369.
48 Ibid., p. 265, n. 373.
49 The Unitarians sought the repeal of the Blasphemy Act of 1698 and to come within the terms of the Toleration Act of 1689, which had only allowed toleration for Trinitarian Dissenters; see G. M. Ditchfield, 'Anti-trinitarianism and Toleration in Late Eighteenth Century British Politics: The Unitarian Petition of 1792', *Journal of Ecclesiastical History*, 42 (1991), pp. 39–67; idem, 'Public and Parliamentary support for the Unitarian Petition, *Enlightenment and Dissent*, 12 (1993), pp. 28–48.
50 *Burke's Speeches*, IV, pp. 52, 56.
51 Ibid., IV, p. 54.
52 Ibid., IV, p. 63.
53 *A Compleat History of the Proceedings of the Parliament of Great Britain against Dr Henry Sacheverell: with his Tryal before the House of Peers for High Crimes and Misdemeanours* (London, 1710), p. 12.
54 B. W. Young, *Religion and Enlightenment in Eighteenth-Century England: Theological Debate from Locke to Burke* (Oxford, 1998), pp. 146–7.
55 Ibid., p. 217.

CHAPTER 7

'The Wisest and Most Beneficial Schemes': William Ogilvie, Radical Political Economy and the Scottish Enlightenment

David Allan

As a professor at King's College in Aberdeen for nearly sixty years, William Ogilvie was an active participant, along with celebrated colleagues like Thomas Reid, George Campbell and James Beattie, in the Aberdeen Philosophical Society (or 'Wise Club'), as well as a prominent member of Scotland's academic community from the 1760s onwards. Yet despite the facts that he had also been Reid's pupil and then studied at Glasgow and Edinburgh when those institutions were at the very height of their intellectual distinction, Ogilvie's relationship with the wider Scottish Enlightenment has gone almost completely unrecognised. This is the more surprising because, while the ideas of the principal Scottish philosophers about the material aspects of human existence have most often been considered as having broadly conservative political implications, Ogilvie's sole publication, *An Essay on the Right of Property in Land* (1781), indicates that inquiries of that kind might also have provoked profoundly radical conclusions about the causes and consequences of social inequality.[1] In Ogilvie's case, moreover, the revolutionary analysis that he constructed would go on to earn him an honoured place in the history of progressive thought. He was later bracketed, for example, with Spence as one of the early 'Agrarian Socialists', paired with Paine as an authentically 'radical social reformer', included by other hagiographers among the 'left-libertarians', and even, in a particularly wrenching mis-contextualisation by Tolstoy, classified simply as an 'Englishman'.[2] What follows therefore attempts to reposition Ogilvie and his peculiar arguments about property, society and government where they actually originated, in the distinctive intellectual environment of the Scottish Enlightenment.[3]

I

Ogilvie was in many ways the archetypal mid-eighteenth-century product of both King's College and Marischal College in Aberdeen – a man with slightly obscure origins in the city's regional hinterland, who achieved such significance as he later acquired by dint of an education at one of its two independent and rival university-level institutions. Born in 1736, he was the only son of James Ogilvie of Pittensear, the owner of a relatively modest ancestral estate near Elgin in Morayshire.[4] Almost nothing is known with any certainty about the son's childhood and upbringing: attendance at Elgin grammar school is strongly suspected but not proven and the only thing we are able to say with confidence is that Ogilvie was soon orphaned and found himself not only inheriting the family property but also taking on responsibility for the support and care of his four sisters. It is also clear that he first matriculated at King's College in 1755. This was the crucial turning point in his life, for it was here that Ogilvie initially fell under the influence of Reid, professor of moral philosophy at the college since 1752. The founder and leading light of the Common Sense school with its strong Aberdonian base, Reid was one of the greatest philosophical thinkers produced by the eighteenth-century Scottish universities as they struggled to contain the wide-ranging threat posed by David Hume's sceptical claims about the nature and limits of human knowledge. It was from Reid that Ogilvie first heard expounded the conventional epistemological and ethical claims of Scottish moral philosophy – about the internal geography of the mind, about the means of perception, about the grounds of human judgement relating to conduct, and so forth.

On graduation in 1759, he initially found a position as a schoolmaster in a north-eastern parish. This was quite a common trajectory for those Aberdeen alumni of the time who harboured academic ambitions. Beattie, for example, had left Marischal in 1753 for a teaching post at Fordoun in Kincardineshire, so Ogilvie's appointment at Cullen in Banffshire merely involved him in setting off down what must have seemed a reasonably well-worn career path. In what was actually a relatively unusual further move, probably indicating exceptional levels of intellectual curiosity, Ogilvie then decided to broaden out his education by continuing his studies elsewhere. Accordingly, he left his job at Cullen after just a year, spending the winter term of 1760–1 at the University of Glasgow and the following year at the University of Edinburgh. The timing of this decision was particularly auspicious. It ensured that Ogilvie can have been one of very few young Scots in a position to exploit a remarkable window of opportunity which briefly opened when Adam Smith, who just three years later would finally relinquish the Glasgow chair of moral philosophy, and Adam Ferguson, who had only been appointed professor of natural philosophy at Edinburgh in 1759, were both active university teachers from whose lectures an ambitious Scottish undergraduate could benefit in quick succession.

Of the two older men, it is obvious that it was Smith whose classes were most closely related to the intellectual preoccupations that later energised Ogilvie's *Essay*. In the years immediately after publishing *The Theory of Moral Sentiments* (1759), Smith's syllabus at Glasgow seems to have delivered on a promise made in the closing paragraph of that work to develop 'an account of the general principles of law and government, and of all the different revolutions which they have undergone in the various ages and periods of society, not only in what concerns justice, but in what concerns police, revenue, and arms and whatever else is the object of law'.[5] The result was what have become known to posterity as the *Lectures on Jurisprudence*, unpublished during Smith's lifetime but adequately documented from subsequently rediscovered student notes and now regarded as a critical element in his comprehensive educational programme, memorably described later in *The Wealth of Nations* (1776) as 'the science of a legislator'.[6] As a result, the *Lectures*, with their insistent focus on the economic and legal history of human society and their aim of providing a framework for identifying effective policy options for modern governments, formed the striking mixture of ideas – not just straightforward moral philosophy but much else besides – to which Ogilvie, when attending Glasgow during the last years of Smith's professorship, would have been exposed.[7]

While Ogilvie was rounding off his studies at Edinburgh, he was formally appointed to an assistant professorship of philosophy at King's. The following year he was advanced to a full chair and began to take classes. With the exception of his transfer to the professorship of humanity (Scottish jargon for Latin) in 1764, this was in fact to be Ogilvie's settled occupation until his death more than five decades later in 1819. Two things, however, are worth adding about the exceptionally long academic career which now stretched before him. One was that, as the early exchange of professorial titles hints, his principal teaching interests soon deviated from moral philosophy and came to focus instead in the field of ancient literature.[8] It is to this decision that he eventually owed his classroom reputation, since his linguistic skills and his translations of Latin texts, produced purely for pedagogic purposes and never published, found great favour among several generations of students at King's. The other significant feature of Ogilvie's tenure was his prominence in college politics, as seen especially in his advocacy of the ultimately doomed proposal in the mid-1780s that King's should merge with Marischal to form a single University of Aberdeen (in effect replicating the very obvious rationalisation imposed by the Covenanting and Cromwellian regimes between 1641 and 1660 and only finally effected by Act of Parliament in 1860).[9] This episode seems to have been wholly typical of Ogilvie's approach to contentious matters of principle. This generally saw him take a stand on what he believed to be the correct course of action on strictly ethical and rational grounds, and then defend it against all-comers. He was also, for example, a vocal critic of his colleagues' misappropriation of bursary funds, and he steadfastly opposed their sale of valuable college properties. Although reportedly a genial and encouraging teacher and much loved by the undergraduates, Ogilvie throughout his time at King's was evidently not remotely afraid of finding himself in a minority. It is not implausible that this proclivity for challenging formidably entrenched interests and staking out coherent counter-arguments in direct opposition to a comfortable consensus played a significant part in the gestation of the *Essay*.

II

Overwhelmingly the most pronounced intellectual influence to have left its imprint on the *Essay* was the tradition of natural jurisprudence. This seminal body of ideas was central to the emergence of incipient social science out of moral philosophy in the broader European Enlightenment. It had already had profound consequences not only for seventeenth-century legal theory in the hands of innovative jurists like Hugo Grotius and Samuel Pufendorf, but also for the emergence of the new political science epitomised above all by Thomas Hobbes. The same philosophical assumptions had established an early, decisive and enduring hold over Scottish minds in particular. This influence is apparent from Viscount Stair's reconceptualisation of Scots law in the *Institutions of the Laws of Scotland* (1681); the adoption of Pufendorf's texts by Gershom Carmichael, professor of moral philosophy at Glasgow at the start of the eighteenth century; the teaching and publications of Carmichael's direct replacement Francis Hutcheson (the so-called 'father of the Scottish Enlightenment'); and those of Hutcheson's own pupil and eventual successor Smith. All told, an especially keen interest had evolved among Scottish thinkers in deriving vital insights into the history and progress of human society and government from an explanatory framework grounded in the existence and operations of fundamental laws of nature.[10] The *Essay* actually makes its direct connections with this rich philosophical heritage very clear, even to the extent of the full title Ogilvie selected: *An Essay on the Right of*

Property in Land, With respect to Its Foundation in the Law of Nature, Its present Establishment by the Municipal Laws of Europe, and The regulations by which it might be rendered more beneficial to the lower Ranks of Mankind.

The *Essay* also contains much of the familiar paraphernalia of an approach to understanding human social history, whose governing assumption was everywhere the objective reality of a 'law of nature'. There is, for example, the customary interest in the ancient Jewish world as described in the opening books of the Old Testament, since what eighteenth-century Scottish philosophers still invariably took to be an authentic documentary account of a paradigmatic early society had long been a staple of natural jurisprudence. The 'institutions of the Mosaical law, respecting property in land', as Ogilvie called them, seemed, after all, particularly useful for demonstrating the founding principles of human society prescribed by God. Indeed, they appeared to confirm that an egalitarian distribution of land, closely in accordance with the dictates of natural law, had been known among the early Jews, introduced, in admittedly unusual circumstances, at the behest of divinely inspired prophets. As Ogilvie argued:

> To that most respectable system an appeal may be made in support of these speculations; for the aim of the Mosaical regulations plainly is, that every field should be cultivated by its proprietor, and that every descendant of Jacob should possess in full property a field which he might cultivate.[11]

For Ogilvie, then, this was not merely an interesting historical occurrence but, precisely because of its great antiquity and rootedness in a society shaped with particular immediacy by the hand of the Creator, a model that could plausibly be followed in any later context: 'Whoever shall consider the probable effect of such an institution in increasing the number of people, will cease to wonder at the uncommon populousness of Judea in antient times', he claimed. 'The same effect might be renewed in that country, could those Agrarian regulations be restored to their force.' Unsurprisingly, Ogilvie also hinted strongly at the possibility of subsequently writing 'more at length of the Mosaical Agrarian, considered as an oeconomical [sic] regulation, in a history of property in land, which may hereafter be offered to the public'.[12]

Like other Scottish philosophers interested in natural jurisprudence, however, Ogilvie's interest in much earlier human societies did not prevent him borrowing relatively freely from other intellectual traditions, among them civic humanism, with its characteristic moralising about the damage to social cohesion and political stability wrought by private interest and especially by material acquisitiveness. Central to civic humanism, with its deep admiration for the classical republics of antiquity, had been enthusiasm both for the formation of citizen militias designed to capture and focus a virtuous public spirit and for sumptuary laws to discourage and restrict individual selfishness. In Scotland this distinctive agenda was in Ogilvie's day most closely associated with Ferguson, who from the 1750s onwards had led an active campaign for the founding of a Scottish militia, while its greatest British exponent had probably been James Harrington, author of *Oceania* (1656), on whom we know Reid had drawn extensively in his lectures.[13]

Accordingly, it is again not surprising to find Ogilvie advancing a case for 'the zealous patriotism of a militia' and also advocating legal restrictions on consumption – the latter because, as he averred, such laws 'might have the most salutary effects on the manners, and character, and even on the prosperity of a people'.[14] He did acknowledge that in contemporary society these might prove unpopular, noting that they 'have been frequently turned into ridicule, and not unjustly, as pretending to maintain an impracticable simplicity, and an unnecessary austerity of manners, among the great body of citizens'. But Ogilvie was nevertheless confident of their merits: 'they deserve a very different estimation', he insisted, 'if considered as means of directing public industry to those exertions which may be productive of the most extensive utility, and most valuable enjoyments to the community at large'.[15]

If this love of ancient constitutional expedients makes Ogilvie sound in places remarkably like Adam Ferguson, then a further aspect of the *Essay* which invites fruitful comparison with the major philosophical thinkers of the Scottish Enlightenment is its striking recourse to an essentially utilitarian justification for public policy. For Ogilvie, in words that appear closely to echo Francis Hutcheson's celebrated claim that 'that Action is best, which procures the greatest Happiness for the greatest Numbers; and that, worst, which, in like manner, occasions Misery', seems to have envisaged his own agrarian reforms, wherever they might be introduced, as satisfying exactly the same principle:

> If in any nation of Western Europe the sovereign were desirous of introducing a system of property in land, wholly consonant to natural justice, and favourable to the greatest happiness of the greatest number of citizens; and if in this undertaking, he found himself under no necessity of paying respect to the prejudices and interests of the present landholders, or any other body of men whatever, he would take for his leading object to increase the number of independent cultivators, and to bring into that favourable situation as great a number of citizens as the extent of his territory would admit.[16]

Given Hutcheson's central place in framing the moral theory of the Scottish Enlightenment and the seminal importance of his ideas about politics and government to both Reid and Smith in particular, it is extremely unlikely that Ogilvie's borrowing here was purely accidental.

Out of this body of commonplaces with widespread currency in eighteenth-century Scottish intellectual life, Ogilvie was able, like several of the country's better-known philosophers, to develop a coherent understanding of society's evolution through successive phases broadly defined by their material characteristics. Again the origins of this type of analysis lay squarely within the grand tradition of natural jurisprudence where, as in Hobbes's famous evocation of a time before concepts of ownership even existed – with 'no Propriety, no Dominion, no Mine and Thine distinct' – the steady improvement in people's living conditions as superior modes of subsistence had emerged and had also brought about of necessity more subtle and sophisticated forms of property law.[17] As Ogilvie maintained:

> the actual system of landed property in the West of Europe is greatly changed, and in some respects greatly improved from what it has formerly been. It has varied its form, with the prevailing character of successive ages; it has been accommodated to the rude simplicity of the more antient [sic] times, to the feudal chivalry of the middle centuries, and to the increasing industry and cultivation of later more tranquil periods: it may now therefore be expected to receive a new modification, from the genius and maxims of a commercial age, to which, it is too manifest that the latest establishment of landed property is by no means adapted ...[18]

A footnote to this description of how ownership systems had evolved through human history also underlined that 'In the progress of the European system of landed property, three stages may be distinguished – the domestic, the feudal, and the commercial', a classic summary of stadial theory that was again very much in keeping with those schemes found in Smith's *Lectures* and in Ferguson's *Essay on the History of Civil Society* (1767).[19]

III

If Ogilvie's indebtedness to natural jurisprudence and immersion in the dominant intellectual currents of the Scottish Enlightenment lent an air of familiarity to several important parts of the *Essay*, however, the bold conclusions he was able to reach most certainly did not. In particular, Ogilvie displayed a willingness to derive explicit natural rights from natural law in a way that was not common in Scotland's intellectual community. As he asserted early in the *Essay*:

> That every man has a right to an equal share of the soil, in its original state, may be admitted to be a maxim of natural law. It is also a maxim of natural law that every one, by whose labour any portion of the soil has been rendered more fertile, has a right to the additional produce of that fertility, or to the value of it, and may transmit this right to other men.[20]

Ogilvie was also adamant that 'an equal share of the soil' was to be understood as an absolute right applicable at all stages in human history, an eternal principle founded on men's undeniable need for subsistence:

> The earth having been given to mankind in common occupancy, each individual seems to have by nature a right to possess and cultivate an equal share. This right is little different from that which he has to the free use of the open air and running water; though not so indispensably requisite at short intervals for his actual existence, it is not less essential to the welfare and right state of his life through all its progressive stages.[21]

It therefore followed that as a fundamental human endowment bestowed by nature, it could neither be taken away by other men nor freely renounced by the individual: 'It is a birth-right', Ogilvie stated categorically, 'which every citizen still retains'.[22]

This startling deduction placed Ogilvie squarely at odds with Smith and Ferguson, and clearly gestured instead towards Jean-Jacques Rousseau's provocative suggestion that men had enjoyed original rights which had been recognised and protected in a pristine state of nature but then lost as society had evolved. Indeed, Ogilvie was convinced that history had seen the steady erosion of certain freedoms and rights, especially those concerned with property ownership: 'In many rude communities, this original right has been respected', he suggested, but 'Wherever conquests have taken place, this right has been commonly subverted and effaced.' Worse, it seemed that as societies passed through successive stages of development this original right had increasingly vanished: 'In the progress of commercial arts and refinement', he concluded, 'it is suffered to fall into obscurity and neglect.'[23] Why this had come about was plain enough to Ogilvie. There were in fact two competing sorts of claims made by men to justify property ownership. One was based on an absolute natural right to an equal share, the other on the labour expended or procured from others when improving it. It was the undue weight given to this latter notion which ultimately explained the habit of advanced societies – those where 'agriculture has made considerable progress' through the application of labour – to pay least regard to the anterior right:

> That right which the landholder has to an estate, consisting of a thousand times his own original equal share of the soil, cannot be founded in the general right of occupancy, but in the labour which he and those, to whom he has succeeded, or from whom he has purchased, have bestowed on the improvement and fertilization of the soil. – To this extent, it is natural and just: but such a right founded in labour, cannot supersede that natural right of occupancy, which nine hundred and ninety nine other persons have to their equal shares of the soil, in its original state.[24]

Directly challenging 'Whatever has been advanced by Mr Locke and his followers', among whom Ogilvie must have numbered Hume, Ferguson and Smith, he considered the conclusion unavoidable that the unequal distribution of landed property was the product merely of human decision enshrined in human law. Its emergence, so far from being defensible in terms of natural right, had been a contravention of nature's decree. It was fundamentally an error for those philosophers writing in the tradition of Locke to have ascribed:

> any such sacred and indefeasible nature, to that sort of property in land, which is established by the regulations of municipal law, which has its foundation in the right of labour, and may be acquired by individuals, in very unequal degrees of extent ...[25]

With inequality in landownership condemned as a breach of men's natural rights and thus, in a sentiment again echoing Hutcheson, as a *prima facie* danger to society, the way lay open for Ogilvie to propose a remedy: a 'progressive Agrarian law'.[26] He insisted that the convention that the sunk investment of labour legitimised the claim to ownership (or more specifically to the value of any improvements) was necessarily outweighed by considerations of the public good as properly pursued by the state: 'Although it may bar the claim of individuals', he maintained, 'it cannot preclude that of the legislature, as trustee and guardian of the whole.'[27] Ogilvie also denied that such a measure, by conferring greater property rights on more people, was without encouraging precedent: 'No impracticable Utopian scheme', he claimed, 'can be said to be suggested, in proposing, that property in land should be diffused to as great a number of citizens as may desire it.'[28] For there was both private and public benefit in increasing the numbers not merely occupying and working the land but also enjoying rights in relation to it. Indeed, the English in particular had shown in recent centuries that 'the land-holder has still found his advantage in communicating to the occupier of the ground, a greater and greater degree of security in his possession, and the public prosperity has kept pace with this good administration of the landholder's private estate'. As Ogilvie therefore suggested of this trend towards conferring secure legal entitlements which made a country's occupiers increasingly more like true proprietors, 'England perhaps owes that power and lustre, by which she surpasses other nations, chiefly to her having preceded them in the prosecution of these changes'.[29]

Nonetheless, Ogilvie was, in the final analysis, reluctant to urge either immediate or complete redistribution. One peculiarity of his argument was a focus on implementation not in Britain, where in any case his own discussion had shown that the empowerment of the occupiers of agricultural land had already proceeded furthest, but rather in other situations where no such progress had yet been seen. Hence Ogilvie actually had more confidence in suggesting implementation in 'certain subordinate states' such as those held by the Russians in Courland, Austria in Lombardy or the European powers in Asia, where the absolute power available to governments operating in an imperial context meant that the upheaval and political danger inherent in imposing the policy would be much less.[30] Another situation in which progress might be made was again strikingly unlike modern Britain – one where an absolute monarch had attained 'such an ascendant over all ranks of their people, that, without hazard they might avow themselves the patrons of the multitude, and supporters of natural justice, in opposition to all the confederated force of the powerful and the rich'.[31] Even so, all that was advisable in such circumstances of enforced change from above was a 'partial Reformation of the Laws respecting Property'. Moderation, in other words, was essential:

> Many schemes of innovation may be thought of, which without amounting to a complete change, or the establishment of the best system of property in land, might yet recommend themselves to the attention of absolute monarchs, as being more suddenly, and therefore more safely to be carried into execution, than any total reformation can be; and productive of very beneficial effects, though not of the best.[32]

Ogilvie even offered a number of alternative reforms that might be profitably imposed in such optimal contexts, including rendering all leases perpetual, converting them into lifetime benefices or simply translating them all into freehold. His approach was again to be purposely undogmatic, noticeably evasive of any precise details: 'These are examples only', he reiterated; 'many other schemes might be easily devised'.[33]

Even in those contexts where Ogilvie was prepared to foresee wholesale redistribution, he was clear that this could only be implemented on something approaching a consensual basis, where:

> all ranks and orders of Men in a state, forgetting for a while their subordinate and particular interests, are disposed with concurring wishes to seek for, and to adopt whatever schemes may contribute most effectually to the public good, and may become the foundations of lasting order and prosperity.[34]

Collective determination to effect thorough-going social and economic change was, however, exceedingly rare – even if Ogilvie, unsurprisingly for a professor of humanity, saw his beloved Romans in the era of the Ten Tables and Athens under Solon as striking examples. What he called this 'happy concurrence of disposing causes' was simply not very likely to arise.[35] He did offer an analysis of the kinds of conditions in which such a 'fortunate situation' might come about. These included not only 'Princes sitting on disputed thrones' and wishing to solicit the active support of the wider populace, but also states that had experienced a genuine political revolution, 'internal convulsions' as Ogilvie conceived them, and in which 'the collective body of the people' captured the government and 'obtained a just re-establishment of their natural rights to independence of cultivation, and to property in land'.[36] Again the historical precedents were deeply discouraging. Britain's 1688 Revolution, the concrete example which sprang most readily to mind, had manifestly produced no such outcome, the population not having been 'taught to understand that they were possessed of any such claim'. Indeed, it was clear that without winning over the people as a whole and promoting widespread support for the necessary measures, Ogilvie's ideas in the *Essay* were unlikely ever to come to fruition. Ultimately, then, and unlike Spence, Ogilvie did not seriously anticipate the full implementation of a worked-out plan for the comprehensive redistribution of landed property and the revolutionising of property law in Britain or anywhere else.[37]

IV

The *Essay*, a unique amalgam of Scottish Enlightenment social theory and radical political speculation, failed even to inspire the constructive debate about property ownership for which Ogilvie had probably more realistically hoped. As one reviewer observed in the *New Annual Register* in 1782: 'There hath been a publication this year of a more general legal nature, that deserves a greater degree of attention than it appears to have met with from the studious part of the world. We mean the "Essay on the Right of Property in Land..."'. Nor was it difficult to see, despite Ogilvie's attempts to deny its Utopian character, why the initial reception was so muted, for as the same reviewer remarked: 'To most readers the author's ideas will seem too speculative; and his plan will, in general, be considered as impracticable'.[38] The *Critical Review* on first publication also clearly recognised the considerable originality and breadth of imagination, acknowledging in particular its 'freedom of philosophical discussion', though it also cautioned the prospective reader that the *Essay* was indeed impossibly idealistic because it aimed 'at a reformation never to be expected in any country where the right of territorial property has once been established'.[39]

Some, however, gradually softened their criticisms, praising Ogilvie's proposals as genuinely enlightened and benevolent: 'This is the reform of a moral philosopher and a gentleman', the work of 'a sage and humane politician', claimed the London clergyman Rev. William Thomson writing in the *Literary Magazine and British Review* more than a decade later.[40] Dugald Stewart, in his lectures on political economy at Edinburgh, also referred admiringly to 'The ingenious author of an Essay on the Right of Property in Land', while Ogilvie's arguments in favour of a fairer distribution of agricultural property clearly made an impression on the young Sir James Mackintosh, who was educated at King's College in the 1780s and with whom his former professor many years afterwards corresponded about possible land reform in British India.[41]

The *Essay* was actually republished in London in both 1838 and 1891, a circumstance which gave it a more extensive nineteenth-century currency than some of what are today viewed as the crowning glories of the Scottish Enlightenment including, for example, Ferguson's works, which were mostly already out of print by then. Ogilvie was of retrospective salience to Victorian opponents of hereditary landlordism, a cause of heightened concern a hundred years after the *Essay*'s first appearance (with manifestations ranging from the land tax proposals of Henry George in the United States and the Aberdeen lawyer D. C. MacDonald, who hymned Ogilvie as 'the Euclid of Land law Reform' and oversaw the 1891 republication, to the so-called 'Highland Land War' in Scotland itself).[42]

Yet Ogilvie's posthumous significance was also evident in the place he subsequently acquired in the intellectual genealogy of socialism, especially as conceived by the Marxists. The influential Georgi Plekhanov, for example, in a discussion published in the *History of Western Literature in the Nineteenth Century* (1913), over-optimistically credited Ogilvie with having 'played a fairly significant part in promoting the development of socialist theory in Britain', an estimation endorsed in F. J. C. Hearnshaw's even more questionable description of Ogilvie's tone as 'communistic' in *A Survey of Socialism* (1928).[43] Given such colourful, anachronistic and, it has to be said, inaccurate profiling, it is perhaps to be expected that the *Essay* should eventually have proven to be a comparatively awkward text for modern students of the Scottish Enlightenment to reclaim. The effort nevertheless remains worthwhile. For in William Ogilvie we can see how the ideas of Scotland's eighteenth-century philosophers could sometimes deliver the most strikingly radical conclusions.

Notes

1 The exact timing of the *Essay*'s publication has proven surprisingly contentious. The title pages of certain extant copies, printed by John Walter of Charing Cross, give 1782, but some copies which record otherwise identical publication details actually carry no date at all. Subsequent uncertainty on this matter vexed Ogilvie himself. In a letter to William Godwin on 28 July 1793, politely chiding the Englishman for stating in print that the *Essay* had appeared in 1791 [sic], its author unambiguously states that it had actually been published 'in 1781. It has never been republished; & it is anonymous': Bodleian Library, MS Abinger c. 2, f. 26r. Initial publication in 1781 is also confirmed by the fact that the *Essay* was evaluated in the *Critical Review*, 52 (1781), pp. 296–8.

2 William Howard Greenleaf, *The British Political Tradition*, 3 vols (London, [1983–7] 2003), II, p. 356; Leslie Macfarlane, 'Socialism and Common Ownership: An Historical Perspective', in Preston T. King (ed.), *Socialism and the Common Good: New Fabian Essays* (London, 1996), p. 27; Peter Vallentyne and Hillel Steiner (eds), *The Origins of Left-Libertarianism: An Anthology of Historical Writings* (Houndmills, 2000), pp. 49–64; Leo Wiener (ed. and trans.), *The Complete Works of Count Tolstoy*, 24 vols (London, 1904–5), XXIV, p. 159.

3 Ogilvie has been treated briefly (though with another painful solecism in the title) in James Eayrs, 'The Political Ideas of the English Agrarians, 1775–1815', *The Canadian Journal of Economics and Political Science*,

18 (1952), pp. 287–302, and was wrongly credited with a programme of 'land nationalization' in Harold Perkin, 'Individualism Versus Collectivism in Nineteenth-Century Britain: A False Antithesis', *Journal of British Studies*, 17 (1977), p. 116. More recently, however, he has been usefully linked to a Scottish radical tradition in Anna Plassart, 'A Scottish Jacobin: John Oswald on Commerce and Citizenship', *Journal of the History of Ideas*, 71 (2010), pp. 263–86, while William Stafford plausibly argues that 'the "Scottish Enlightenment" produced no other text of comparable social radicalism' in his *Socialism, Radicalism and Nostalgia: Social Criticism in Britain, 1775–1830* (Cambridge, 1987), p. 2.
4 The biographical survey here draws heavily on Lionel Alexander Ritchie, 'Ogilvie, William (1736–1819)', in H. C. G. Matthew and Brian Harrison (eds), *Oxford Dictionary of National Biography* (Oxford, 2004).
5 Adam Smith, *The Theory of Moral Sentiments* (London, 1759), p. 551.
6 Adam Smith, *An Inquiry into the Nature and Causes of the Wealth of Nations*, 2 vols (London, 1776), II, p. 51.
7 I am grateful to Archive Services at the University of Glasgow for help with Ogilvie's experiences at the institution in the winter of 1760–1.
8 Paul B. Wood, *The Aberdeen Enlightenment: The Arts Curriculum in the Eighteenth Century* (Aberdeen, 1993), p. 156.
9 David Stevenson, *King's College, Aberdeen, 1560–1641: From Protestant Reformation to Covenanting Revolution* (Aberdeen, 1992), pp. 120–3.
10 Knud Haakonssen, *Natural Law and Moral Philosophy: From Grotius to the Scottish Enlightenment* (Cambridge, 1996); Thomas D. Campbell, 'Francis Hutcheson: "Father" of the Scottish Enlightenment', in R. H. Campbell and A. S. Skinner (eds), *The Origins and Nature of the Scottish Enlightenment* (Edinburgh, 1982), pp. 167–85.
11 William Ogilvie, *An Essay on the Right of Property in Land* (London, [1781]), p. 208.
12 Ibid., pp. 208–9.
13 Haakonssen, *Natural Law*, p. 220.
14 Ogilvie, *Essay*, pp. 108, 48.
15 Ibid., p. 209.
16 Francis Hutcheson, *An Inquiry into the Original of Our Ideas of Beauty and Virtue* (London, 1726), pp. 177–8; Ogilvie, *Essay*, p. 141.
17 Thomas Hobbes, *Leviathan* (London, 1651), p. 63.
18 Ogilvie, *Essay*, p. 57.
19 Ibid., p. 204.
20 Ibid., pp. 17–18.
21 Ibid., pp. 11–12.
22 Ibid., p. 12.
23 Ibid., p. 14.
24 Ibid., pp. 16–17.
25 Ibid., p. 15. Ogilvie's place in the Lockeian tradition is touched on in M. Goldie (ed.), *The Reception of Locke's Politics: Volume 6 – Wealth, Property and Commerce, 1696–1832* (London, 1999), p. 266.

26 Ogilvie, *Essay*, p. 85. Hutcheson had very briefly noted the same problem and suggested an identical solution, again probably drawing on Harrington: 'some publick interests of societies may justify such Agrarian Laws as put a stop to the immoderate acquisitions of private citizens which may prove dangerous to the state' in his *System of Moral Philosophy*, 3 vols (London, 1755), I, p. 327.
27 Ogilvie, *Essay*, p. 16. On this important Lockeian distinction, see Noel Thompson, *The Real Rights of Man: Political Economies for the Working Class, 1775–1850* (London, 1998), pp. 15–16.
28 Ogilvie, *Essay*, p. 195.
29 Ibid., p. 194.
30 Ibid., p. 64.
31 Ibid., pp. 64–5.
32 Ibid., p. 68.
33 Ibid., p. 70.
34 Ibid., pp. 71–2. Here Ogilvie neatly reverses a point of Hutcheson's, for whom an agrarian law was hypothetically a precondition rather than a consequence of participative constitutions: *System*, II, p. 259.
35 Ogilvie, *Essay*, p. 72.
36 Ibid., pp. 97–9.
37 H. T. Dickinson, *Liberty and Property: Political Ideology in Eighteenth-Century Britain* (London, 1977), pp. 267–8; T. M. Parssinen, 'Thomas Spence and the Origins of English Land Nationalization', *Journal of the History of Ideas*, 34 (1973), pp. 135–41.
38 *The New Annual Register*, 2 (1782), p. 217.
39 *Critical Review*, 52 (1781), pp. 296–8.
40 *Literary Magazine and British Review*, 12 (1794), pp. 458–9.
41 Sir William Hamilton (ed.), *Collected Works of Dugald Stewart*, 10 vols (Edinburgh, 1854–60), IX, p. 281; Jane Rendall, 'The Political Ideas and Activities of Sir James Mackintosh (1765–1832): A Study in Whiggism between 1789 and 1832' (unpublished PhD dissertation, University College, London, 1972), pp. 7–8; Kitty Datta, 'James Mackintosh, Learned Societies in India and Enlightenment Ideas', in Jennifer J. Carter and Joan H. Pittock (eds), *Aberdeen and the Enlightenment* (Aberdeen, 1986), pp. 40–51.
42 William Ogilvie, *Birthright in Land* (London, 1997), p. 27; M. Beer, *The Pioneers of Land Reform* (London, 1920), pp. v–vi.
43 Georgi Plekhanov, *Selected Philosophical Works*, 3 vols (2nd edn, Moscow, 1976), III, p. 537; F. J. C. Hearnshaw, *A Survey of Socialism: Analytical, Historical and Critical* (London, 1928), p. 176.

CHAPTER 8

Thomas Spence and James Harrington: A Case Study in Influence

Stephen M. Lee

This essay will attempt to identify the extent to which the political thought of Thomas Spence (1750–1814) was influenced by the works of James Harrington (1611–77). In his introduction to *The Political Works of Thomas Spence*, Harry Dickinson noted that Spence 'was much influenced not only by the Bible, but by the idealised societies of Thomas More's *Utopia* and James Harrington's *Oceana*', and 'accepted James Harrington's thesis that political power was derived from the possession of property, especially landed property'.[1] Other scholars have also identified the influence of Harrington, although they have been divided over its extent. Malcolm Chase argued that 'much of the distinctiveness of Spence's thought was derived ... from ... James Harrington', most particularly in his 'concern to isolate property in land as the key to political power'.[2] Chase, in addition, noted that both Spence and Harrington also:

> confidently shared a belief that landed property was capable of a meaningful and enduring redistribution. Likewise, they were dismissive of the claims of mobile property to form the basis of political citizenship or national fortune or stability. The terms in which this belief was expressed by Spence suggest a close acquaintance with Harrington's work.[3]

As further evidence of this 'special affinity', Chase highlighted the similarity between the names of the 'allegorical societies' that the two authors imagined (Oceana and Crusonia/Spensonia), noted that Spence read from Harrington's work at his trial in 1801, and reminded the reader that in *Pig's Meat* – Spence's weekly journal that ran from 1793 to 1795 and consisted largely of extracts from other writers – the writer most often quoted was Harrington.[4] Earlier work had drawn similar connections, and G. I. Gallop stated that 'James Harrington was a major influence on Spence', while Olive Rudkin identified 'one writer who had a real influence upon Spence, and he is James Harrington'.[5]

Thomas R. Knox, however, was more cautious and, while he conceded that Harrington is the only writer towards whom Spence might possibly display a 'hint of a significant debt', he argued that in general Spence used a somewhat limited knowledge of English political theorists 'to legitimate, not to inspire' his own ideas.[6]

Overall, with the partial exception of Chase, the direct or indirect influence of Harrington on Spence has been asserted rather than demonstrated in a literature that has been more concerned with Spence's own influence on later radicals.[7] This essay therefore aims to provide a more systematic account of the relationship between Harrington and Spence. Any such inquiry must begin with some brief consideration of the methodological problems to which the concept of 'influence' gives rise. Quentin Skinner has given detailed attention to the problems of attempting to identify the influence of one writer or text on another and highlights a danger especially relevant to the Harrington/Spence example:

> An argument in one work ... may happen to remind the historian of a similar argument in an earlier work, or may appear to contradict it. In either case the historian may mistakenly come to suppose that it was the intention of the later writer to refer to the earlier, and so may come to speak misleadingly of the 'influence' of the earlier work.[8]

While Skinner acknowledges that 'the concept of influence, while extremely elusive ... is far from being empty of explanatory force',[9] he is concerned to establish more rigorously the foundations of influence:

> what the necessary conditions would have to be for helping to explain the appearance in any given writer *B* of any given doctrine, by invoking the 'influence' of some earlier given writer, *A*. Such a set of conditions would at least have to include (i) that there should be a genuine similarity between the doctrines of *A* and *B*; (ii) that *B* could not have found the relevant doctrine in any writer other than *A*; (iii) that the probability of the similarity being random should be very low (i.e., even if there is a similarity, and it is shown that it could have been by *A* that *B* was influenced, it must still be shown that *B* did not as a matter of fact articulate the relevant doctrine independently).[10]

Furthermore, in earlier observations, Skinner had perceptively argued that:

> The claim to have discovered an influence of P_1 on P_2 becomes ... a remark neither about P_1 nor P_2 but about the observer himself. The observer in effect asserts that in studying P_2 he is sometimes reminded

of P_1. This may, however, represent nothing more interesting than an implied confession of ignorance. It might be that if the observer had also studied the ideas or events P_3, P_4, P_5, ... P_n some of them would have reminded him of P_1 even more strongly. It is in any case clear that on this formulation it will be impossible to assign any unambiguous meaning to the concepts of influence and inner connectedness as explanatory hypotheses, short of a complete knowledge about all of the relevant items in the aggregate of historical information.[11]

With Skinner's rigorous analysis of the concept of influence in mind, it is possible to structure an inquiry into the nature and extent of any possible influence of Harrington on Spence around a number of subquestions. Are there any similarities between the ideas of Harrington and the ideas of Spence? If there are, could Spence have got them from anywhere other than Harrington or could he have come up with them independently? And, finally, does the fact that a number of writers on Spence have been reminded, as we have seen, of the ideas of Harrington as they strove to understand Spence have any relevance in a discussion of any putative influence of Harrington on Spence?

I

With regard to the similarities between Harrington's ideas and those of Spence, commentators have largely focused on the issue of land and its relation to political power. Particular emphasis is often placed upon the alleged similarity of Harrington's and Spence's plans for land redistribution in their respective ideal commonwealths.[12] Harrington thought it a principle of good government that there should be an agrarian law that ensured no individual or oligarchy could monopolise political power as a consequence of a too unequal division of land within the commonwealth:

> An equal agrarian is a perpetual law establishing and preserving the balance of dominion, by such a distribution that no one man or number of men within the compass of the few or aristocracy can come to overpower the whole people by their possession of lands.[13]

Moreover, Harrington clearly thought that it was possible to use mechanisms such as the laws of inheritance or marriage to break up larger landholdings.[14] This aimed to create what Pocock has called 'a democracy of landholders – that is, a society where a *demos* ... of landed freemen held land in relative equality' with the distribution of 'political authority in the diversified and balanced ways that created a self-stabilising *politeia*'.[15] It should be noted here that Harrington did not attack the principle of private property or its unequal distribution but rather he wished to ensure that private property was not too unequally distributed.

Spence and his famous 'Land Plan' also proceeded from the premise that unequal political power was derived from unequal economic power, specifically from the unequal distribution of landed property. His solution to this problem was to do away with individual landed property and to reorganise society by getting the inhabitants of every parish in the country to form themselves into what Dickinson called 'parochial corporations', which would take over all the land within the parish. Land would be rented out, as would other resources such as lakes or mines, but the parish would retain ownership in common.[16] On the face of it and despite the differences between the two authors (including, most notably, Spence's effective abolition of private ownership of fixed property), there is a case for potential influence insofar as both authors sought to create a politically improved commonwealth through a reform in the way that land is held and distributed.

II

For the sake of argument, let us allow that Skinner's first test has been met. Did Spence, however, get his ideas directly from Harrington's work (tests two and three of Skinner's trio)? The fullest analysis to date of the possible links between Harrington's and Spence's ideas on land has been provided by Chase, and some of the dangers to which historians are prey and to which Skinner has pointed are evident in his analysis:

> Much of the distinctiveness of Spence's thought was derived not from Locke but from his contemporary James Harrington, a subtler and ostensibly more unusual source of inspiration. Direct references to Harrington occur only in the writing of Spence's London years. His influence, however, is more appropriately considered as part of the ideological context in which Spence grew to political maturity ... There are indeed elements common to Spence and Harrington which should more properly be considered as the legacy of the country party ideology to Spence, though their appeal may well have been reinforced by his reading of Harrington.[17]

This passage exhibits a tension between the desire to pin down a specific origin for Spence's ideas, namely Harrington, and the awareness of the inadequacy of such a reductive notion of influence. Chase is too good a historian to be unaware of the extent to which Harrington's ideas had entered the political culture of England in the century and a half since he flourished, and yet he still appears to cleave to what Skinner might call a 'mythological' explanation by arguing for a direct influence.[18]

Spence developed the essentials of his 'Land Plan' at an early stage of his career in Newcastle as a consequence of the impact of the Newcastle Town Moor affair in the early 1770s. In the aftermath of this affair, on 8 November 1775, Spence gave a lecture to the Newcastle Philosophical Society called *The Real Rights of Man*.[19] This lecture contained the details of Spence's 'Land Plan', details that he would spend the rest of his life elaborating.[20] It would be seventeen years before Spence moved to London and began to publish extracts from Harrington's works in his journal *Pig's Meat*, and he would only make direct reference to Harrington in his own work once, in *The Important Trial of Thomas Spence* (1803).[21] In this work he gave an account of his 1801 trial for sedition and recounted how he quoted verbatim from *The Examination of James Harrington, Taken in the Tower of London by the Earl of Lauderdale* – the first work of Harrington's he had quoted in *Pig's Meat*.[22]

It would appear, therefore, that while there is a certain resemblance between the ideas of Harrington and Spence on land distribution, there is little reason to conclude that Skinner's other conditions are met. Spence could easily – given the extent to which Harrington's ideas had entered the vocabulary of English political thought – have got them from his reading of other authors or, indeed, developed them independently. We are left with the impression that, to adapt Skinner's words, historians are simply asserting that in studying Spence they are sometimes reminded of Harrington.

As it has been widely noted, however, the author most commonly quoted in *Pig's Meat* was in fact Harrington. This is undoubtedly the case, as the following table (see Table 8.1) of the five most cited authors in *Pig's Meat* makes clear:[23]

Table 8.1 Authors cited in *Pig's Meat*

Author	Number of separate appearances in *Pig's Meat*, I–III
James Harrington	24
John Trenchard and Thomas Gordon, *Cato's Letters*	13
George, Lord Lyttelton	10
Richard Lewis, *The candid philosopher*	9
Joel Barlow	8

If one is to believe Spence's attributions, fourteen of these twenty-four passages come from 'Harrington's Oceana' and two from 'Harrington's Oceana and his other works'. By comparing the excerpts in *Pig's Meat* with the 1771 Toland edition of Harrington's works, however, one can precisely identify the passages used by Spence in terms of the specific original works by Harrington. An interesting picture emerges:[24]

Table 8.2 Sources for Harrington citations in *Pig's Meat*

Work	Number of citations
The Prerogative of popular Government	12
[John Hall], *The Grounds and Reasons of Monarchy*	4
Political Aphorisms	2
A System of Politics delineated in short and easy Aphorisms	2
The examination of James Harrington	1
A Word concerning a House of Peers	1
The Commonwealth of Oceana	1
The Art of Lawgiving	1

In fact, only one passage is from *Oceana* itself and those historians who believe that Spence was indebted to Harrington's ideas for a landed democracy advanced in *Oceana* for aspects of his 'Land Plan' would appear to have been misled by Spence's reference to 'Harrington's Oceana', which appears to have been shorthand for Toland's edition of *The Oceana and Other Works*. In fact, Spence made greatest use of Harrington's *Prerogative of Popular Government*, a defence by Harrington of the ideas expressed in *Oceana* prompted by the attacks on it since its publication. Moreover, the second most frequent source was not, in fact, by Harrington but by John Hall, albeit habitually published in all Toland's editions of Harrington's works.

III

What can we say about the purported influence of Harrington on Spence? There are certainly no grounds for believing that Spence derived his ideas for his famous 'Land Plan' directly from Harrington. The plan was formulated in the early to mid-1770s and the earliest reference to

Harrington in Spence's work comes in the form of extracts in *Pig's Meat* in the early 1790s. The most recent edition of Harrington's works published in Spence's lifetime was in 1771, but apart from a chronological conjunction there are no grounds for believing that Spence read it prior to developing his own plan. It is true that *Pig's Meat* purports to contain passages collected by Spence 'in the course of his reading for more than twenty years', but again there is no evidence that he actually read Harrington prior to conceiving the 'Land Plan'. Moreover, it was not to *Oceana* that Spence appears to have been drawn but to *The Prerogative of Popular Government*, which does, nevertheless, defend some of Harrington's views on land as expressed in *Oceana*. It would appear to be the case, as historians such as Chase have recognised, that Harrington's country party ideas had so entered English political discourse that Spence need not have read Harrington and been directly influenced by him to arrive at similar positions. As Knox has written, Spence used the ideas collected in *Pig's Meat* to legitimate his previously worked out position.[25]

Where, then, did Spence get his ideas? The immediate danger here, of course, is that having found Harrington (P_1 as it were) wanting as a source of influence on Spence's ideas we desperately cast around looking for some other writer or writers (P_2, P_3, P_4, ... P_n) who might have influenced him instead, only to find ourselves faced with the exact same problem with the details changed. We might look, for example, to the figure of Rev. James Murray (1732–82). When living in Newcastle upon Tyne, Spence's family attended Murray's Presbyterian chapel, and Murray defended Spence against expulsion from the Newcastle Philosophical Society in the aftermath of his lecture in 1775. In particular, Murray posed eighteen questions to Spence's opponents, many of which concerned issues relating to land and which Spence added to later editions of his lecture and also included in *Pig's Meat*.[26] In addition, Spence included three extracts from Murray's *Sermons for the General Fast Day* (1781) in *Pig's Meat*.[27] Interestingly, however, Spence makes no use of Murray's most explicit treatment of the issue of land ownership, which is contained in the fourth sermon of his *New Sermons for Asses* (1781).[28]

We might also expand our inquiry from the influence of one preacher to that of a sect as a whole, namely the followers of John Glas (1695–1773) (known as Glasites or Sandemanians). Spence's father and brother were Glasites and it has been suggested by Knox and Dickinson that Spence himself came under the influence of Glasite ideas, particularly those regarding property.[29] A recent history has summarised these ideas:

> Glasites did not hold property in common, nor were members compelled to contribute their money or property into any kind of common fund

for even redistribution ... [but] Glas maintained that every member is bound to consider his worldly wealth at the service of the church, especially in its ministering to needy brethren.[30]

This is suggestive of possible influence, but again we lack any actual evidence and Spence made no explicit references to the ideas of the Glasites.

We are probably on safer ground if we look at the political milieu in which Spence grew up in Newcastle upon Tyne and the North-east of England. In an important investigation, Dickinson analysed the vibrant political culture that developed there in the late eighteenth century.[31] Beginning with the stimulus provided by the Middlesex election case in 1768–9, during which the propaganda issued by John Wilkes and his followers in the Society for the Supporters of the Bill of Rights appeared extensively in the local press, radicals in the North-east began to challenge local oligarchies, as Wilkes had done at the national level. This led to the development of a number of debating clubs, one of which was the Philosophical Society, founded in 1775 and at which (as noted earlier) Spence gave his incendiary lecture on the rights of man. James Murray was also an active participant in this culture of public political debate, and he and Spence were particularly active in the campaign against the enclosing of the local common land known as the Town Moor. The campaign was successful and the passing of the Newcastle Town Moor Act in June 1774 against the wishes of the corporation was a victory for the freemen against the local oligarchy. The timing is interesting here, as this campaign occurred in the early 1770s, presumably at the same time as Spence was developing the ideas that became his controversial lecture, *The Real Rights of Man*, given in 1775.

This, crucially, gets us to the issue underlying the fruitless search for influence: is it because Thomas Spence was a self-educated, poor, often marginalised figure that we assume that he must have received any complex ideas that he had from somebody else more 'appropriate' such as Harrington or Murray? If that is the underlying assumption behind the persistent desire to locate the source of Spence's ideas in the thoughts of someone else, then it is a classic example of what Edward Thompson called 'the enormous condescension of posterity'.[32] Instead, we should suggest that Spence's 'Land Plan' might be a product of the fact that as a marginalised autodidact he was able to think things through from the perspective of his own experiences and situation in society, free from the overbearing influence of other thinkers. By putting Spence himself back at the centre of his own work, we restore an agency to him that is downplayed by an obsessive hunt for the sources of his ideas and reaffirm the dangers that historians face when they fall under the mythology of influence.

Table 8.3 *Comparison of Pig's Meat, I–III (1793–5) with The Oceana and other works of James Harrington, with an account of his life by Iohn Toland (1771) and The political works of James Harrington, ed. J. G. A. Pocock (1977)*

Pig's Meat	Title of extract (with typography preserved)	Possible source in *Oceana etc.* (1771)	Pocock (1977)
I.79-81	*A valuable Collection of general political principles, or fundamental truths in Government: Extracted from* HARRINGTON'S OCEANA *and his other works.* [Portions of this Collection will frequently be inserted in the Course of this Publication.] *An extract from the examination of James Harrington, when confined in the Tower, by the Earl of Lauderdale,* &c.	*The examination of James Harrington, taken in the tower of London by the earl of Lauderdale, Sir George Carteret, and Sir Edward Walker*, p. xxx	pp. 858-59
I.83-5	*Continuation of Extracts from* HARRINGTON'S OCEANA, *and his other works.*	[John Hall], *The Grounds and Reasons of Monarchy*, pp. 3-4 (two extracts)	n/a
I.96-8	GENERAL POLITICAL APHORISMS OR MAXIMS. FROM HARRINGTON'S WORKS.	*Political Aphorisms* [92-4, 97-9, 102 (part), 104 (part), 106, 109, 110-18, 120], p. 488-90	pp. 774-78
I.114-18	*Whether the Balance of Dominion in Land be the natural cause of Empire?* FROM HARRINGTON'S OCEANA.	*The Prerogative of popular Government*, pp. 226-28	pp. 404-6
I.126-8	A GOVERNMENT OF CITISENS IS INVULNERABLE. FROM HARRINGTON'S OCEANA.	*The Prerogative of popular Government*, pp. 256-7	pp. 441-43
I.212-13	POPULAR ASSEMBLIES UNDERSTAND ONLY THEIR OWN INTERESTS. *From Harrington's Oceana.*	*The Prerogative of popular Government*, pp. 263-4	pp. 450-51
I.272-74	GENERAL POLITICAL APHORISMS, OR MAXIMS. *From* HARRINGTON'S WORKS.	*Political Aphorisms* [1, 5, 11, 14-18, 23-26, 36, 38, 63-70, 85 (presented as two separate aphorisms), 86-9], pp. 483-84, 486-8	pp. 762-66, 770-71, 773-74

Pig's Meat	Title of extract (with typography preserved)	Possible source in *Oceana etc.* (1771)	Pocock (1977)
II.106-8	FUNDAMENTAL POLITICAL APHORISMS OR MAXIMS. [*From Harrington's System of Politics.*]	*A System of Politics delineated in short and easy Aphorisms* [I.14-17; II.4-6; IV.21, 26; V.3, 18], pp. 465-66, 469-70, 472	pp. 834-35, 838-39, 842
II.108-110	PRIVATE INDIVIDUALS MAY PLAN MODELS OF GOVERNMENT, [*From Harrington's Oceana.*]	*The Prerogative of popular Government*, pp. 219-20	pp. 395-96
II.140	COMMONWEALTHS capable of raising the greatest Armies in Proportion to Territory. [*From Harrington's Oceana.*]	*The Prerogative of popular Government*, p. 258	p. 444
III.120-21	THE AMBIGUITY OF KINGLY TITLES (*From Grounds and Reasons of Monarchy in* HARRINGTON'S OCEANA.)	[John Hall], *The Grounds and Reasons of Monarchy*, pp. 6-7 (two extracts)	n/a
III.139-40	ENGLAND IS A COMMONWEALTH. [*From* HARRINGTON'S *Works.*] Dated Feb. 20, 1659	*A Word concerning a House of Peers*, pp. 441-2	p. 704
III.169-70	Invention as much the Property of an Individual, as Judgment is of an Assembly. [*From* HARRINGTON'S OCEANA]	'Epistle to the Reader', *The Prerogative of popular Government*, p. 214	pp. 390-91
III.171	REMARKABLE OBSERVATIONS OF EMINENT PHILOSOPHERS ... *Fourthly. Of* HARRINGTON	*The Prerogative of popular Government*, p. 299	p. 495
III.181-2	SUCCESSION GENERALLY FOUNDED BY USURPERS. (*From Grounds and Reasons of Monarchy in* HARRINGTON'S OCEANA.)	[John Hall], *The Grounds and Reasons of Monarchy*, pp. 10-11 (with slight modifications)	n/a
III.187	*Governments take their Forms according to the Balance of Property.* (*From* HARRINGTON'S OCEANA.)	*The Prerogative of Popular Government*. p. 122	p. 398

Pig's Meat	Title of extract (with typography preserved)	Possible source in *Oceana etc.* (1771)	Pocock (1977)
III.192-93	POLITICAL APHORISMS, OR, MAXIMS RESPECTING RELIGION. (*From* HARRINGTON'S *system of* POLITICS.)	*A System of Politics etc.*[VI. 8 (part), 9-10, 16-21, 28], pp.474-76	pp. 845-46
III.195-7	LANDED PROPERTY ONLY FOUNDATION OF EMPIRE. (*From* HARRINGTON'S OCEANA.)	*The Commonwealth of Oceana*, pp. 37-8	pp. 163-65
III.258-9	AN EQUAL COMMONWEALTH NEED NOT FEAR SEDITION. (*From Harrington's Oceana*)	*The Prerogative of popular Government*, pp. 242-3	pp. 424-25
III.269-71	HARRINGTON's ANSWER TO THREE OBJECTIONS AGAINST POPULAR GOVERNMENTS.	*The Prerogative of popular Government*, pp. 356-7 (abbreviated)	pp. 564-66
III.274-76	REPUBLICS ARE AS MUCH JURE DIVINO AS KINGSHIPS. (*From Grounds and Reasons of Monarchy in* HARRINGTON'S OCEANA.)	[John Hall], *The Grounds and Reasons of Monarchy*, pp. 5-6	n/a
III.279-80	GOD INTENDED A COMMONWEALTH AMONG THE ISRAELITES BY DIVIDING THE LAND AMONG ALL PEOPLE. (*From Harrington's Oceana*.)	*The Prerogative of popular Government*, pp. 272-3	pp. 462-63
III.280-82	THE DANGER OF SUFFERING TOO LONG CONTINUANCE OF THE PUBLIC SERVANTS IN OFFICE. (*From Harrington's Oceana*.)	*The Prerogative of popular Government*, pp. 295-6 [Actually not by Harrington but a quote from Macchiavelli inserted by Harrington; identified as *Discorsi*, III, 24 by Pocock (p. 491n3)]	pp. 490-91
III.282-3	WHETHER MEN OR MONEY BE THE NERVE OF WAR. (*From Harrington's Art of Lawgiving*.)	*The Art of Lawgiving*, p. 430	p. 690

Notes

1 H. T. Dickinson (ed.), *The Political Works of Thomas Spence* (Newcastle, 1982), pp. vii, xiv.
2 Malcolm Chase, *'The People's Farm': English Radical Agrarianism 1775–1840* (Oxford, 1988), pp. 32–3.
3 Ibid., p. 33.
4 Ibid., p. 34; T. M. Parssinen, 'Thomas Spence and the Origins of English Land Nationalization', *Journal of the History of Ideas*, 25 (1973), p. 140, n. 19.
5 G. I. Gallop (ed.), *Pigs' Meat: The Selected Writings of Thomas Spence, Radical and Pioneer Land Reformer* (Nottingham, 1982), p. 28; Olive D. Rudkin, *Thomas Spence and His Connections* (New York, 1966), p. 19.
6 Thomas R. Knox, 'Thomas Spence: The Trumpet of Jubilee', *Past and Present*, 76 (1977), p. 79, n. 8.
7 See, for the best example, Iain McCalman, *Radical Underworld: Prophets, Revolutionaries and Pornographers in London, 1795–1840* (Cambridge, 1988).
8 Quentin Skinner, 'Meaning and Understanding in the History of Ideas', *History and Theory*, 8 (1969), p. 25.
9 Skinner, 'Meaning and Understanding', p. 25.
10 Ibid., p. 26.
11 Quentin Skinner, 'The Limits of Historical Explanations', *Philosophy*, 41 (1966), p. 212.
12 See, for example, Chase, *People's Farm*, p. 34: 'Generally, as one seeks out affinities between Spence and Harrington, it is the purpose and character of their agrarian reforms which arguably are most significant.'
13 James Harrington, *The Commonwealth of Oceana and a System of Politics*, ed. J. G. A. Pocock (Cambridge, 1992), p. 33.
14 Ibid., p. 101.
15 J. G. A. Pocock, *The Machiavellian Moment: Florentine Political Thought and the Atlantic Republican Tradition* (Princeton, 1975), pp. 387–8.
16 Dickinson (ed.), *Political Works*, p. xii.
17 Chase, *People's Farm*, p. 32.
18 Skinner, 'Meaning and Understanding', p. 26.
19 Its original title would appear to have been *Property in Land, Everyone's Right* (see the homepage of the Thomas Spence Society: http://thomas-spence-society.co.uk/index.html [accessed 20 March 2015] for the recent discovery of an original printed version).
20 Dickinson (ed.), *Political Works*, pp. ix–x. See also T. M. Parsinnen, 'Thomas Spence', p. 137, n. 10.
21 Chase offers this as evidence for the influence of Harrington on Spence (*People's Farm*, p. 34), but given its singular nature it could be taken as the opposite. There is also one other interesting indirect reference to Harrington in Spence's work. Spence was a language reformer and

he produced a version of his 1803 work *The Constitution of Spensonia* in phonetic spelling to which he gave the title *Dh'e K'onst'itush'un 'ov Sp'ensone'a, A Kŭntre ĭn Fare Lănd, Sĭtuatĕd bĕtween Utope'a 'and Oshean'a: Brŏŏt frŏm dhĕns bi K'apt. Sw'alo* [*A Country in Fairy Land, Situated between Utopia and Oceana: Brought from thence By Capt. Swallow*] (London, 1803?).

22 Dickinson (ed.), *Political Works*, pp. 92–103.
23 The periodical was published in collected form as: *One Pennyworth of Pig's Meat; or, Lessons for the Swinish Multitude* (London, 1793); *Pigs' Meat; or, Lessons for the Swinish Multitude* (London, 1794); *Pigs' Meat; or, Lessons for the People* (London, 1794–5) [hereafter *Pig's Meat*, I–III]. Despite the differing place of the apostrophe in vols II and III and the fact that, given its Burkean origins, there must be more than one pig, the most commonly used form is *Pig's* rather than *Pigs'*. The table gives a cumulative total of all separate passages used by Spence, but takes no account of the cumulative length of these passages.
24 See the Appendix to this article for a detailed comparison of the works identified as being by Harrington in *Pig's Meat*, I–III with James Harrington, *The Oceana and Other Works of James Harrington, with an Account of his Life by John Toland* (London, 1771) and J. G. A. Pocock (ed.), *The Political Works of James Harrington* (Cambridge, 1977). The 1771 edition of Toland was the last to appear prior to Spence's career as a polemicist, though it is entirely possible that he used other editions or intermediary sources to compile his extracts.
25 Knox, 'Thomas Spence', p. 79, n. 8.
26 Ibid., pp. 79–81; Dickinson (ed.), *Political Works*, pp. xii–x; Thomas Spence, *The Rights of Man, as Exhibited in a Lecture, Read at the Philosophical Society, in Newcastle* (London, 1793), pp. 36–8; *Pig's Meat*, III, pp. 240–1.
27 *Pig's Meat*, I, pp. 165–7; II, pp. 23–8, 74–6.
28 James Murray, *New Sermons for Asses. By the Author of Sermons for Asses* (London, 1781), pp. 77–102.
29 Knox, 'Thomas Spence', p. 79; Dickinson (ed.), *Political Works*, p. vii.
30 John Howard Smith, *The Perfect Rule of the Christian Religion: A History of Sandemanianism in the Eighteenth Century* (Albany, 2008), p. 59.
31 H. T. Dickinson, *Radical Politics in the North-East of England in the Later Eighteenth Century* (Durham, 1979).
32 E. P. Thompson, *The Making of the English Working Class* (Harmondsworth, 1968), p. 12.

CHAPTER 9

Thomas Spence, Children's Literature and 'Learning ... Debauched by Ambition'

Matthew Grenby

One of the most infamous phrases of the late eighteenth- and early nineteenth-century 'war of ideas' was Edmund Burke's characterisation of the people as a 'swinish multitude'. It was an insult so revealingly contemptuous that those opposed to Burke's views seized on it with glee: men like Thomas Spence, whose periodical *One Penny Worth of Pig's Meat: Lessons for the Swinish Multitude* (1793–5) cast Burke's insult back in his face. Spence's reputation has oscillated dramatically in the two hundred years since his death in 1814. Having been so influential that an Act of Parliament was passed specifically prohibiting 'All societies or clubs calling themselves Spencean or Spencean Philanthropists', and influencing a long line of radicals including the Chartist leaders and Karl Marx, Spence came to be regarded as an eccentric extremist.[1]

It was Harry Dickinson (like Spence, a scion of the North-east of England) who, by producing the first modern edition of Spence's political works in 1982, enabled and perhaps obliged historians to take Spence's ideas seriously.[2] As Dickinson's edition shows, Spence repeatedly deployed Burke's scornful epithet to reveal the inherent self-interest of the landlord class, the object of Spence's ire since his first political writings in the mid-1770s. What is often forgotten, however, is that Burke's infamous 'swinish multitude' barb was used in the context of scholarship and education. 'Along with its natural protectors and guardians,' Burke had written, '*learning* will be cast into the mire, and trodden down under the hoofs of a swinish multitude.'[3] In this essay, I want to argue that Spence would have found this particularly provocative. A teacher himself, Spence recognised how important children's education was to social and political renewal. Further, the claim I want to advance here is that his understanding of education's potential was inspired at least in part by his exposure, before his move from Newcastle to London in around 1787, to a surprisingly radical children's literature.

Dickinson's edition included the first modern reprinting of one of Spence's more unusual works, *A Supplement to the History of Robinson Crusoe, Being the History of Crusonia, or Robinson Crusoe's Island,*

Down to the Present Time, published in Newcastle by Thomas Saint in 1782. Dickinson, in fact, reproduced a 'new edition' in conventional English, the tract having first been published earlier that same year in the reformed, phonetic 'Crusonian' language that Spence had already developed, as *A S'upl'im'int too thĭ Hĭstĭre ŏv Rŏbĭnsĭn Kruzo*. Dickinson did not, however, reproduce the entire text, omitting three short stories that follow the main section. In the *S'upl'im'int* Spence had appended a story called 'An Hĭstĭre ŏv thĭ Riz ănd Progrĕs ŏv Lĭrnĭng, ĭn Lĭlĭpŭt, Braut ovĭr ĭn thĭ Shĭp Swălĭ, bi Mâstĭr Rămbĭl'. In the 'new edition', he changed the title of this section, adding the coda 'And the Changes it produced there in the Manners and Customs', and included two further short stories, 'The History of the Mercolians, communicated by Master Brolio of Lilliput' and 'An Account of what passed on a journey with old Zigzag'.

Spence himself has sometimes been identified as the author or these three stories, and they have been seen as illustrations of his political thought. Francis Place, for instance, wrote in his manuscript notes for a memoir of Spence that, like the 'supplement to Robinson Crusoe ... the Learning of Lilliput and the History of the Mercolians are pictures of what he [Spence] supposed would be the practice and condition of people under his system'.[4] The early biographers and some modern critics have made the same assumption.[5] In fact, they were not by Spence. All three stories were appropriations from titles published in London in the 1750s and 1760s by the pioneer of children's literature, John Newbery. 'The Rise and Progress of Learning in Lilliput' and 'The History of the Mercolians' were from Newbery's *The Lilliputian Magazine*, the first children's periodical, published in three parts in 1751 and 1752. 'A journey with old Zigzag' was from *The Valentine's Gift*, published by Newbery probably in late 1764 or early 1765. Spence was no plagiarist. Throughout his career, he reprinted snippets of texts that supported his case, notably in *Pig's Meat*. His appropriation of excerpts from Newbery's children's books was an early example of his practice of argument-by-bricolage. But it can also reveal much about both the nature of early children's literature and the development of Spence's thinking.

I

Spence, born in 1750 in Newcastle, was in exactly the right place at the right time to be exposed to the 'new' children's literature being developed by Newbery. Although Newbery had started publishing for children in the mid-1740s and although his works were advertised in the Newcastle press,[6] Spence would have been too young, and too poor, to meet with these children's books when they first appeared. However, it is highly probable that Spence encountered Newbery's publications in his twenties, with the debate over the enclosure of the Newcastle Town Moor just crystallising his political opinions, through the Newcastle printer and bookseller Thomas Saint.

In the eighteenth century Newcastle was one of the most important centres for print culture in England outside London, and Saint was one of the enterprising printers who helped to make it so. From the early 1760s, he published a wide range of material (including Spence's *Property in Land Every One's Right* and *Grand Repository of the English Language* in 1775) and even experimented with his own books for children. Newbery died in 1767 and was succeeded by rival sets of heirs, and it was sometime after then that Saint began a thorough programme of pirating children's books, setting them in new editions, with new illustrations for the northern market. Between 1777 and 1785, Nigel Tattersfield has found that Saint published at least twenty-four Newbery piracies in Newcastle (among a total of forty-five children's books, including five from another London publisher, John Marshall). At first he attempted to disguise what he was doing with false imprints. Later he became more blatant. Saint also acted as agent for a much more profitable commodity distributed by Newbery and his successors, their range of patent medicines, the most celebrated of which was the infamous Dr James's Fever Powders. So long as Saint continued to bring in handsome profits for the Newberys from the medicines, Tattersfield speculates, his literary piracies were ignored or perhaps even given the Newberys' sanction.[7]

Some of what Spence found in the children's books published by Newbery would have had instant appeal, and may even have had a role in forming his views and the way he would go on to express them. From the anonymous *Valentine's Gift*, Spence took 'Some Account of Old Zigzag, and of the Horn Which He Used to Understand the Language of Birds, Beasts, Fishes, and Insects'. This was a series of fables with a consistent political edge. Zigzag hears the bee berate the wasp for his lack of industry, for instance. But the wasp answers back that 'Your property is not your own', and forcefully argues that there is little point in labouring 'for the thief will come in the night, that tyrant man will steal on you in the dark, and murder you, and set fire to your house, in order to rob you of your food. Under the dominion of tyrants, property is never secure.' Likewise, the cow laments to the ploughman that 'I have ploughed your ground for you, got your corn, carried it to market, and done all I could to make you happy, and now you are going to murder me.' But cows 'were made for the use of man', protests Zigzag:

> So you all say indeed, replied the Ox; but I can see no reason for it. You men are but tenants of the earth as well as we; and I don't no [sic] why one creature should not live as well as another.[8]

It is the language as much as the sentiment that makes this sound so Spencean. Throughout his career, Spence employed animal imagery – the angry hog and his self-characterisation as 'free as a cat' on his tokens, for instance, or the lions, tigers, hyenas, wolves and foxes ('Bloody Tyrants') being overthrown by the united cattle to bring in a 'Reign of Justice and Peace' in one of his fables.[9] Alastair Bonnett has observed that Spence identified 'with animals as a repository of incorruptible freedom and defiance' and 'found within the animal kingdom the kind of unchanging, primordial integrity that he wished to find in people'.[10] It is this, presumably, that drew Spence to poach 'Old Zigzag'. Indeed, the 'gaffer rook' Zigzag overhears seems to out-Spence Spence, remonstrating that 'We have master rooks and madam crows who lounge about and live upon the labours of others', always complaining of ill-health only 'because they will not work and be well'.[11] That such 'Spencean' material appeared in a children's book emphasises that early children's books were not always prim and pious works of moral and didactic tendency. Rather they could often be caustic and subversive and, as shown by the other two stories Spence appropriated, they could even engage with specific political contexts.

The Lilliputian Magazine, from which Spence took these two other stories, contained a mixture of material, from riddles to bible stories and songs to drastically abridged novels. Its authorship remains obscure, though Christopher Smart – known as a poet but also a performer, journalist, dissident, religious maniac and Newbery's stepson – certainly contributed some material and may have written much more.[12] 'A History of the Rise and Progress of Learning in Lilliput' was one of its four short utopian tales, begun in the first part of the *Magazine* and continued in the second. It is set in Lilliput under the reign of 'a morose, ill-natured, illiterate' and warlike king, Abiho, 'universally hated for his cruel and inhuman disposition'. Under his reign grows up a precociously learned boy named Billy Hiron. His 'scheme for the cultivation of learning', proposed when he was only ten, is rejected by Abiho. However, Abiho soon dies and his young son Miram ascends the throne. He ends his father's wars and is thus left 'at full liberty to reform some vices in the state; and to encourage virtue, learning and commerce'. Adhering to Billy Hiron's principles, 'liberty sprung up' and 'the prince and the people, [and] the whole community was exceedingly happy'.[13]

It is difficult to resist reading this as political allegory, particularly when we recall its publication date. The *Magazine*'s frame story, giving an account of the putative 'Society' that publishes it, is dated 26 December 1750. But advertisements in the London newspapers record that the first part probably appeared in early March 1751.[14] Just then

George II was dangerously ill, largely confined to his bed and, according to a contemporary report, he had '3 or 4 mortal disorders' and 'cannot recover'.[15] Inevitably then, the apparently dying George II seems the model for the expiring Abiho in Lilliput. Abiho is ill-natured, uncultivated and warlike. George II (according to Lord Hervey, a member of his intimate household) 'often used to brag of the contempt he had for books and letters' and was known for his 'brusqueries to everybody by turn'.[16] And because he led the country into the War of the Austrian Succession (1740–8) and had to deal with protracted Jacobite rebellions, it might easily be said of him, as it was of Abiho, that his 'pride and ambition led him into continual wars with the neighbouring nations and domestic quarrels with his own subjects'.[17]

In the event, it was not George II but his son, Frederick, Prince of Wales, who died, unexpectedly, on 20 March 1751. The succession of Miram in Lilliput was perhaps connected, though the precise chronology is problematic, since the first part of the *Lilliputian Magazine* (which probably included the first part of 'Rise and Progress of Learning') was advertised as being published on 'this day' on 2, 5 and 7 March (this latitude giving some indication of why Newbery's advertisements are not always reliable), which is to say several days before Prince Frederick's sudden demise. Yet the comparison is striking. Frederick's death left his twelve-year-old son, George (later George III), as his heir. Miram is described as 'a very little boy when he ascended the throne' of Lilliput. Both were associated with books, George having been the dedicatee of (and depicted in) various children's books in the 1740s and Miram having read 'the best books he could procure'.[18]

Whether or not the author of 'Rise and Progress of Learning' was writing in a world in which Prince George had suddenly become the immediate heir to the throne is unclear; what is clear is that the death of a cruel and ignorant king was being imagined – a radical act, even if not in the precise sense of the law of High Treason (in which 'to imagine the king's death' meant deliberately to plot it). So too was his replacement by a young and very different prince who could usher in a new age of peace and cultivation. Attributing 'Rise and Progress of Learning' to Christopher Smart would help to explain this political tendency, for Smart (according to his most recent biographer) was a supporter of Prince Frederick and a central member of the Leicester House movement and, following Frederick's death, probably identified the young George, Prince of Wales as a 'likely source of patronage'.[19] But thirty years later, it was doubtless not the localised politics of the early 1750s that appealed to Spence, but the dramatisation of an iniquitous regime's fall and of society's regeneration by two young people, an infant king and his precocious advisor.

Spence also had other reasons to appropriate 'Rise and Progress of Learning'. His *S'upl'im'int* was designed as a school book which could support his extraordinary spelling reform. He had noticed that the notoriously unphonetic spelling of English prevented ordinary people from reading and thus from learning about, and contributing to, their society. Its effect was thus politically and socially repressive. Whoever wrote 'Rise and Progress of Learning in Lilliput' shared this concern with language and aimed to broaden access to learning. In the second instalment of the *Magazine* it is explained how Master Hiron, recognising 'that the language of the *Lilliputians* was irregular, and difficult to be understood', established an 'alphabet of letters, and regulated their sounds'. In one sense this is Spencean *avant la lettre*. In another, it would have been a provocation to Spence, since what follows is a fairly conventional presentation of the letters of the standard English alphabet and their sounds, singly and when combined. 'Rise and Progress of Learning' records how a defective language (the 'Etrolan' dialect of Lilliputian) was replaced, under the guidance of the King (presumably Miram) by English, which, once learned, opens up the road to social mobility and a better world: 'by these twenty-six letters ... little boys and girls can do very surprizing things, and learn a great deal in a very little time, if they please'. And 'learning is the road to preferment, to riches, to honour, and even wisdom itself'.[20]

Spence responded with wholesale alterations. He ran the two parts of 'Rise and Progress' together and presented not Lilliputian, but English, which 'the Kings' and those 'at Court' had 'endeavoured to ... establish throughout their Dominions', as the language that was in dire need of reform, since:

> Their Spelling too was all confused, being without Rule or Order, and the only sure Maxim they had laid down was, that all Words which could be sounded different Ways were to be written according to the hardest, harshest, longest, and most unusual Sound; so that a Life-time was little enough to learn their Spelling in.

Thus Billy Hiron 'established the Crusonian Alphabet and Manner of Spelling' (that is to say, Spence's reformed language, in which the *S'upl'im'int* was originally printed).[21] This is the thirty-two-year-old Spence at his most self-congratulatory, presenting himself as a second Billy Hiron, reformer of language, political prodigy and benign liberator of a failing nation.

The same quasi-messianic theme is at the core of the third story that Spence appropriated, called 'The History of the Mercolians'. The Mercolians are the inhabitants of a rich, strong nation located on an island in the Lilliputian sea. Notably like the British, they 'had by their industry, trade, and commerce, acquired immense riches' and had made other nations 'their slaves and dependents'. However, with all this affluence, they became corrupt: 'They grew proud, insolent and idle' and 'The only use they made of their riches was to purchase them new invented pleasures.' The state falls, overwhelmed by its former dependents. 'Such was the fate of the MERCOLIANS; and may this be a warning to all future states.'[22]

Again, what stands out is the apparent enmeshment in contemporary politics. Besides growing 'effeminate' and generally decadent, three specific causes of the Mercolians' fall are given: that 'they chose their generals and officers from a foreign people'; that 'they took counsel of strangers'; and that 'They made a law to naturalise the slaves and refuse of other nations.'[23] That Britain relied too heavily on 'an international fraternity' of mercenaries for its generals was a common eighteenth-century complaint.[24] The French Huguenot John Ligonier, who rose to become commander-in-chief of the British army, was not untypical, and took much of the blame for a series of defeats in the War of Austrian Succession. The 'counsel of strangers' could have many applications, possibly referring to Princess Augusta of Saxe-Gotha, wife of Prince Frederick, and whom Henry Pelham controversially sought to appoint as regent, in the event of George II's death, to her young son Prince George. Or it might refer to Samson Gideon, 'the greatest of mid-eighteenth century loan contractors', who had supported the regime during the wars and was to be caught up at the centre of the debate on the 'Jew Bill' in 1753.[25] *The Lilliputian Magazine* was first published before the Jewish Naturalization Act, so the revealing reference to the naturalisation of 'the slaves and refuse of other nations' cannot pertain to it directly. Yet it was surely a reference to the equally vitriolic if lesser-known general Naturalization Bills of 1747 and 1751. These were controversies that generated a large paper war: pamphlets, ballads, newspapers, prints and, apparently, even children's books.[26] It is also notable that Smart wrote against the general Naturalization Bills in some of his 1751 journalism.[27]

It was what happens next in Mercolia that would have interested Smart. Some of the 'best families' of Mercolia set up a new state on another island, led by a fourteen-year-old boy named Turvolo.[28] Under his guidance, this new state becomes a utopia, strikingly egalitarian. Turvolo builds temples of Fame and of Virtue. Knowing that 'worth and honour are confined to no particular class of people', Turvolo insists that the Temple of Fame he establishes, reachable only by way of the Temple of Virtue, should be decorated with the 'names of all those who were good men, whether ploughmen, tradesmen, or whatever else' and goes on to underline his point: 'Nor did either honour or infamy descend from the father to the son, for every man was to win his own laurels, and be accountable for his own actions *only*.'

Once more, we could read this in the light of contemporary politics. As shown in the engraving that accompanies the text, the temples' domed, circular form (a 'tholos') is reminiscent of the Temple of Ancient Virtue, built to the design of William Kent at Stowe in 1737. Turvolo's temples also fulfil a similar function to the Temple of British Worthies built at Stowe in 1734–5 as a pantheon for great men of all ranks (particularly radicals). Stowe was the seat of Richard Temple, first Viscount Cobham, and was a centre of political opposition and associated with Prince Frederick's party. Mercolia may then offer a continuation of the attack on George II begun in 'Rise and Progress of Learning'. However, more evidently Spencean (and certainly going well beyond the views of the Leicester House party) was the other law introduced by Turvolo, that, every four years, all inhabitants 'bring their money into the public treasury, from which an equal distribution was again made, to each person his share', those who have made money in each cycle receiving nothing save 'the thanks of the community'.[29]

Such a radical redistribution of wealth went further than almost all eighteenth-century utopian writing, though it evidently had its roots in the idea of the 'jubilee' set out in Leviticus (25: 8–17), which ordained an economic redistribution and cancelling of debts after every fifty years. As Malcolm Chase has shown, the jubilee had featured in English radical thought from Bunyan (and intriguingly, as Clement Hawes has noted, Smart made much of the idea in his later religious verse).[30] Spence (despite Christopher Hill's view that he was the first to secularise Gerard Winstanley's idea of a religious millennium based on the common ownership of land) certainly enthusiastically adopted the idea of the jubilee (as we might expect from someone brought up as in the strictly Presbyterian Glasite sect).[31] He included a hymn called 'Thĭ Unĭvĭrsĭl Jubĭle' (to be sung to the tune of 'God Save the King') in the *S'upl'im'int*: it promised a new age with no taxes and no landlords.

What is curious then is that one of the very few revisions Spence made to 'The History of the Mercolians' was to cut out the passage detailing the quadrennial redistribution of the community's goods, replacing it with a rather bland description of the Mercolians' electoral processes. Why would Spence omit this specific aspect of the Mercolian history, given that he supported the redistribution of property? For the same reason, no doubt, that he replaced the method developed by Billy Hiron for teaching language in 'Rise and Progress of Learning', namely that he had himself developed what he considered a more feasible and far-reaching method. Just as Spence spurned Hiron's reforming but too timid plan to make reading easy, so he rejected the idea of the *recurring* jubilee set out in Mercolia, for it ran counter to the *one-off* event that he envisaged. As he would observe later, 'once possessed of land' people 'do not easily give it up, but are very tenacious of their property'. That being the case, 'One hearty revolution and one Jubilee will do the business for ever.'[32] Paradoxically then, this omission of the redistributive plan from 'The Mercolians' does more to suggest that he was inspired by what he read in *The Lilliputian Magazine* than a direct repetition would have been.

II

What is surely certain is that Spence did not appropriate material from Newbery's publications merely to bulk out his 1782 book. He seems to have been inspired by them in a number of ways. The subtitle of the *S'upl'im'int*, 'Publĭshĭd ... fŏr thĭ agreĭbil Pĭruzil ŏv Rŏbĭnsĭn Kruzo'z Frĕndz ŏv aul sĭziz', for instance, imitates Newbery's famous formulation 'Children of All Sizes' (as used in the full title of *Valentine's Gift*). His adoption of Defoe's *Robinson Crusoe* as the framework for his utopian thinking imitates the intertextual use of Swift's Lilliput for the same purpose in *The Lilliputian Magazine*. And just as 'Old Zigzag' exhibited the possibilities of using the fable form for social critique, so 'Rise and Progress of Learning' and 'The Mercolians' demonstrated the power of a kind of 'friendly' utopianism that Spence was to deploy not only in the *Supplement* but in subsequent works such as his *Description of Spensonia* (1795). Spence's reliance on the idea of the return to a 'Golden Age' perhaps has its origins in Newbery too. The subtitle of the *Lilliputian Magazine* explained that it was designed to be:

> An Attempt to mend the World, to
> render the Society of Man more
> Amiable & to establish the Plainness,
> Simplicity, Virtue & Wisdom of the
> GOLDEN AGE
> much Celebrated by the
> Poets and Historians.
> Man in that Age no Rule but Reason knew,
> And with a native bent did Good pursue: -
> Unforc'd by Punishment, unaw'd by Fear, -
> His Words were Simple & his Soul sincere.

The echo in Spence's *Rights of Infants* (1797) is impossible to miss (as is the animalist imagery, which, with its 'tam'd tyger', inevitably reminds us of William Blake's 1795 *Songs of Innocence and of Experience*):

> The Golden Age, so fam'd by men of yore,
>   Shall now be counted fabulous no more.
>   The tyrant lion like an ox shall feed,

And lisping Infants shall tam'd tygers lead:
With deadly asps shall sportive sucklings play,
Nor ought obnoxious blight the blithesome day.
Yes, all that prophets e'er of bliss foretold,
And all that poets ever feign'd of old,
As yielding joy to man, shall now be seen,
And ever flourish like an evergreen.
Then, Mortals, join to hail great Nature's plan,
That fully gives to Babes those Rights it gives to Man.[33]

In Newbery's text the Golden Age, celebrated by 'poets and historians', was in the past, but its values could be recaptured. In Spence's, a past Golden Age, imagined by 'poets' and 'prophets', was a mere fiction, but a new, real Golden Age could actually be brought into being. And even if Spence's *Rights of Infants* was not necessary the early step towards the UN Convention on the Rights of the Child that some have claimed, it is difficult not to wonder how much his decisions to illustrate political freedom with images of the young ('lisping Infants', 'sportive sucklings') was influenced by an early immersion in children's culture.[34]

Beyond these specific debts, the fundamental ethos of Newbery's enterprise surely finds an echo in Spence too. If we ask how, in Newbery's works, a new Golden Age was to be achieved, the answer is clear: education. The entire Newbery 'project' was founded on the notion that instruction, of the sort his books provided, could lead to personal advancement and a better society. What is more, the idea of education in Newbery's publications was radically egalitarian: 'a good Man, may be born anyhow, and anywhere; of any Parents, and in any Country', explained the preface in *The Renowned History of Giles Gingerbread* (1765). Although this drew on the Lockean concept of the child's mind as a *tabula rasa*, it also prefigured the radical contention of Thomas Paine, that Nature 'scatters' wisdom 'among mankind': 'It rises in one to-day, in another to-morrow, and has most probably visited in rotation every family of the earth, and again withdrawn.'[35] Many Newbery narratives exemplify this, but none more explicitly than the preface of *The Lilliputian Magazine*, which includes a fable describing an inadvertent exchange of the eggs from an eagle's and a crow's nest. The fable shows 'the surprising force and benefit of education', readers are told: 'The young eagles, who were by accident hatch'd under a crow, grovel on the ground, and look no higher than their supposed mother; while the young crows, who had the advantage of being nurtured under the eagle, soar aloft, and over-look their fellow-creatures.'[36]

We note here the decidedly Spencean animal metaphor, but we should also recognise the continuance into Spence's thought of this faith in the levelling power of education as a means of social renewal. It should not surprise us. Spence was proud to present himself as a 'teacher' in the titles of and advertisements for his early publications. His dedication to a reformed language that would liberate the 'laborious part of the people' is well known.[37] He thought of his *S'upl'im'int* (according to an advertisement in Saint's *Newcastle Courant*) primarily as 'a Reading Made Easy or First Book for teaching English upon' and reported that he had used the book in his lessons 'with the greatest ease and pleasure to himself and scholars'.[38] Spence even proposed that the *S'upl'im'int* would be only the first instalment of a full suite of educational books ('I ĭntĕnd too print both Tĕstĭmĭnts, ănd Bibĭlz, Praĭr-books, ănd such uthĭr Books ăz mi Frĕndz … rekwir'[39]), replacing the 'ordinary Road' of 'Horn-Book, Primer, Psalter, Testament, and Bible' that John Locke had recommended in 1693 and which still largely held sway in schoolrooms.[40] And in his description of Crusonia he was precise about the educational provision on offer:

> every parish has a free-school, with the best of teachers, as also a public library, containing copies and translations of all the best books in the world, so that everyone may read and inform himself as far as he pleases … There is also a national university, which every parish is allowed to keep one at, where all human learning is taught to perfection; and this one, is chosen by ballot out of the most promising youths.[41]

Moreover, Spence openly avowed that it was education that would bring about his 'Golden Age'. In the material he added to his conventional spelling version of 'Rise and Progress of Learning', as well as a description of how his 'Crusonian' language was adopted in Lilliput, he set out its *effects*:

> We must not omit the important Revolution occasioned in the Customs, as well as Manners, of Lilliput, by this Introduction of Learning. As they could now learn as much in a Month, as formerly in a Year, the very poorest soon acquired such Notions of Justice, and Equity, and of the Rights of Mankind, as rendered unsupportable, every Species of Oppression, however antiquated, or common. The Customs of Crusonia, became familiar along with the Language; and Landlords appeared despicable and burthensome, in Proportion as the Happiness of being without them was perceived; and the least Ill-treatment from them was now borne with the greatest Uneasiness and Impatience.[42]

Other late eighteenth-century writers were also persuaded by the power of education to bring social change (William Godwin and Mary Wollstonecraft, for example), but few went so far as Spence in envisaging that the 'Introduction of Learning' would lead directly to political revolution. And the effect on individuals would be just as profound. In Crusonia, he promised:

> you may frequently hear the fond mother caressing her darling boy, and crying he will be an admiral, general, senator, or any great officer she pleases to mention, and yet none can contradict it; as he may, for ought anybody knows, be one or all that she prophesies, one after another, if his merit be sufficient. This is great encouragement for parents to bring up their children properly, and indeed makes our youth, as was observed of Jephthah's children, each one resemble the children of a king.[43]

This, as we have seen, was exactly the promise of Newbery's children's books. In effect, in both Newbery and Spence, education acts as a kind of 'jubilee' in the Levitical sense, promising a continual redistribution of rank as children, educated meritocratically, generation by generation renew (and literally rejuvenate) the social hierarchy.

III

Here, then, is what Burke would stigmatise as 'learning ... debauched by ambition', that is to say, education deployed as a strategy for social and perhaps political change, trampling (in Burke's terms) the 'nobility and clergy ... under the hoofs of a swinish multitude'. Spence may have gone further than Newbery, promising not only wealth and prestige but also the high offices of state ('admiral, general, senator') to the meritorious child, whatever his background. But the underlying ethos was identical. '[E]ducation', wrote the 'Author' in the dialogue that opens *The Lilliputian Magazine*, 'is a matter of such vast importance, that our happiness and misery (and in some measure) the welfare of the kingdom and government must rest upon it.' This being the case, Newbery's 'Author' went on, 'what care ought not to be taken, to unloose the minds of children, from the fetters of habit and custom'?[44]

This point – that education could loosen the 'fetters of habit and custom' and secure the 'welfare of the kingdom and government' – was picked up by Spence. It remains impossible to determine the precise extent to which he was indebted to Newbery's works, which he probably encountered in Saint's piracies of the 1770s or early 1780s. But juxtaposing Newbery's publications and Spence's writings, as this essay has done, demonstrates their affinity. It highlights the remarkable radicalism of mid-eighteenth-century children's literature, and it emphasises how important education was as a strand of Spence's utopian thinking.

Notes

1 57 Geo. III c. 19. The Chartist George Julian Harney proposed in 1850 that a statue of Spence should replace the figure of Earl Grey on the column erected in the centre of Newcastle upon Tyne following the Great Reform Act, while Marx named Spence as an English communist in *The German Ideology* (1846/7); Malcolm Chase, 'Paine, Spence, Chartism and "The Real Rights of Man", in Alastair Bonnett and Keith Armstrong (eds), *Thomas Spence: the Poor Man's Revolutionary* (London, 2014), pp. 14, 22.
2 H. T. Dickinson (ed.), *The Political Works of Thomas Spence* (Newcastle, 1982).
3 L. G. Mitchell (ed.), *The Writings and Speeches of Edmund Burke. Volume VIII: The French Revolution 1790–1794* (Oxford, 1989), p. 130 [emphasis added].
4 British Library, Add. MS 27,808, f.170r, Francis Place, 'Collection for a Memoir of Thomas Spence and the Spenceans'.
5 See, for example, Olive D. Rudkin, *Thomas Spence and His Connections* (London, 1927), p. 32; Marcus Wood, *Radical Satire and Print Culture 1790–1822* (Oxford, 1994), pp. 219–20; Robert W. Rix, 'Thomas Spence's Spelling Reform', in Bonnett and Armstrong (eds), *Thomas Spence*, p. 97.
6 For example, The *Lilliputian Magazine* was advertised in the *Newcastle Courant* on 2 March 1751.
7 Nigel Tattersfield, 'Saint or Sinner? Thomas Saint of Newcastle upon Tyne, printer, publisher and pirate', paper delivered at the Children's Book History Society symposium, 'Publishing for Children in the Hand-Press Era', London, 11 May 2013.
8 [Anon.], *The Valentine's Gift: or, a Plan to Enable Children of All Sizes and Denominations to Behave with Honour, Integrity, and Humanity. Very Necessary in a Trading Nation* (London, 1777), pp. 46, 51–2.
9 Thomas Spence, *A Suitable Companion to Spence's Songs: A Fable* (London, n.d.), pp. [i]–[ii].
10 Alastair Bonnett, 'Spence and the Politics of Nostalgia' in Bonnett and Armstrong (ed.), *Thomas Spence*, p. 84.
11 *Valentine's Gift*, pp. 66–7.
12 For a discussion, see M. O. Grenby (ed.), *Little Goody Two-Shoes and Other Stories Originally Published by John Newbery* (Basingstoke, 2013), pp. xii–xv.
13 'The Lilliputian Magazine', in Grenby (ed.), *Little Goody Two-Shoes and Other Stories*, pp. 18–21.
14 The second number followed in late June, and a third in mid-August 1752. A collected edition in one volume was then advertised for the Christmas market in 1752. This single volume was intermittently published until the late 1780s, and it is only in this form that the texts survive. *Whitehall Evening Post*, 2 and 7 March 1751; *London Daily Advertiser and Literary Gazette*,

29 June 1751; *London Evening Post*, 15 August 1752; *Public Advertiser*, 20 December 1752. See also Jill E. Grey, 'The Lilliputian Magazine – A Pioneering Periodical?', *Journal of Librarianship*, 2 (1970), 107–15.
15 Quoted in Robin Eagles, 'No more to be said'? Reactions to the Death of Frederick Lewis, Prince of Wales', *Historical Research*, 80 (2007), 348.
16 Andrew C. Thompson, *George II* (New Haven, CT, 2011), p. 98.
17 'Lilliputian Magazine', p. 20.
18 See Andrea Immel and Brian Alderson (eds), *Tommy Thumb's Pretty Song-Book* (Los Angeles, 2013), pp. 11, 97, 108.
19 Chris Mounsey, *Christopher Smart, Clown of God* (Cranbury, NJ, 2001), pp. 116, 167.
20 'Lilliputian Magazine', p. 63.
21 Thomas Spence, *A Supplement to the History of Robinson Crusoe, Being the History of Crusonia, or Robinson Crusoe's Island* (Newcastle, 1782), pp. 40–1.
22 'Lilliputian Magazine', pp. 45–6.
23 'Ibid., p. 46.
24 John Brewer, *The Sinews of Power: War, Money and the English State 1688–1783* (London, 1989), pp. 55–6.
25 Frank Felsenstein, *Anti-Semitic Stereotypes: A Paradigm of Otherness in English Popular Culture, 1600–1830* (Baltimore, 1995), p. 206.
26 See Daniel Statt, 'The City of London and the Controversy Over Immigration, 1660–1722', *Historical Journal*, 33 (1990), 45–61.
27 See Mounsey, *Christopher Smart*, pp. 116, 124.
28 The political power of children seems to have had a particular appeal to Spence. As well as his adoption of the stories of Billy Hiron and Turvolo, he included an old narrative, 'The History of the Rise and Fall of Masaniello', describing a Neapolitan children's revolt, in his periodical *Pig's Meat*, 3 (1795).
29 'Lilliputian Magazine', pp. 46–8.
30 Malcolm Chase, 'From Millennium to Anniversary: The Concept of Jubilee in Late Eighteenth- and Nineteenth-Century England', *Past and Present*, 129 (1990), pp. 132–47. Clement Hawes, *Mania and Literary Style: The Rhetoric of Enthusiasm from the Ranters to Christopher Smart* (Cambridge, 1996), pp. 194–5.
31 Christopher Hill, *Puritanism and Revolution: Studies in Interpretation of the English Revolution in the 17th Century* (London, 2001), p. 49. On Spence's abiding religiosity, see Malcolm Chase, *The People's Farm: English Radical Agrarianism 1775–1840* (London, 2010), p. 46.
32 Thomas Spence, *The Rights of Man, as Exhibited in a Lecture, Read at the Philosophical Society, in Newcastle, To Which is Now First Added, an Interesting Conversation, Between a Gentleman and the Author, on the Subject of his Scheme* (London, 1793), p. 26.
33 Dickinson (ed.), *Political Works*, p. 52.

34 R. S. White is surely right to conclude that, in *Rights of Infants*, children are 'the occasion of an argument rather than the end of an argument' in *Natural Rights and the Birth of Romanticism in the 1790s* (Basingstoke, 2005), p. 210.
35 *The Renowned History of Giles Gingerbread: A Little Boy who Lived upon Learning* (London, [1766]), p. 4; Thomas Paine, *Rights of Man*, Part II, in Philip S. Foner (ed.), *The Complete Writings of Thomas Paine* (New York, 1945), p. 367.
36 'Lilliputian Magazine', pp. 5–6.
37 Spence, preface to *The Grand Repository of the English Language* (1775), quoted in Joan Beal, *English Pronunciation in the Eighteenth Century* (Oxford, 2002), p. 4.
38 Quoted in Keith Armstrong (ed.), *Bless'd Millennium: The Life & Work of Thomas Spence* (Tyne and Wear, 2000), p. 11.
39 Thomas Spence, *A S'upl'im'int too thĭ Hĭstĭre 'ov Robĭnsĭn Kruzo, bĭng th'i H'ist'ire 'ov Kruzonea, ŏr R'ob'ins'in Kruzo'z Il'ind* (Newcastle, 1782), p. iii.
40 John Locke, *Some Thoughts Concerning Education* (London, 1693), p. 186; and see M. O. Grenby, *The Child Reader 1700–1840* (Cambridge, 2011), pp. 41–2.
41 Dickinson (ed.), *Political Works*, p. 13.
42 Spence, *Supplement*, pp. 41–2.
43 Dickinson (ed.), *Political Works*, p. 13.
44 'Lilliputian Magazine', p. 6.

Part III

The Long and Wide 1790s

CHAPTER 10

British Radical Attitudes towards the United States of America in the 1790s: The Case of William Winterbotham*

Emma Macleod

'While the governments of most countries in Europe are perfectly despotic, and while those which are not actually such, appear to be verging fast towards it, the government of America is making rapid strides towards perfection ...'[1] So wrote William Winterbotham (1763–1829), the Plymouth Baptist preacher, from Newgate prison where he had been jailed for four years (1793–7) and fined £200 for allegedly seditious content in two sermons he preached in November 1792.[2] The government of America, he continued, perhaps with some feeling, 'being contrary to all the old governments, in the hands of the people, they have exploded those principles by the operation of which civil and religious disqualifications and oppressions have been inflicted on mankind ...' While Winterbotham was confined, and in order to help meet some of the expenses of his conviction, he entered into various publishing ventures with his fellow political prisoners, the publishers James Ridgway, Daniel Holt and Henry D. Symonds.[3] His most ambitious work was *An Historical, Geographical, Commercial, and Philosophical View of the American United States,* which was published in four volumes in 1795, and from which the opening quotation is taken – no small achievement for a journeyman silversmith, the son of a fuller, who had had little formal education.[4]

It is not surprising that British radicals – about whose thinking and activities Harry Dickinson has written so perceptively and so humanely – continued to admire and be fascinated by the American political example after American independence, especially during the oppressive 1790s.[5] They had sympathised with the colonial case against British government

---

* I am grateful for the discussions on earlier versions of this paper contributed by the graduate seminar in British history in the long eighteenth century at the University of Oxford and the Baptist Historical Society; and to the *Baptist Quarterly* for their permission to reprint here much of the material published as 'Civil Liberties and Baptists: William Winterbotham of Plymouth in Prison and Thinking of America', *Baptist Quarterly*, 44 (2011), pp. 196–222.

policy in the decade before the war and they had applied these arguments to the British situation, making the case for reform at home as well as independence for America. They had opposed the British war against the revolutionary Americans and they now found in the new United States of America a totem, an inspiration and, in some cases, an asylum from the increasingly politically repressive Britain of the 1790s. While the French Revolution was exciting but unpredictable and, increasingly, a dangerous model to espouse, the case of America could much more easily be employed to demonstrate the viability of representative government. Much of the historical literature examining British radical connections with and opinions upon the United States has tended to concentrate on those who eventually emigrated there.[6] Winterbotham's *View of America* offers an opportunity to consider the views of one of those who remained in Britain. Although his trial and imprisonment have been previously discussed in the context of 1790s alarmism, notably by Michael Durey and Ralph Manogue, his *View of America* has generally only been the subject of passing comment, with the recent exception of a fine chapter by Wil Verhoeven.[7] It demonstrates the fascination that America held for British radicals beyond Paine, Priestley and Price, although Winterbotham did come into prolonged contact with various leading radicals through his Newgate imprisonment.[8] A second British edition of Winterbotham's *View of America* was published as soon as 1799, also in four volumes: he had not misjudged the British market for publications on America.[9] This essay explores his political analysis of the new republic.

I

Winterbotham's radical credentials are relatively easily established, although the sermons for which he was convicted are not obviously seditious and the witnesses who helped to convict him were clearly questionable. The fact that he was a Dissenter doubtless made his situation more precarious.[10] His downfall may have been caused partly by his earlier interference in local politics, however, and, as his grandson's *Sketch* says, the sermons were 'certainly imprudent'.[11] The first sermon in particular makes his advanced radicalism apparent. In this sermon, preached on the national fast-day held on 5 November 1792 to commemorate the foiling of the Gunpowder Plot on 5 November 1605 and the landing of William of Orange at Torbay on 5 November 1688, Winterbotham stated that the French Revolution was a cause for rejoicing. He also argued, in terms highly reminiscent of Richard Price's *Discourse on the Love of our Country* (1789), that the implications of the Glorious Revolution of 1688 had been that:

First, all government originates with the people.

Secondly, The people have a right to cashier their governors for misconduct.

Thirdly, The people have a right to change the form of their government if they think it proper to do so.[12]

While he made it clear that the worst political evils of the present day were caused by the abuse of 1688 principles, he also emphasised that the Revolution settlement itself was imperfect.[13] The title page of the published version of the two sermons, throwing caution to the winds now that he was already convicted, carried an epigram which honoured the radical Whig scourges of the Stuart kings, John Hampden and Algernon Sidney, gave warning of the potential downfalls of monarchs from the examples of Charles I and James II, and concluded that 'The people make the laws and laws were made for kings.'

Moreover, although his name has faded from view historically, his case was noticed and honoured by some of the leading radicals of the 1790s. It is true that he was not pictured in any of Richard Newton's prints of the political inmates of Newgate in 1793, although these portrayed an otherwise comprehensive roll-call of these men and their visitors.[14] Thomas Paine, however, cited Winterbotham's *View of America* in his *Letter to George Washington* (1796).[15] Major John Cartwright bracketed him with the more harshly treated, and more lastingly famous, Thomas Muir and Thomas Fyshe Palmer in writing about the worst radical 'martyrdoms' of the period.[16] Joseph Priestley, whose cause Winterbotham had defended in the first of his two offensive sermons, a year after Priestley's property had been destroyed in the Birmingham riots, was finally persuaded to emigrate to America by Winterbotham's fate, and he supported Winterbotham staunchly during his four-year prison sentence.[17] The Unitarian minister Theophilus Lindsey, Priestley's great friend, provided critical moral and spiritual support and, through a wealthy member of his congregation, substantial financial support to Winterbotham.[18] The list of subscribers printed at the front of the *View of America* includes such well-known radical Dissenting names as Dr John Aikin, Benjamin Flower, Rev. Andrew Kippis and Gilbert Wakefield.[19]

What has been questioned, however, is the extent to which Winterbotham's *View of America* contains his own opinions. The best-known fact about the *View* is that it was heavily plagiarised.[20] The practice of pirating American publications in London was common, as other American writers could testify in the 1790s; and it is also true that most early histories of the American Revolution, on both sides of the Atlantic, as Page Smith put it, 'drew heavily and without specific citation' from other sources.[21]

In fact, Winterbotham did not attempt to hide the fact, but he freely admitted in the preface that he had 'not only borrowed [the] ideas [of others], but, where he had not the vanity to conceive himself capable of correcting it, he has adopted their language', to such an extent that he was often unable to know his own 'few connecting sentences' from the work he had borrowed. An examination of Winterbotham's declared list of sources is instructive. It is not surprising that it includes eminent botanists, explorers, geographers and cartographers. Much of the work, whose expressed *raison d'être* was educational, is taken up with geographical, social, physical and botanical concerns. In his illuminating study, Verhoeven reads even these sections of the *View of America* as a utopian enterprise and 'a displaced critique of the political establishment in Britain'.[22] But historical discourse also forms an important part of the *View* and here it is interesting that Winterbotham's sources represent a range of political stances. No doubt this is partly a reflection of what sources were available by 1794 and also that these represented some of the most eminent authorities. It does, though, suggest that Winterbotham must have had to make certain editorial choices in deciding whose views to reflect, where judgement, rather than plain fact, was offered. Durey has suggested that Winterbotham was something of a 'shooting star, briefly significant for only a few short months from the end of 1792 until his two trials for sedition in July 1793'.[23] If we accept, however, that the political comment contained in his *View of America* involved more than a simple work of indiscriminate plagiarism, it too is worth critical reflection.[24]

A range of radical opinion was represented by the works of the Abbé Raynal, who supported the popular right to consent to taxation and the right to revolt; Benjamin Franklin, a francophile, who supported a wide franchise, and the separation of property and the rights to vote and hold public office; Thomas Jefferson, the Democratic-Republican leader who became the third American president in 1801; Joel Barlow, the radical poet and journalist; the American land speculator Gilbert Imlay; and the French revolutionary, Jacques Pierre Brissot. Federalist opinion – more moderate, but still liberal by British standards – was represented by the historian Jeremy Belknap, who deeply distrusted democracy; John Adams, the second President of the United States (1797–1801), whose works attacked French revolutionary principles and praised powerful executives, including monarchs; the American historian David Ramsay; and Benjamin Rush, who had criticised the 1776 constitution of Pennsylvania because it gave too much power to popular rule. The Scottish historian William Robertson might be described as a conservative liberal, who supported the gradual spread of civil liberty but always subject to social hierarchy. Winterbotham's sources also represented both sides of the divide over slavery, if not very evenly: Raynal, Franklin, Belknap, Ramsay, Rush and Brissot were vocal abolitionists; Jefferson, who, though he famously proclaimed all men to be 'created equal' and professed to detest slavery, nevertheless kept slaves; and Bryan Edwards, the British politician and historian of the West Indies, was a planter and defender of his interest group against the abolitionist lobby in the British Parliament.

Moreover, most of Winterbotham's declared sources offered less in the way of sustained discussion of the political condition of America after 1782, and there is therefore comparatively little obvious overlap or 'plagiarism' from them in his work in this regard. While, therefore, as one critic of his *View* put it, Winterbotham had 'never [been] out of this kingdom in his life',[25] it seems fair to treat his political comments on the independent United States of America as more genuinely his own, though they were no doubt much influenced by the discussions he had with his fellow political inmates in Newgate, many of them followers of Thomas Paine. (It is difficult to believe that he had not read Paine's *Rights of Man*, although he did not cite it.) The rest of this essay will discuss Winterbotham's observations on the American constitution, paying particular attention to the views he expressed on representative government, social equality and religious liberty.

II

British radicals did not, of course, hold homogeneous opinions about the independent United States of America.[26] Scholars such as Colin Bonwick and Richard Twomey have emphasised such factors as the socio-economic background of individual radicals and whether or not they had personal links with American politicians to explain the range of their views.[27] By the mid-1790s, there was a still more conspicuous explanation for the more sophisticated, certainly more detailed grasp of American politics held by some radicals. Those who had emigrated to America cared far more about what they saw as American party politics and were more critical of the new federal constitution of 1787, while those who remained at home generally expressed admiration for the Federalist supporters of the Washington and Adams administrations as much as they did for Jefferson's Democratic Republicans and did not differentiate much between the two. Not surprisingly, Winterbotham's views reflected the home camp on these issues, while perhaps his London artisan background, and his political companions in Newgate, pushed him to the more radical end of the home spectrum.[28]

For Winterbotham, the American example clearly demonstrated the enormous advantages of popular sovereignty. He acknowledged that scripture did not prescribe any one form of government, and that monarchy could be benign and reformist. However, he believed that it was easily corrupted, and that aristocracy was idle and prone to 'vice, ignorance, and folly'.[29] Popular sovereignty, on the other hand, he thought might be called 'the *Panacea* in politics':[30]

> [H]ere then we contemplate the government springing from its right source; originating with the people, and exercised under the guidance of a constitution formed agreeable to their sovereign will.[31]

By contrast, European constitutions all originated in governments which had been established by conquest and usurpation, and the traditional bulwarks and symbols of British liberties – Magna Carta, Habeas Corpus and the Bill of Rights – had all been won gradually and with difficulty by the people.[32] The proof of the practical benefits of a properly representative form of government could be seen in the 'rising importance, and rapid improvements of the United States'.[33] And the American willingness to keep reforming their constitution could only add to its longevity and merits. Echoing Paine, Winterbotham praised the American people for 'discarding the contemptable [sic] arguments that would render innovation formidable [and] raising a new and more perfect system'.[34]

His judgement of the specific provisions of the new constitution of 1787 was one of thoughtful optimism.[35] Its principal effect was to redistribute some of the power previously held by individual states to the central government; its great merit was that it did so without reducing popular sovereignty. Winterbotham nevertheless had criticisms to offer. In his judgement, liberty was not sufficiently safeguarded in a number of respects. He had strong words for what he considered to be the inadequate number of representatives: 'Owing to the small number of members in the house of representatives, there is not the substance, but the shadow only of representation.'[36] Furthermore, the powers of Congress in general, and the Senate and the President in particular, were in some respects too great and unconstrained. He disapproved of the fact that the members of the Senate were elected by the state legislatures, not directly by the people. Judicial procedures between state and federal governments were not satisfactory; there was no security for the powers currently reserved to individual state governments; and there was as yet no legal preservation of the liberty of the press, or the right to trial by jury in civil causes, nor was there a legal ban on maintaining a standing army during peacetime.[37] Nevertheless, Winterbotham thought that these flaws were surprisingly few and easily remediable, and that it should be recalled that the Americans had no previously worked example in the construction of a confederate republic to guide them.[38]

Winterbotham had clearly read some of the most important recent works on various aspects of the United States and had a fairly detailed grasp of the machinery of the new constitution. While he was certainly aware of the beginning of the polarisation of American politics by the 1790s and of the main issues at stake, however, he did not obviously take sides himself.[39] His preface was dated 21 January 1795, so the book seems to have been completed before Jefferson's supporters in America – and especially the British radicals in exile there – turned against President Washington personally for having signed the Jay Treaty with the British government into American law during the summer of 1795 and, therefore, as they saw it, having descended into partisan politics on the side of the Federalist party.[40]

Mark Philp has argued that the language of classical republicanism – a broader and less radical philosophy than the specific goal of ending monarchy, which stressed instead mixed government, civic virtue and the dangers of commerce – was abandoned in England during the 1790s. By the 1790s, on both sides of the Atlantic, the term 'republican' had come instead simply to refer to representative government.[41] Arthur Sheps suggests that the specifically anti-monarchical element of the modern understanding of republicanism also became widespread in the 1790s.[42] Durey argues that Winterbotham became less Lockean and more Paineite during his four years in Newgate, on the basis of the footnotes he added to the published versions of his sermons.[43] This would not be surprising, given the company he kept in prison, though his views that the monarch was chosen by Parliament on behalf of the people, and that King, Lords and Commons alike should be regarded as but men, and as accountable to the laws as any other men, formed part of the grounds for his prosecution in 1792–3.[44] The republicanism of Winterbotham's *View of America* was, if anything, less radical than that to be found in his sermons of November 1792 as published in 1794, in which his criticism of monarchy was much stronger,[45] but it is certainly true that the *View of America* is solidly in favour of representative government.

Part of the beauty of American republicanism for Winterbotham was what he called its 'equality of situation'. He suggested that the great majority of men in America were economically independent, with only a few who were very rich and also few who were absolutely dependent on others.[46] This was partly explained by American circumstances: America was a land of second chances partly because there was physical and economic space for a man who had tripped up to rise again; 'and the less unfortunate stumbler [there] looks round at leisure, and without dismay, for some more profitable path to be pursued', while England was both physically and economically overcrowded.[47] As Verhoeven points out, Winterbotham even went to the length of recommending to potential emigrants three townships in Kentucky which did not yet exist, and none of which ever actually did come into existence, despite his inclusion of maps noting their locations, and their town plans.[48] However, he also explained the American inclination towards social egalitarianism by the republican tendency, as he put it, to estimate 'a man more at what he *is*, and less at what he *seems*'.[49] Winterbotham's own artisan background was doubtless a factor in his support for a greater degree of social equality, and his Baptist worldview may also have contributed.[50]

Winterbotham was therefore also highly critical of the institution of chattel slavery, the obvious exception to social egalitarianism in America. He quoted (without attribution) Jefferson's *Notes on Virginia* (1782): 'It is impossible to be temperate and to pursue this subject through the various considerations of policy, of morals, of history, natural and civil. We must be contented to hope they will ultimately force their way into every one's mind.'[51] Other British radicals also admired the relative egalitarianism of American society, but it is striking how infrequently chattel slavery was discussed in British radical writings on America in the 1790s.[52] Michael Durey shows that British radical emigrants to the United States often found themselves adapting to their new environment, sometimes to the extent of owning slaves. It was easier for a radical living in Britain, such as Winterbotham, to remain unblinkingly opposed to slavery. Durey also found that emigrants who were influenced by Calvinism and evangelical theology were more likely to continue to condemn slavery; and British Baptists in the late eighteenth century strongly opposed slavery and the slave trade.[53] Winterbotham's own brother had been converted through 'an African then preaching in London amongst the Calvinstic Methodists'.[54]

While he had emphasised the African victims of slavery in his second November 1792 sermon, however, Winterbotham spent as much space in the *View of America* expounding the damage that slavery did to civil society in general as he did lamenting its cruelty to the slaves themselves.[55] Moreover, he betrayed his own prejudice in promoting the view that silk production was not well suited to the nature of labourers in the most southerly States, 'who, being blacks, are not careful or skilful'.[56] He also claimed that the presence of a sufficient number of anti-slavery Americans, even in the slaveholding states, mitigated against the evil effects of slavery on the general *mores* in America:

> In countries where slavery is encouraged, the ideas of the people are, in general, of a peculiar cast; the soul often becomes dark and narrow, and assumes a tone of savage brutality. Such at this day are the inhabitants of Barbary and the West-Indies. But, thank God! nothing like this has yet disgraced an American State. We may look for it in Carolina, but we shall be disappointed.[57]

Winterbotham's desire to praise the new American republic was strong enough to outweigh even his concern to condemn the practice of slavery.

The disproportionate representation of Dissenters among the ranks of British radicals, and the enshrining of religious freedom in the American federal and state constitutions, meant that American religious liberty was treated enthusiastically in radical writings on the new republic, although in fact neither the typical American practice of religion nor some state rights to religious liberty were quite as liberal as many British radicals imagined or immigrants expected.[58] Winterbotham thoroughly approved of the separation of church and state in America:

> Religion, or what is called an establishment in Europe, has had and continues to have its share in rivetting in the fetters of ignorance ... What can be a greater presumption, or a higher pitch of arrogance, than presuming to arraign or judge of the sentiments of men, the propriety of which is to be determined before a tribunal in Heaven? It is an insult too gross to merit a comment.
> In America this evil has ceased to exist, the monster is destroyed, the unnatural alliance ... is broken ...[59]

Unusually for an orthodox Dissenter, Winterbotham wanted complete freedom not only for all 'church sects' but also for any 'society of religious persons whatsoever', though he did not specify the breadth of liberty he demanded more precisely than this.[60] He continued to practise what he preached in Britain long after his release from prison, signing petitions for Catholic emancipation as well as supporting the repeal of the Test and Corporation Acts for Protestants.[61]

III

Winterbotham was not above writing about the new republic with what might be read as a certain air of British condescension: 'Judging ... from its present promising infancy, we are encouraged to hope, that, at some future period, not far distant, it will, in every point of view, be respectable.'[62] Predominantly, however, he warmly promoted the United States of America. First, it was an example to Britain and the other European nations. '[T]he revolution in the late British American colonies', he wrote, 'bids fair ultimately not only to occasion the emancipation of the other European colonies on that continent, but to accomplish a complete revolution in all the old governments of Europe.'[63] A practical, worked example, as Paine had pointed out in the second part of his *Rights of Man*, had much more force than books on the subject. 'It renders this truth evident,' Winterbotham wrote, 'that the people have a right to do what they please, with regard to the government.'[64] Second, he praised the United States as 'an asylum' for 'the persecuted in France or England, ... where their lives, property and liberty are secure; where they may almost say, the wicked cease from troubling, and the weary are at rest.'[65] This was a well-established British radical conception of the American republic, following Paine's *Common Sense* in 1776, which had depicted America as an asylum for the very principle of liberty.[66] Third, Winterbotham argued that America was also a good prospect for economic migrants. Verhoeven has argued persuasively that the *View of America* is 'best seen as a thinly veiled plea in favor of emigration to America ... an unadulterated sales pitch aimed at persuading the book's readers to take up lots in the future capital of the United States'.[67] And yet Winterbotham himself did not participate in the 'exodus of British radicals' to America after his release from prison. After Winterbotham was released from Newgate on 26 November 1797, he married Mary Brend of Plymouth, a defence witness at his trial, and returned to minister at the Baptist chapel in Plymouth until 1804, when he moved to Shortwood Baptist Church in Gloucestershire. Here, according to his grandson, he maintained a keen interest in campaigns for religious liberty, parliamentary reform, free trade and the abolition of slavery.[68]

While radical emigrants to the American republic gradually recognised that they were living in a reality rather than a utopia, those such as Winterbotham who remained in Britain had fewer constraints on their vision.[69] Like him, radicals such as Price, Sharp and John Thelwall all expressed mild concern with some aspects of life in America, and others were dismayed by the passage of the Alien and Sedition Acts in 1798. But these were the anxieties of those who wished keenly to see perfection in the new republic, and the dominant opinion of British radicals was one of deep admiration for the new system of government established across the Atlantic, especially once they had become disillusioned with the revolution in France in the aftermath of the Terror.

American influence was frequently cited by British state prosecutors in the treason and sedition trials of 1793–5. For most radical (rather than predominantly economic) emigrants to America, however, their removal was a matter not of their own choosing but caused by their defeat at home.[70] Perhaps Winterbotham, who had not in fact mentioned America in either of his offensive sermons, viewed it rather as an intellectual escape from his confinement in Newgate than as a realistic prospect for himself. He did not comment directly on the British system of government in the *View of America*, but his advanced radical opinions were nonetheless made very plain in the work, courageously so in the context of his own imprisonment. In his *View of America*, despite its extensive plagiarism, he proposed his own thorough approval of the new United States of America.

Notes

1 William Winterbotham, *An Historical, Geographical, Commercial, and Philosophical View of the American United States, and of the European Settlements in America and the West-Indies*, 4 vols (London, 1795) III, p. 281.
2 William Winterbotham, *The Trial of Wm. Winterbotham, Assistant Preacher at How's Lane Meeting, Plymouth* (London, 1794), p. 132.
3 Ralph A. Manogue, 'The Plight of James Ridgway, London Bookseller and Publisher, and the Newgate Radicals 1792–1797', *The Wordsworth Circle*, 27 (1996), pp. 158–66; idem, 'James Ridgway and America', *Early American Literature*, 31 (1996), pp. 264–88; *Critical Review*, 15 (September 1795), pp. 87, 95.
4 W. H. Winterbotham, *The Rev. William Winterbotham: A Sketch*, privately printed (London, 1893), pp. 1, 5–6.
5 For example, see H. T. Dickinson, *Liberty and Property: Political Ideology in Eighteenth-Century Britain* (London, 1977), pp. 195–269; idem, *British Radicalism and the French Revolution 1789–1815* (Oxford, 1985); idem, *The Politics of the People in Eighteenth-Century Britain* (Basingstoke, 1995), pp. 190–254; idem, '"The Friends of America": British sympathy with the American Revolution', in Michael T. Davis (ed.), *Radicalism and Revolution in Britain, 1775–1848* (Basingstoke, 2000), pp. 1–29; idem, 'Richard Price on reason and revolution', in William Gibson and Robert G. Ingram (eds), *Religious Identities in Britain, 1660–1832* (Aldershot, 2005), pp. 231–54. On the radicals' continuing fascination with America, see Arthur Sheps, 'The American Revolution and the Transformation of English Republicanism', *Historical Reflections*, 2 (1975), pp. 3–28; David A. Wilson, *Paine and Cobbett: The Transatlantic Connection* (Kingston and Montreal, 1988), ch. 3; Mark Philp, 'The Role of America in the "Debate on France" 1791–5: Thomas Paine's Insertion', *Utilitas*, 5 (1993), pp. 221–37.
6 See, for example, Frank Thistlethwaite, *The Anglo-American Connection in the Early Nineteenth Century* (Philadelphia, 1959); Richard J. Twomey, *Jacobins and Jeffersonians: Anglo-American Radicalism in the United States, 1790–1820* (New York, 1989); Michael Durey, *Transatlantic Radicals and the Early American Republic* (Lawrence, 1997). Colin Bonwick, *English Radicals and the American Revolution* (Chapel Hill, 1977) is an important exception; see also Emma Macleod, *British Visions of America, 1775–1820: Republican Realities* (London, 2013).
7 Michael Durey, 'William Winterbotham's Trumpet of Sedition: Religious Dissent and Political Radicalism in the 1790s', *Journal of Religious History*, 19 (1995), pp. 141–57; for Manogue, see n. 3; Wil Verhoeven, *Americomania and the French Revolution Debate in Britain, 1789–1802* (Cambridge, 2013), pp. 199–238.
8 Michael T. Davis, Iain McCalman and Christina Parolin, '"Patriots in Prison": Newgate Radicalism in the Age of Revolution', in Davis, McCalman and Parolin (eds), *Newgate in Revolution: An Anthology of Radical Prison Literature in the Age of Revolution* (London, 2005), p. xvi; Verhoeven, *Americomania*, pp. 205–7.

9   Two American editions were also published in New York and Philadelphia in 1796, 'with additions and corrections'.
10 Durey, 'Winterbotham's Trumpet of Sedition', pp. 152–3; Macleod, 'Civil Liberties and Baptists', pp. 196–201. See also the *Critical Review*, 11 (1794), pp. 224–5 and Henry F. Whitfield, *Plymouth and Devonport: In Times of War and Peace* (Plymouth, 1900), p. 440.
11 Winterbotham, *Sketch*, p. 25; William Cobbett and T. J. Howell (eds), *Complete Collection of State Trials, continued from the Year 1783 to the Present Time*, 33 vols (London, 1816–26), XXII, col. 871; G. E. Welch, 'Municipal Reform in Plymouth', *Transactions of the Devonshire Association*, 96 (1964), p. 325; Verhoeven, *Americomania*, pp. 201–2; *Critical Review*, 11 (June 1794), p. 225.
12 W. Winterbotham, *The Commemoration of National Deliverances, and the Dawning Day: Two Sermons, preached November 5th and 18th, 1792: at How's Lane Chapel, Plymouth* (London, 1794), p. 16; Richard Price, *A Discourse on the Love of Our Country* (London, 1789), p. 34.
13 Winterbotham, *Two Sermons*, pp. 32, 16, 25–6; Durey, 'Winterbotham's Trumpet of Sedition', p. 152.
14 David Alexander, *Richard Newton and English Caricature in the 1790s* (Manchester, 1998), pp. 36–8, 62 n. 85, 120–1.
15 Philip S. Foner (ed.), *The Complete Writings of Thomas Paine*, 2 vols (New York, 1945), II, p. 718, n. 15.
16 John Cartwright, *The Constitutional Defence of England, Internal and External* (London, 1796), p. 98. See also idem, *The State of the Nation; in a series of letters to His Grace the Duke of Bedford* (Harlow, 1805), pp. 30–1.
17 Joseph Priestley, *The Present State of Europe compared with Antient Prophecies; A Sermon, Preached at the Gravel Pit Meeting in Hackney, February 28, 1794, being the Day Appointed for a General Fast* (London, 1794), pp. xvii–xviii; R. E. Schofield, *The Enlightened Joseph Priestley: A Study of his Life and Work from 1773 to 1804* (University Park, PA, 2004), p. 323, n. 17.
18 Durey, 'Winterbotham's Trumpet of Sedition', p. 155; Winterbotham, *Sketch*, p. 38.
19 Winterbotham, *View of America*, I, p. viii.
20 Manogue, 'Ridgway and America', p. 275, n. 16, 27; Bonwick, *English Radicals*, p. 295, n. 15.
21 Manogue, 'Ridgway and America', p. 267; Bonwick, *English Radicals*, pp. 221–2; Page Smith, 'David Ramsay and the Causes of the American Revolution', *William and Mary Quarterly*, 17 (1960), pp. 52, 59–60.
22 Winterbotham, *View of America*, I, p. vi; Verhoeven, *Americomania*, p. 209.
23 Durey, 'Winterbotham's Trumpet of Sedition', p. 144.
24 And see Verhoeven, *Americomania*, p. 212.

25 *Look Before You Leap or, a Few Hints to such Artizans, Mechanics, Labourers, Farmers and Husbandmen, as are Desirous of Emigrating to America* (London, 1796), p. xiv.
26 For this aspect of radical ideologies, see Mark Philp, 'The Fragmented Ideology of Reform', in Philp (ed.), *The French Revolution and British Popular Politics* (Cambridge, 1991), pp. 50–77.
27 Richard J. Twomey, 'Jacobins and Jeffersonians: Anglo-American Radical Ideology, 1790–1810', in Margaret Jacob and James Jacob (eds), *The Origins of Anglo-American Radicalism* (London, 1984), pp. 284–99; Bonwick, *English Radicals*, pp. 217–18, 224–5, 231.
28 Winterbotham, *Sketch*, pp. 2–3, 8–12; Durey, 'William Winterbotham's Trumpet of Sedition', pp. 144–50.
29 Winberbotham, *Two Sermons*, p. 41; idem, *View of America*, I, pp. iv–v and III, p. 286.
30 Winterbotham, *View of America*, I, p. 232.
31 Ibid., I, p. 238.
32 Ibid., I, pp. 238–9. Contrast this with David Ramsay, *The History of the American Revolution*, 2 vols (London, 1791), I, p. 356, where Ramsay's emphasis is rather on those who granted the concessions in Europe than on those who won them.
33 Winterbotham, *View of America*, I, pp. 238–9; see also I, pp. 231–3, 235, 239–60 and III, pp. 283–4, 294–5, 299.
34 Ibid., I, pp. 238, 584–5. See Paine's *Rights of Man, Part One* (London, 1791) in Foner (ed.), *Complete Writings*, I, pp. 250–4.
35 Winterbotham, *View of America*, I, p. 587. There is a passage here lifted from Ramsay, *History of the American Revolution*, II, pp. 342–3.
36 Winterbotham, *View of America*, I, p. 224.
37 Ibid., I, pp. 233–5, 585, 224–6.
38 Ibid., I, pp. 585–7, 224–6.
39 Ibid., III, pp. 335–6.
40 Durey, *Transatlantic Radicals*, pp. 236–40.
41 Mark Philp, 'English Republicanism in the 1790s', *Journal of Political Philosophy*, 6 (1998), pp. 235–62. See also his 'Time to Talk', in Philp, *Reforming Ideas in Britain: politics and language in the shadow of the French Revolution, 1789–1815* (Cambridge, 2013), pp. 287–311, on the difficulty of drawing precise conclusions regarding people's ideological commitments from their use of political language in the 1790s.
42 Sheps, 'The American Revolution and the Transformation of English Republicanism'.
43 Durey, 'Winterbotham's Trumpet of Sedition', pp. 154–5.
44 Winterbotham, *Two Sermons*, pp. 20, 37; Cobbett and Howell (eds), *State Trials*, XXII, cols 825, 845–6, 869–70.
45 Winterbotham, *Two Sermons*, pp. 16–25, 32–3, 36–7, 44.
46 Winterbotham, *View of America*, III, pp. 285–6.
47 Ibid., III, p. 302.

48 Verhoeven, *Americomania*, pp. 215, 226.
49 Ibid., p. 301. For works exploring similar themes, see Robert Bage, *Man As He Is* (1792) and William Godwin, *Things As They Are, or, The Adventures of Caleb Williams* (1794).
50 Note the resonance of 1 Samuel 16:7: 'for man looketh on the outward appearance, but the LORD looketh on the heart'.
51 Winterbotham, *View of America*, III, p. 110; Thomas Jefferson, *Notes on the State of Virginia* (Richmond, VA, 1782), p. 300.
52 For substantial discussion of this issue, see Christopher Leslie Brown, *Moral Capital: Foundations of British Abolitionism* (Chapel Hill, 2006), pp. 126–34; Anthony Page, '"A Species of Slavery": Richard Price's Rational Dissent and Antislavery', *Slavery and Abolition*, 32 (2011), pp. 53–73; Anthony Page, 'Rational Dissent, Enlightenment and Abolition of the Slave Trade', *Historical Journal*, 54 (2011), pp. 741–72; Macleod, *British Visions of America*, pp. 146–7, 142–4.
53 Durey, *Transatlantic Radicals*, pp. 283–7; Raymond Brown, *The English Baptists of the Eighteenth Century (1689–1815)* (London, 1986), pp. 102, 118, 121–2, 127, 136.
54 Winterbotham, *Sketch*, p. 13.
55 Winterbotham, *Two Sermons*, p. 51; idem, *View of America*, I, pp. 206–7.
56 Winterbotham, *View of America*, III, p. 292.
57 Ibid., III, p. 254 and I, pp. 207–8.
58 Durey, *Transatlantic Radicals*, pp. 188–9ff.; Bonwick, *English Radicals*, ch. 7.
59 Winterbotham, *View of America*, III, p. 282.
60 Ibid., III, p. 281.
61 Winterbotham, *Sketch*, p. 48; Durey, 'Winterbotham's Trumpet of Sedition', pp. 154–5; Winterbotham, *Two Sermons*, p. 33.
62 Winterbotham, *View of America*, I, p. 204.
63 Ibid., I, p. iv.
64 Ibid., I, p. iv–v, 232 and III, p. 283; Foner (ed.), *Complete Writings*, I, p. 353–4.
65 Winterbotham, *View of America*, I, pp. v–vi and III, pp. 295–331. A slightly odd allusion to Job 3:17, which refers to the rest offered by the grave.
66 Foner (ed.), *Complete Writings*, I, pp. 19, 31.
67 Verhoeven, *Americomania*, pp. 212, 215.
68 Winterbotham, *Sketch*, pp. 48–9.
69 On the emigrants, see Durey, *Transatlantic Radicals*, p. 211 and chs 6 and 7.
70 Sheps, 'The American Revolution and the Transformation of English Republicanism', pp. 17–18; Durey, *Transatlantic Radicals*, pp. 134, 163, 165.

CHAPTER 11

Was there a Law of Sedition in Scotland? Baron David Hume's Analysis of the Scottish Sedition Trials of 1794

Atle L. Wold

On 13 January 1794, Maurice Margarot of the London Corresponding Society stood before the bar at the High Court of Justiciary in Edinburgh charged with the crime of sedition. Margarot was one of the very few English delegates who had been present at the so-called British Convention, organised by the Scottish branch of the radical society the Friends of the People, and held in Edinburgh in November and the beginning of December 1793. Together with his fellow Englishman Joseph Gerrald, and William Skirving of the Edinburgh Friends of the People, Margarot had taken on a leading role at the Convention. It was for this that he had been put on trial. In the opening stages of the trial, Margarot presented a challenge to the judges and the prosecution which initiated a discussion about sedition as a crime under Scots law both in his trial and those of other Convention delegates. Margarot stated:

> I beseech your lordship, to point out the law which makes sedition a crime, and also, that which shows the punishment that is due to it. I understand some people think sedition so well understood, as not to need explanation. I differ from them: I say it is not merely the authority of a judge that is sufficient; he must lay his finger upon the law-book, and point out to the subjects that they may know where to find it when they are not before the judge.[1]

In the trial, Margarot's challenge was understood to raise a question: which statute under Scots law made sedition a crime in Scotland? Margarot's focus was thus on *written* law, and his view seemed to be that if no such statute could be produced, then sedition should not be accepted as a crime in Scotland and the case would have to be abandoned. Certainly, when seen from the point of view of an Englishman such as Margarot, the situation in Scotland must have appeared rather odd. Whereas English law provided for the possibility of charging a defendant with 'seditious libel', it had been made clear by the time of

Margarot's trial that there was no statute under Scots law which used the term 'sedition'.²

Margarot had himself been a witness at the immediately preceding trial of his co-delegate William Skirving, and in his summing up at the end of the trial, the presiding judge on the bench, the Lord Justice Clerk Lord Braxfield, had stated: 'by the penal law of Scotland, it [sedition] is a crime very different from the law of England; for it is not necessary to have any act of parliament for it'.³ There was, in other words, no statute passed by the pre-union Scottish Parliament using the word sedition. Nor had English law been introduced, as it had for the crime of treason through an Act of 1709 (which thereby abolished the old Scottish law of treason).⁴ Moreover, the judges and lawyers had not been able to identify any previous trials of sedition in Scotland, meaning that there was no case law or precedent on which they might rely in the absence of a relevant statute.⁵

Did this mean that there was no law of sedition in Scotland and that, consequently, the trials went ahead without any proper legal basis for the charge? If so, it would certainly amplify the already well-established view of the Scottish sedition trials of the 1790s as grossly unfair – near miscarriages of justice even – and marked by biased judges who were prepared uncritically to accept the prosecution case and thus assist the government's attempt to silence political radicals through the use of the court system.⁶ Having experienced the inconclusive debates on sedition which took place during Skirving's trial – where the main emphasis had been placed on the argument that sedition had to be a crime in Scotland because it had been recognised as a crime 'by the common law of every civilized government upon earth, from the earliest records to the latest period', as the Lord Advocate Robert Dundas put it – Margarot was determined to force the issue of bringing forward a more precise definition of sedition under Scots law.⁷

In the absence of statute and case law, however, the Scottish legal tradition provided an opportunity to seek answers in 'authoritative writings' on Scots law, and that is precisely what was done in both Margarot's trial and in two subsequent trials at the High Court in Edinburgh. The focus of this essay is on such authoritative writings: firstly, to examine their use in the trials; and secondly, to explore the subsequent analysis of the trials conducted by the learned legal scholar Baron David Hume shortly afterwards.⁸

I

Starting in earnest in the seventeenth century and continuing into the eighteenth century, a tradition developed in Scotland whereby learned legal scholars produced treatises on Scots law.⁹ The purpose of these treatises was to clarify the contents of Scots law through the unification of its constituent parts: customary, feudal, Canon, Roman and statute law. Scots law was thus seen to be based on a number of different sources, of which statutes passed by the Scottish Parliament were but one. The aim of many of those who wrote treatises on law was to present a unified *national* Scottish law based on these many sources. One of the most influential writers of the seventeenth century, James Dalrymple, first Viscount Stair, had arguably aimed to 'differentiate the law of Scotland from that of other countries' through his *Institutions of the Law of Scotland* (1681), a treatise which was later 'accorded the status of a formally binding source, equivalent in authority to the decisions of the higher courts'.[10] Authoritative writings were thus seen to describe and explain what characterised Scots law as distinct from the law of other countries and could be used as a source of law in the courtroom.

Treatises such as Stair's *Institutions* were often modelled on Justinian's *Institutes* in terms of structure and usually aimed to address the totality of Scots law. For that reason, they came to be denoted as *institutional* writings in the nineteenth century.[11] Such sources should be kept distinct from other legal literature, most of which (textbooks on law, for example) did not have the authoritative status of institutional writings. In present-day Scots law, only a very few works are counted as institutional.[12] Authoritative writings could thus be seen to form a part of Scots *common* law (that is, those aspects of the law of Scotland which were not explicitly part of the statutes). In relation to statute and case law, such treatises held a third position, with statute law as 'first in the hierarchy of authority'.[13] While authoritative writings had not obtained the formalised position of institutional writings on Scots law by the 1790s, it was clear that resort to such works as a source of law was accepted in the sedition trials by all parties who were familiar with Scots law (which Margarot, of course, was not). This became apparent in the response to Margarot's challenge.

Speaking for the prosecution, the Solicitor-General Robert Blair quickly appealed to authoritative writings and began by reaching for a truly ancient authority. 'Sedition was made a crime not by any statute, but by the common law of Scotland,' Blair stated, 'and if the gentleman wishes for authority, I refer him to the book called "Regiam Majestatem," where sedition is expressly stated to be a crime.'[14] *Regiam Majestatem* was a later-medieval legal text, probably compiled sometime between 1295 and 1320, and based heavily on an English legal text known as *Glanvill*. It was thus not a typical authoritative work of the kind that was written by Scottish scholars in the seventeenth and eighteenth centuries but nevertheless shared some central features with them, most notably that it was believed to have been compiled in order to 'set out the existing law of Scotland'.[15] Not all scholars held *Regiam* to be a central work on Scottish law. Stair, for one, had dismissed the text as forming 'no part of our law',[16] but Blair insisted that it was 'the oldest book that we have upon the law of Scotland'.[17] The purpose of appealing to it must therefore have been to demonstrate that sedition had been a part of Scots law for a very long time.

Although further references were made to *Regiam* from time to time in the trials, the main focus came to be placed on more recent sources and primarily on the two central authorities of Sir George Mackenzie and John Erskine. Of the two, Mackenzie would seem the more obvious choice of reference because – in addition to publishing a more typical institutional kind of treatise of Scots law in *The Institutions of the Law of Scotland* (1684) – Mackenzie had also authored the only thesis entirely devoted to the criminal aspect of Scots law. His coverage of criminal law in *The Laws and Customs of Scotland in Matters Criminal* (1678) was therefore a more extensive treatment than could typically be found in institutional works. Nevertheless, in a book covering more than four hundred pages, the crime of sedition was addressed on merely two pages (as compared to twenty for the crime of treason) and arguably did not give the courts very much to work with. Sedition, Mackenzie stated in the opening passage:

> is a commotion of the people without authority, and if it be such as tends to the disturbing of the government ... it is treason; but if it only be raised upon any private account it is not properly called treason, but it is with us called a convocation of the lieges.

Sedition was thus closely related to treason, but the two crimes should nevertheless be seen as distinct in that 'to raise men against the prince is treason', whereas 'to raise them against public order or discipline ... is sedition'. The vital question was whether there had been any design or attempt to kill the king and, for that reason, 'sedition may be accompanied with qualities which may raise it to treason', Mackenzie concluded.[18] In other words, if a decision was made to attack the monarch, what started off as sedition would quickly become treason. At least three central points emerge from Mackenzie's analysis: first that sedition was *called* a 'convocation of the lieges' in Scots law; second that it involved an (illegal) *commotion* of the people; and third that it was directed against the *public peace*, though without that involving an attack on the king's person. Mackenzie did state that the word 'sedition' was used in the *Regiam Majestatem*, which he saw as an important source of Scots law, but otherwise the implication here seems to be that sedition was not a concept commonly used in the Scottish legal practice.

How could this understanding of sedition be applied in trials against political radicals in the 1790s? The prosecution, judges and defence all resorted to Mackenzie from time to time. In the trial of Sinclair, for example, Robert Dundas cited Mackenzie's definition of sedition as a 'commotion of the people' and asked a rhetorical question: when the British Convention 'met for the express purpose of resisting the parliament of these kingdoms, and continued to meet until they were dispersed by the civil magistrate', was that not precisely what Mackenzie had meant by a 'seditious convocation'?[19] By contrast, Adam Gillies for the defence in the trial of Gerrald referred to Mackenzie's definition and argued that since the British Convention had *not* led to any 'commotion of the people' – which he understood to mean a *rising* of the people – then it followed that it was not seditious.[20] Despite the position of Mackenzie's *Laws and Customs* as the 'only book of criminal law which we lawyers acknowledge as of authority', as Robert Dundas stated in the trial of Margarot, it was, however, John Erskine's definition of sedition which came to play the more central role in the trials.[21]

II

By 1794, John Erskine's *An Institute of the Law of Scotland* was the most recent authoritative treatise on Scots law.[22] Published posthumously in 1773, Erskine's was a typical Scottish institutional work, in that it aimed to discuss Scots law as a whole. For that reason, perhaps, criminal law, and more specifically the category he denoted as 'crimes against the state', was dealt with fairly briefly. Moreover, just as Mackenzie had done, Erskine focused mainly on the law of treason, covering sedition in just a couple of short paragraphs. Erskine nevertheless presented some important distinctions. The crime of sedition, he argued, could be defined as consisting in 'raising commotions and disturbances in the state', a point which was clearly in line with Mackenzie's view.[23] He then proceeded to draw up a distinction between *real* and *verbal* sedition, which Mackenzie had not mentioned, and these were concepts which were debated at length in the Scottish courtrooms.

Real sedition, Erskine stated, 'is inferred from an irregular convocation of a number of people, without lawful authority, tending to obstruct or trouble the peace of the community'. If such 'commotions' were 'aimed directly against the sovereign or state', they were to be regarded as high treason, but if they were raised 'merely to redress some supposed grievance', it would be a matter of (real) sedition. Verbal sedition, by contrast, consisted in the 'uttering of words tending to sedition, or the breeding of hatred and discord between the king and his people' and – of crucial importance in the political trials of the 1790s – was a crime 'which in our statutes gets the name of leasing-making'. What Erskine meant by 'our statutes' appeared to be laws passed by the Scottish Parliament prior to the union of 1707, and what his analysis seemed to demonstrate was that only one of the two forms of sedition which he identified – verbal sedition – was covered by a statute, but then under a different name, that of leasing-making. Mackenzie had also addressed the crime of leasing-making, but then as a form of verbal injury, or libel, and he had not linked it to sedition in the way Erskine did.[24]

This was an important difference. Erskine's distinction thus seemed to suggest that verbal sedition – or leasing-making – was to do with *words*, spoken or written, whereas real sedition had to involve some kind of *physical action*. This analysis caused a variety of problems in the courtroom. Did the differentiation into real and verbal sedition mean that they should be treated as two distinct crimes, and how was the relationship between sedition and leasing-making really to be understood? Moreover, was the decision to charge the delegates with sedition a matter of a simple mistake caused, perhaps, by ignorance on the part of the prosecution, which ought to have set up a charge of leasing-making instead – as the nineteenth-century legal scholar Lord Cockburn would later claim – or was it deliberate?[25] When pressed on this matter by the defence, the prosecution was certainly very adamant that the charge was *not* one of leasing-making.

Blair was the first to appeal to Erskine. In his attempt to define the crime of sedition, Blair began by stating that 'as to a definition of sedition ... there are many crimes of so complex and so vague a nature, that it is hardly possible to give a general definition to comprehend them all'. Despite this degree of 'vagueness', however, 'if a definition is wanted of the crime charged against that gentleman, I will read him Mr Erskine's definition of it in his first institute'.[26] Thus, while sedition had been a crime under Scots common law since the writing of *Regiam* at least, Blair seemed to argue, its precise definition *now* was that provided by the most recent authoritative writing on Scots law. The issue had not, however, been fully settled by Blair's explanation.

In the subsequent trial against Charles Sinclair, the junior counsel for the defence, Archibald Fletcher, challenged the court to clarify the point in the major proposition of the indictment which stated that 'sedition is a crime'. Did this mean that the panel was accused of real or verbal sedition? This was important, Fletcher claimed, because if the charge was one of real sedition, then it was common law which applied, whereas if the charge was one of verbal sedition – that is, leasing-making – then it was statute law which applied.[27] This had to be the case, Fletcher insisted, because there existed a specific statute on leasing-making dating from 1703, and statute law would take precedence over common law.[28] In his response, the Solicitor-General accepted the division of sedition into real and verbal, but stated that 'the facts charged here amount to both verbal and real sedition'. He then proceeded to cite Erskine's definition of real sedition, but stated that 'the charge here made is not leasing-making'. Indeed, he insisted that 'sedition and leasing-making are by no means synonymous terms', and that 'an act may be leasing-making which is not sedition, and an act may be sedition which is not leasing-making'.[29]

Where did this leave verbal sedition? Was it not to be understood as leasing-making in the way Erskine claimed and consequently to be treated as a common law crime? And if so, did it mean that Erskine had to be abandoned as a source of law on this particular issue? Blair did not address these issues, and the subsequent debate in Sinclair's (short) trial did not really seem to resolve them either. Increasingly, the prosecution and the judges came to focus on real sedition as opposed to leasing-making, leaving the whole issue of verbal sedition aside, so much so that Lord Braxfield eventually claimed that the 'distinction of verbal and real sedition' had 'misled the counsel for the panel'. Moreover, Braxfield came close to dismissing Erskine when he stated: 'Leasing-making is not always sedition; it is in fact, properly, a species of verbal injury, and is treated and arranged as such by Sir George Mackenzie.'[30]

The issue was raised again by Gillies in the trial of Joseph Gerrald, when he tried to convince the court that the charge of sedition – which had been stated in 'vague and general terms' in the indictment – could not be 'construed' to mean 'any thing more than verbal sedition, or leasing-making'.[31] To this, James William Montgomery for the prosecution stated that while it 'is very true both verbal and real sedition are known to the laws of this country', the charge at hand was 'not leasing-making, but real sedition; a crime well known to our laws long before the existence of any statute'.[32] He then proceeded to cite Erskine's definition, before embarking on a long argument to show that Gerrald's activities at the British Convention had amounted to real sedition. Placing so much emphasis on real sedition, however, seemed to open up a void, and one of the judges, Lord Henderland, felt the need to close this. 'I can conceive verbal sedition as criminal, as dangerous, as any that can be committed by actions', Henderland stated, because:

> Suppose a man to run into the streets, and call out 'To arms! to arms! kingly power is useless; it is cumbersome, it ought to be laid aside. Parliament is venal and corrupt. Let us name a body of our own to assume the power which they have improperly taken. Rouse and assert your rights.'

Surely, Henderland argued, if this kind of statement was followed by an actual rising, it would be treason, but 'suppose nobody follows him, is there no criminality? ... Can any man doubt that this would be a sedition totally different from any thing that I can conceive with respect to leasing-making?'³³ Henderland's position thus seemed to be based on two main arguments: first that sedition could also take on a verbal form, and that this had to be acknowledged; and second that this verbal kind of sedition had to be kept clearly distinct from leasing-making. How this latter point was to be reconciled with Erskine's definition was, however, open to conjecture, and was not addressed by Henderland. In the end, the attempts made by the defence to turn the charge into one of leasing-making failed and convictions were reached for the crime of sedition.

III

Was this really a satisfactory outcome of the debate on sedition as a crime under Scots law? One scholar who felt the need to address the whole question of sedition and leasing-making was David Hume, the nephew of the famous philosopher. At the time of the trials in 1794, Hume held the post of professor of Scots law at the University of Edinburgh, as well as that of sheriff of Linlithgowshire (he would later, in 1822, become a Baron of the Exchequer).³⁴ A popular and well-renowned teacher of law, Hume addressed criminal law in a series of summer lectures in the 1790s. These lectures formed the basis for his *Commentaries*. While the focus on criminal law alone meant that *Commentaries* was not an institutional work in the strict sense, it is nonetheless considered an authoritative work on Scots law now, and replaced Mackenzie as the main authority on criminal law.³⁵

A first and important point to make with respect to Hume's analysis is that he accepted the trials of 1794 as forming new precedent. For that reason, he did not really question the validity of either the proceedings in court or the outcome, but rather seemed to think that the trials had clarified the situation. In their wake it was possible to give a clear definition of sedition as a crime under Scots law. Hume's work is arguably not, therefore, the right source to consult if the purpose is to determine whether or not these trials constituted a miscarriage of justice. Nevertheless, it can be argued that he was able to trace some of the apparent confusion in the trials to weaknesses in Erskine's definition, and to present a more coherent and persuasive explanation of the nature of sedition as a crime under Scots law.

He began by addressing leasing-making. This particular crime could be traced back to a fifteenth-century statute which stated that leasing-makers are characterised as 'inventors and tellers of rumours "whilk may ingender discorde betwixt the King and his people"'.³⁶ Since then, however, the nature of the crime had been further defined through the act of 1703 and, combined with the 'course of practice' since then, leasing-making should now be understood as 'a verbal injury levelled against the King, and is construed in the law to be done out of malice and evil disposition, entertained against him'.[37] This could take the form of 'the invention of such rumours, stories, and allegations with respect to his Majesty, as are to his prejudice or dishonour', or to question his 'moral character' by accusing him of adultery or describing him as a 'common liar'.[38] Leasing-making was, in other words, directed against the king's *person* and his reputation, and was therefore a crime which could be characterised as 'a high and aggravated sort of *slander*' upon the king. This made it different from sedition because sedition, Hume argued:

> is a crime of a far wider and more various description, as well as of a deeper character, which may equally be committed in relation to any of the other powers, orders, or parts of the public constitution of the land, or to any class or division of the society of its inhabitants, and without the use of special calumnies or slanders against the King, or any other individual: as by the forming of combinations, the taking of resolutions, the circulation of doctrines and opinions, or, in general, the pursuit of any *course of measures and actions*, such as tends to resistance of the Legislature or established Government, or to the new modelling of the State without the authority of law.[39]

Whereas leasing-making essentially consisted in the 'defamation of the King', Hume stated, sedition was a much graver crime in that it was a *'measure and proceeding*, which tends *directly* to occasion a breach between Prince and People, *and is taken by the author for no other purpose'*.[40] It could be committed in a variety of ways such as by 'deed, word, or writing', and in the following discussion Hume presented examples of sedition, covering just about all the different kinds of radical activities which had taken place in Scotland in the first half of the 1790s.[41] Precisely because the *purpose* of the delegates at the British Convention had not been merely to pass slurs on the king or his family, but also to undermine the government of the land, Hume seemed to argue, leasing-making was not the crime they had committed. What then of the distinction between real and verbal sedition and Erskine's view that verbal sedition was synonymous with leasing-making? In Hume's opinion, Erskine's analysis was 'inaccurate' on several counts.

With respect to real sedition, Hume argued, Erskine had confounded it with the 'crime of riot or convocation of the lieges; inasmuch as he holds it to be committed … by an actual commotion only, or breach of the peace'. It was important to make this clear distinction between sedition and rioting, because 'sedition is a State crime; which is levelled against the Government, structure of laws, or political order of the land', and 'if any *hostile* rising ensue, the offender shall be guilty of no lower crime than treason'.[42] It was possible to imagine many kinds of riots, Hume held, which were not spurred on by any seditious purpose – meal mobs plundering grain stores, for example – while the printing and publishing of a pamphlet attacking the government was an act of *real* sedition, precisely because the author had 'taken a most material *step* or *measure* towards disturbing the tranquillity of the State'.[43] But if the writing and publishing of a pamphlet was real sedition, what would then constitute verbal sedition? Again, Hume took issue with Erskine's view of verbal sedition as equalling leasing-making.

Admittedly, there were cases when leasing-making and sedition could be seen to 'coincide', for example in a 'tendency to lessen the due reverence of the Sovereign with his people', but since sedition was 'done on a project of disturbing the State', while leasing-making emanated 'out of a special dislike to the Prince on the throne as a person', they were not 'convertible terms'. The crucial point was again the *purpose* or *intention* held by the perpetrator of the deed. Moreover, even if one accepted the division into real and verbal sedition (and Hume did not dismiss this out of hand), it was, he argued, of little practical use. It was not 'from the form wherein the mischief is conveyed' that sedition could be identified, 'but from the nature and substance of the thing itself'.[44] A speech given at a radical meeting, for example, was as 'real' an act of sedition as the organising of a convention, if it was spurred on by an intention of subverting the British state. It was this underlying intention – and not the medium through which it was expressed – which was central to the question of sedition. The main points that emerged from Hume's analysis, therefore, were that the old Scottish crime of leasing-making was not relevant for the political trials of the 1790s and that sedition should be understood as essentially one kind of crime.

IV

Hume's interpretation received an endorsement by the Advocate Depute at Edinburgh, John Burnett, just over a decade after he had first published his work.[45] Burnett, who himself had taken part in one of the trials of the 1790s as prosecutor in the trial of Thomas Fyshe Palmer in 1793, supported Hume's analysis in all major respects, but also added one important element. In Burnett's opinion:

> Mobs and convocations, arising from some local or private grievance, either real or imagined, may *ultimately* tend to a general purpose, and their proceedings may create a general disquiet and alarm, though there is no intention to subvert the government, or endanger the person of the King.[46]

At first glance, Burnett's argument appears to reduce the importance of *intention* in the definition of sedition. If an action – which had initially been taken to address 'some local or private grievance' but without any intention of challenging the political regime – escalated out of control and turned into a threat against the political system, then, according to this statement, it had to be seen as seditious regardless of the perpetrator's intention. It is, however, possible to see Burnett's point in a different light. If, in a trial for sedition, the defence insisted that the defendant had never intended anything but to present remedies for some perceived flaws in the existing political system and that this did not amount to a desire to topple the *entire* system as such, then the prosecution could retort that, since the actions which had been taken could *tend* to or *lead* to such a threat to the system, the act was, nonetheless, seditious. This could be claimed because the defendant should have *realised* what was the real tendency of his actions. Sedition could thus be proved by the *tendency* of the act, as well as by the *intention* behind it. Burnett's view was considerably slanted in favour of the government and of that crown prosecution of which he himself had been a member less than twenty years before publishing his work.[47] When the Whig Lord Cockburn proceeded to write about the same topic some forty years later, however, it was an altogether different perspective on the trials which emerged in his *Examination*. Despite Cockburn's critical view of the trials, however, he does not seem to have disagreed with Hume and Burnett's analyses of the crime of sedition under Scots law:

> My notion of sedition then is, that it is the publication of any sentiment intended and calculated materially and speedily to obstruct or weaken the legal authority of the State ... Their *tendency* and their *design* must be got at.[48]

Although research has questioned the quality of Cockburn's analysis of Hume, the fact that commentators of such divergent political views could come to an agreement on the nature of a *political* crime suggests that a consensus had eventually been reached.[49]

Notes

1 William Cobbett and T. J. Howell (eds), *Complete Collection of State Trials, continued from the Year 1783 to the Present Time* [hereafter: *State Trials*], 33 vols (London, 1816–26), XXIII, col. 616.
2 On the question of sedition as a crime under English law, see F. K. Prochaska, 'English State Trials in the 1790s: A Case Study', *Journal of British Studies*, 13 (1973), pp. 64–82; Philip Harling, 'The Law of Libel and the Limits of Repression, 1790–1832', *The Historical Journal*, 44 (2003), pp. 107–34.

3 *State Trials*, XXIII, cols 588–9.
4 7 Anne c. 21.
5 A point made by Henry Cockburn in his *An Examination of the Trials for Sedition which have hitherto occurred in Scotland*, 2 vols (New York, [1888] 1970), I, pp. 1–2.
6 The literature on the sedition trials is extensive but, to date, the most comprehensive work remains John Barrell, *Imagining the King's Death: Figurative Treason, Fantasies of Regicide 1793–1796* (Oxford, 2000).
7 *State Trials*, XXIII, col. 536.
8 Baron David Hume, *Commentaries on the Law of Scotland respecting the Description and Punishment of Crimes*, 2 vols (Edinburgh, 1797).
9 John W. Cairns, 'Institutional Writings in Scotland Reconsidered', *The Journal of Legal History*, 4 (1984), p. 89.
10 Ibid., p. 90; J. D. Ford, 'Dalrymple, James, first Viscount Stair (1619–1695)', in H. C. G. Matthew and Brian Harrison (eds), *Oxford Dictionary of National Biography* (Oxford, 2004); D. M. Walker, *The Scottish Legal System* (Edinburgh, 1992), pp. 109–14.
11 John W. Cairns, 'Historical Introduction', Kenneth Reid and Reinhard Zimmermann (eds), *A History of Private Law in Scotland*, 2 vols (Oxford, 2000), I, pp. 170–1; Cairns, 'Institutional Writings', pp. 76–81, 98–102.
12 Walker, *Scottish Legal System*, pp. 452–7. In Scotland, a work becomes institutional when it is 'recognised by the Scottish courts as specially authoritative'; Cairns, 'Institutional Writings', p. 102.
13 Cairns, 'Historical Introduction', p. 68. Common law was held to include the customs and traditions which had developed over time within the Scottish legal tradition, including 'feelings of natural justice', and natural law. It was thus possible to point to other countries and argue that, since sedition was considered a crime 'in all well-governed realms', it had to be a criminal offence in Scotland too, just as murder or theft was; see note 7 above.
14 *State Trials*, XXIII, col. 617.
15 Walker, *Scottish Legal System*, p. 92; Cairns, 'Historical Introduction', pp. 42–5.
16 Walker, *Scottish Legal System*, p. 92; John W. Cairns, 'Scottish Law, Scottish Lawyers and the Status of the Union', in John Robertson (ed.), *A Union for Empire: Political Thought and the British Union of 1707* (Cambridge, 1995), p. 253.
17 *State Trials*, XXIII, col. 617.
18 Olivia F. Robinson, *The Laws and Customs of Scotland in Matters Criminal by Sir George Mackenzie* [hereafter: Mackenzie, *Laws and Customs*] (Edinburgh, [1678] 2012), p. 54.
19 *State Trials*, XXIII, col. 791.
20 Ibid., XXIII, cols 841–5.
21 Ibid., XXIII, col. 681.

22 John Erskine, *An Institute of the Law of Scotland*, 2 vols (Edinburgh, [1773] 1989).
23 Erskine, *Institute*, II, pp. 1186–8. For a further discussion of Erskine's treatment of criminal law, see John W. Cairns, 'John Millar's Lectures on Scots Criminal Law', *Oxford Journal of Legal Studies*, 8 (1988), pp. 387–91.
24 Mackenzie, *Laws and Customs*, pp. 225–6.
25 Cockburn, *Examination*, I, pp. 245–6.
26 *State Trials*, XXIII, cols 617–18.
27 Ibid., XXIII, col. 784.
28 *Acts of the Parliaments of Scotland*, 11 vols (London, 1814–44), XI, 16 September 1703, no. 4, 'Act anent Leesing Makers and Slanderers'.
29 *State Trials*, XXIII, cols 786–8.
30 Ibid., XXIII, col. 800.
31 Ibid., XXIII, cols 828, 841.
32 Ibid., XXIII, cols 853, 855.
33 Ibid., XXIII, col. 890.
34 John W. Cairns, 'Hume, David (bap. 1757, d. 1838)', in Matthew and Harrison (eds), *ODNB*.
35 Walker, *Scottish Legal System*, pp. 453–4.
36 Hume, *Commentaries*, II, p. 79.
37 Ibid., II, p. 82.
38 Ibid., II, pp. 82, 85.
39 Ibid., II, pp. 96–7 [emphasis in the original].
40 Ibid., II, p. 99 [emphasis in the original].
41 Ibid., II, pp. 484.
42 Ibid., II, p. 492. On the first point about a convocation of the lieges, Hume also seemed to take issue with Mackenzie's definition of sedition, while his second point on treason was more in line with that presented in *Laws and Customs*.
43 Ibid., II, p. 493 [emphasis in the original].
44 Ibid., II, pp. 495, 496.
45 John Burnett, *A Treatise on Various Branches of the Criminal Law of Scotland* (Edinburgh, 1811).
46 Ibid., p. 240 n. 2 [emphasis in the original].
47 For an example of Burnett's pro-government views, see Burnett, *Treatise*, pp. 260–1.
48 Cockburn, *Examination*, I, pp. 14–15.
49 John M. Pinkerton, 'Cockburn and the Law', in Alan Bell (ed.), *Lord Cockburn: A Bicentenary Commemoration 1779–1979* (Edinburgh, 1979), pp. 104–23.

CHAPTER 12

The Vilification of Thomas Paine: Constructing a Folk Devil in the 1790s

Michael T. Davis

On 29 July 1797, the *London Evening Post* reported on the tragic events of a suicide that had taken place four days earlier. The victim was John Atwood, a baker from Upper Bristol Road in Bath, who had attempted to hang himself in the previous month but was prevented by the rope breaking. However, on the fateful day there was to be no redemption. During the course of that day, Atwood 'had ran after his wife with a knife, swearing he would kill her', but she was able to pacify him and eventually left him 'tolerably quiet' before attending to business in town. While she was away, Atwood 'shut the maid out of doors, and tied himself up' to a rafter in his house.[1] During the Coroners' examination, the maid – Elizabeth Batchelor – provided a witness statement, noting how she 'perceived frequent symptoms of insanity' in Atwood for the three months prior to his death and how she believed the victim 'was at the time of his so hanging himself ... not of sound mind but lunatic and distracted'. The Coroners' jury agreed and it was ultimately decided that Atwood's suicide was the consequence of him 'not being of sane mind, memory or understanding'.[2] Some newspapers, however, added a twist to this tragedy. The *Oracle and Public Advertiser*, for instance, declared Atwood had been reading Thomas Paine's *Age of Reason* on the morning he committed suicide. The victim's desperation was said to be the result of the 'fumes of intoxication working upon a mind rendered callous by having imbibed such abominable principles'. According to this report, the 'unhappy derangement of mind' experienced by Atwood 'had been occasioned by the fatal impressions made by the perusal of Paine's pernicious doctrine'.[3]

As a trans-Atlantic figure, it seems the capacity for Paine to transfix the minds of men and lead them to perform horrid acts with dreadful endings was not confined to Britain. In Delaware, a physician named Theodore Wilson was allegedly bewitched by Paine in a similar way to Atwood. Wilson was married with two children, but he 'was infected with the most shameful and uneasy of all diseases, an incurable lust after strange women'.[4] The cause of Wilson's 'disease' was said to be the *Age of Reason*, which he first read at the age of twenty-five when he was prepared 'to swallow with delight ... [Paine's] bold slanders of the bible'.[5] Enchanted by Paine's ideas, Wilson pursued Nancy Wiley, the wife of a tavern-keeper in Lewistown and who 'was blest, or rather as it turned out, was curst, with an extraordinary portion of beauty'.[6] Their affair continued for some time until one day in 1799 Mrs Wiley's husband discovered her on the sofa and in the lap of Wilson, 'leaning her cheek against his bosom, he fondly encircling her in his arms and printing *burning kisses* on her lips'.[7] Afterwards, in the presence of his wife, Wilson tried to repent his transgression by burning the *Age of Reason* and 'saying at the same time, "*cursed book! it was you that helped to undo me!*"'.[8] In the end, the curse of Paine could not be broken and Wilson 'had his brains blown out' by his lover's husband.[9]

Both the Atwood and Wilson narratives are deliberate conservative constructions designed to foster anti-Paine sentiments, drawing on several common elements to articulate moral and didactic tales about the dire consequences of reading Paine. The evil effects begin with the psychological impact of Paine's writings which mesmerise men, creating a desperate and deranged state of mind – a form of political madness that makes the subject lose all sense of control. In the late eighteenth century, such a hysterical condition had homological links with attributes of incivility and was used by conservative commentators to dichotomise 'us' from 'them' and 'good' versus 'evil'.[10] Moreover, as Roy Porter points out, observations of insanity in this period were 'meant to be instructive, and the miseries ... hammered home as object lessons to impressionable youngsters'.[11] By all accounts, losing one's mind was the most dreaded disease in this period and one that was believed to dehumanise the individual by rendering their behaviour the same as a wild beast.[12] Only a miserable life could follow from such an infliction, as one eighteenth-century writer observed:

> to attack his fellow creatures with fury like a wild beast; to be tied down, and even beat, to prevent his doing mischief to himself or others; or, on the contrary, to be sad and dejected, to be daily terrified with vain imaginations; to fancy hobgoblins haunting him; and after a life spent in considerable anxiety, to be persuaded that his death will be the commencement of eternal punishment.[13]

In the Atwood and Wilson anecdotes, the loss of mental reasoning was just the beginning of Paine's destructive influence. Both men lose their lives in gruesome performances, enacting their final personal demise and using an ending of death to play on what was the greatest mortal fear of Britons during the eighteenth century.[14] And ultimately the most enduring impact was the levelling of the core of society – the family unit – with the widowed and distraught wives of Paine's victims left alone to raise young children.

I

These elements of the Atwood and Wilson narratives were intentionally evocative, charged with emotion and serving to represent Paine as not only an unworthy citizen but also a genuine threat to society. Paine is identified as an evil force, capable of possessing minds through his writings and bewitching the subject to carry out immoral and destructive acts. Somewhat ironically, by connecting Paine with the loss of a person's mind, anti-radical commentators had contributed to what reformers recognised as a fabricated discourse that was symptomatic of conservative madness. The radical satirist Charles Pigott saw 'writing books full of obscurity and mysticism, filled with extravagant fictions and false rhetoric' as a key definition of 'madness' and something to which loyalists were prone.[15] But the Atwood and Wilson anecdotes were much more than hollow conservative fantasies or, as Pigott put it, the product of 'an over-heated brain with disappointed ambition'.[16] They were an integral part of conservative intervention in the space of public opinion, a deliberate tactic to address Paine and construct an anti-Paine fear in social consciousness. Indeed, the strategy of defaming and denigrating Paine was the preferred approach of his British critics. Contemporary written responses to Paine were sometimes serious ideological critiques but, as Harry Dickinson points out, most conservative propagandists preferred malicious condemnation: 'Afraid that sober arguments might persuade readers that there was at least some merit in Paine's works, they turned to abuse and vilification in order to persuade readers there was much to fear and nothing to praise in these writings.'[17]

Indeed, this construction of fear had an important sociological purpose. As Frank Furedi notes: 'Fear serves as a cultural metaphor to express claims, concerns, values, moral outrage and condemnation.'[18] The suspicion and dread of Paine was in many ways an all-pervasive and all-consuming aspect of counter-revolutionary culture in the 1790s, as a moral panic was raised and sustained to identify and validate him as an amoral agent and deviant in society.[19] Stanley Cohen asserted that societies 'appear to be subject, every now and then, to periods of moral panic', during which time a 'condition, episode, person or group of persons emerges to become defined as a threat to societal values and interests'.[20] The press plays a critical role in facilitating and sustaining a moral panic, with the nature of the perceived threat 'presented in a stylized and stereotypical fashion by the mass media' and as the 'moral barricades are manned by editors, bishops, politicians and other right-thinking people'.[21] A critical phase in the developmental cycle of a moral panic involves the amplification of fear through false exaggerations and distortions as well as predictions of dire consequences of the threat.[22] In this process, coded images of deviants are produced as those who transgress an evaluated norm are identified as the targets of anxiety, hostility, restraint and retribution. The construction of these deviant identities creates personas of 'otherness', whereby scapegoats are stigmatised as folk devils. They become disvalued members of society, stripped of their political, social and moral legitimacy and confined to the margins. In that space, folk devils exist as 'visible reminders of what we should not be' and are instantly recognised as 'unambiguously unfavourable symbols'.[23]

Part of this symbolisation involves cultivating folk devils as wicked and depraved social types. As one scholar notes, folk devils are 'the personification of evil ... which are stripped of all positive characteristics and endowed with pejorative evaluations'.[24] Jeffrey Alexander suggests such characteristics and evaluations are used to locate members of society on the grid of civil culture through the use of an elaborate symbolic code. The 'worthy' are defined by the attributes on the positive side of the symbolic set, while the identities of the 'unworthy' are shaped and informed by the negative side, which represents, as Alexander explains:

> the 'worst' in the national community, it embodies evil. The objects it identifies threaten the core community from somewhere outside it. From this marginal position, they present a powerful source of pollution. To be close to these polluted objects ... is dangerous. Not only can one's reputation be sullied and one's status endangered, but one's very security can be threatened as well. To have one's self or movement be identified in terms of these objects causes anguish, disgust, and alarm.[25]

This symbolic code reveals 'the skeletal structures on which social communities build their familiar stories, the rich narrative forms that guide their everyday, taken-for-granted political life'.[26] In the 'familiar stories' constructed by conservatives in the 1790s, Paine was nothing less than an evil wrongdoer.

Indeed, by identifying Paine as the binary opposite of a moral citizen, loyalists were able to define the moral boundaries of what they considered to be the respectable core of society: 'Deviant forms of behaviour, by marking the outer edges of group life, give the inner structure its special character and thus supply the framework within which the people of the group develop an orderly sense of their own cultural identity.'[27] To represent Paine as evil had deep political meaning and ramifications. As social psychologists suggest, evil people have trouble maintaining control over their emotions and evil represents the 'antithesis of order, peace, and stability'.[28] As the definitions of respectability were tightened in the 1790s, calm, reasonable, rational and sane were the personal attributes required of a worthy and active citizen. By implication, those who became immersed in the excitable and evil politics of Paine were relegated to the margins of society by loyalists and denied a place in the political nation.

II

And this was a political nation that loyalists considered to be threatened by Paine. In the over-reactionary counter-revolutionary culture of the 1790s, Paine was often deplored as the source of all disorder and instability. Interestingly, however, some contemporaries attempted to deflate the revolutionary influence of Paine by suggesting there was actually no real threat at all. In November 1792 – at a time when *Rights of Man* was enjoying enormous success and circulation – the *World* newspaper reflected upon Paine's 'endeavour to gull John Bull with the supposed advantages of *Air Balloon Governments*'.[29] This is a potent metaphor in the context of the early 1790s. At this time, air ballooning was a cultural phenomenon that captured the popular imagination – in much the same way as the *Rights of Man*.[30] When deconstructed further, there were other analogies implied between air balloons and Paine's pamphlet: both appeared to have substance but were in fact hollow, and both seemed buoyant but were rudderless. The *Rights of Man* – like an air balloon – was something of a disguise and it was suggested in the *World* that Paine had 'little chance with the deception' because 'English sincerity is not so easily entrapped. If the French are mad, and want *Chaos* to come again, thank God the English are not so: they are satisfied with one good master.'[31]

Yet, it was chaos that most conservative commentators predicted would flow from the ideas of Paine. In 1791, within a few months of the first part of the *Rights of Man* being published, the *Evening Mail* made a tongue-in-cheek list of the 'warranted' consequences of Paine's doctrine that included dethroning the monarch; overturning Parliament; pulling down the courts of law; murder; arson; and rape. If those destructive consequences of the *Rights of Man* were not enough, and 'in order to crown the whole and give surrounding empires an example of British freedom', it was suggested that the navy of England be moored in one place to 'let Paine set the whole ablaze by lighting a fireship with *Magna Carta*, and directing it to the body of the fleet in honour of the *Rights of Man*'.[32] Imagining Paine as an arsonist gave him the dubious distinction of being placed in a select class of criminals – along with those convicted of murder, rape and treason – facing the death penalty. And, in an age of scarce fire-fighting resources, it was an image designed to connect what one scholar notes as a 'considerable fear and condemnation'[33] of an act of destruction with the calamitous politics of Paine.

This was not the only time that loyalists fantasised about Paine as an incendiary. On the evening of 9 May 1792, a *'pair of breeches* then on fire, but not in flames' was discovered in the toilet of the House of Commons and the press reported the incident as a deliberate machination to destroy the building.[34] By the end of the month, some newspapers were reporting the 'real cause' was a Scottish Member of Parliament who was 'not much in the habit of using ... *flannel* drawers' and was 'taken rather suddenly ... when, in his haste, he forgot his drawers, and absolutely dispatched his business therein'. In this 'disagreeable predicament', he decided to conceal the 'disaster in the ceiling over the water-closet'.[35] As the so-called 'Breeches Plot' thickened, the focus shifted away from this embarrassing accident when Isaac Cruikshank pictured Paine as the ringleader of a plot to destroy Parliament in a caricature called *Mad Tom's First Practical Essay on the Rights of Man* (1792) (Fig. 12.1). As an accused sans-culotte, Paine was thought to have no need for his breeches and – supported by the reformist brewer Samuel Whitbread, and an intoxicated Richard Brinsley Sheridan, who was a sitting Member of Parliament at the time – Paine set fire to his own straw-filled trousers while exclaiming: 'Now for a Deed that will outdo my Pen.'

Figure 12.1 Isaac Cruikshank, *Mad Tom's First Practical Essay on the Rights of Man* (1792). © Trustees of the British Museum

Cruikshank envisaged Paine as much more than just the destroyer of the House of Commons. In the image *Wha Wants Me* (1792) (Fig. 12.2), Paine trampled under his feet all the ideals and virtues of the British nation: obedience to the laws; justice; personal security; private property; loyalty; morality; and happiness. Yet Paine was offering his services to bring liberty and equality to the nation, prepared for a fight and carrying on his back a bundle of weapons labelled 'Levelling Instruments'. Simmering in the heat haze rising from his inflamed mind were the practical realities for any nation that embraced Paine's doctrine: anarchy; murder; treason; rebellion; atheism; misery; famine; and injustice.

With a proud stance and a wry smile, Paine seemed rather pleased with these disastrous outcomes. Some conservative commentators suggested that Paine's indifference to – or even his glorification of – his

Figure 12.2 Isaac Cruikshank, *Wha Wants Me* (1792). © Trustees of the British Museum

pernicious principles extended from the fact he had nothing to lose. The *World* newspaper in July 1792, for instance, stated what was considered a truism *'that every man will fight for what is dear to him'* but 'Paine has no property, so he cannot fight for that'.³⁶ Several months later, the *Public Advertiser* made a similar observation:

> What little we know of Mr Paine as an inhabitant of this country is, that he has not one inch of land, nor one shilling's worth of property in it, consequently would risk nothing should he succeed in throwing it into confusion. So far we can only consider him absolutely indifferent as to our national prosperity or adversity.³⁷

In the late eighteenth century, there was an intrinsic connection between property and social status as well as political rights. As Harry Dickinson points out: 'The ownership of sufficient property to render a man independent was still seen as the ideal basis for the franchise.'³⁸

According to the *Public Advertiser*, however, Paine was considered to be much worse than someone merely without property: he was also a traitor. It made reference to Paine having 'acted in concert with our enemies'and, following his election to the French National Convention in September 1792, he was seen as 'exerting his endeavours to promote the prosperity of those whom ... we should have called our natural enemies'.³⁹ Given the relationship between Britain and France was 'one of the most intense, most troubled, and most significant in modern times'⁴⁰ and the two nations were on the brink of war when this column was published, the passage can be read as an expression of historical animosity and contemporaneous rising tensions. But it was also drawing on the suspended terror of revolutionary conspiracies in Britain during the 1790s. In fact, conspiracy theories were so pervasive throughout the entire eighteenth century that some scholars point to a 'conspiratorial mode' during this period.⁴¹ As Michael Taylor states: 'Over the course of the long eighteenth century, fear of conspiracy had become commonplace and the clandestine plot was an integral part of British and European political cultures. In the postrevolutionary decade, recourse to conspiracy was a natural means of explaining trauma and of focusing current paranoia.'⁴²

To imagine Paine engaging in conspiracy was a way of channelling conservative energies as well as a means of conflating and inflating public paranoia. Some conservative propagandists not only presented the threat of Paine conspiring with others as a phenomenon confined to the temporal world but one that sometimes involved supernatural agents. There are examples of Paine depicted in caricature in council with a demon, which informs the notion of Paine as a folk devil and evokes his evilness. For instance, in *The Friends of the People* (1792), Isaac Cruikshank

Figure 12.3 Isaac Cruikshank, *The Friends of the People* (1792).
© Trustees of the British Museum

showed Paine – sitting on the right on a barrel of gunpowder and with a dagger in his hand – facing Joseph Priestley (Fig. 12.3). On the wall were hung illustrations of historical as well as contemporary moments and symbols of subversion and terror: a lynching; the assassination of the King of Sweden in 1792; the execution of Charles I; Wat Tyler; and the guillotine. Joining the two men was a smiling demon, with the trio surrounded by weapons, as well as books of which the contents contain such ruinous outcomes of this nefarious conspiracy as rebellion, downfall of royalty and – to ensure the message was clear – a double dose of treason and massacres. Such associations of Paine with a demon were a pictorial trope favoured by loyalist caricaturists during the 1790s and which endured well after Paine's death.[43]

It was a simple but effective way of distinguishing 'good' from 'evil', which was also a polarity commonly captured in conservative literature. In an anonymous broadside issued in 1792, the Devil took on the role of father to a deliberately misspelt 'Tom Pain' and together with 'the damn'd French rascals' they 'swore ... to drive us all to hell and damnation'.[44] In the same year, *Intercepted Correspondence from Satan to Citizen Paine* was published, in which the Devil appears as Paine's 'warmest and most congenial associate' and advises him to follow his advice, among which is 'sowing the glorious seeds of Dissention and Rebellion among mankind'.[45] And another publication transformed Paine into the mentor for a 'thin, pale-faced fellow' who sometimes meets a group of strangers at a public house that call him 'Mr Mac'Serpent' – a thinly veiled reference to the snake as the embodiment of the Devil and a symbol of chaos.[46]

Although some contemporaries seemed almost willing to concede to the apparent contradiction of Paine's 'evil genius',[47] more often – as John Barrell puts it – he appeared 'as the arch-agent, the Pandora of evil and irresponsibility in the great narrative of revolution'.[48] Certain loyalist commentators believed the lid on Paine's box of curses was opened due to the social class to which his works appealed. In a letter published in the *Morning Post* on 29 May 1794, one correspondent complained of how Paine 'abuses very violently all Systems of Religion' in the first part of the *Age of Reason* and goes on to say: 'It appals me with horror when I consider the evil tendency and pernicious effects that may arise, if a Publication of such a nature is allowed to pass unrefuted, particularly when I reflect on the description of people who may peruse it.'[49] Two years earlier, when the *Rights of Man* was newly published, a similar reflection was made on Paine's audience: 'Mr Paine ... writes against the Government, under which we have risen superior to all difficulties, and cries aloud for reform; proposing such, principally, as are most likely to obtain the support of the lower order of inhabitants of this country.'[50] And it was a point not lost by the visual satirists of the period. The engraver, William Grainger, produced a print in 1793 of Paine in a sylvan scene and captioned: '"Hear and improve", he pertly cries: "I come to make all nations wise"'. In one hand, raised above his head, is a copy of the *Rights of Man* and around him a group of interested monkeys pejoratively representing the social status and intelligence of those who read Paine.

III

Yet, not everyone believed the British public would ignorantly accept Paine's ideas. In fact, one writer in the *Diary or Woodfall's Register* – identified as 'Detector' – went so far as to disclaim the *Rights of Man* had any wicked capacity:

> no evil possibly can arise to the community from Paine's answer to Mr Burke's excellent performance. The opinion is insidious, contemptible, ludicrous, and pusillanimous. No work was ever more esteemed than Mr Burke's, nor more generally reprobated than Paine's. Happily the human race are not born to be abstract reasoners; they have a strong bias to delight in good actions, and abhor such as are obnoxious.[51]

This was not, however, an attempt to construct an anti-panic about Paine. Rather it was a pointed tactic of contempt aimed at debasing the author of the *Rights of Man* and the credibility of the ideas presented in that work. And contempt was something that was heaped upon Paine in large quantity by his critics, especially when it came to his personal character and appearance.[52] As Corinna Wagner notes: 'Anti-Painites contended that his solitariness, his drunkenness, his dirtiness, his animalistic features, and his sexual deviance were all physical manifestations of his mutinous politics ... Through the efforts of his political enemies, his allegedly diseased, alcoholic, sexually dysfunctional, pocked, and dirty body became the signifier of his true intentions'.[53] These visions of Paine were largely cultivated by malicious biographies written by his opponents, *ad hominem* attacks that tended to repeat scurrilous falsehoods one after another.[54]

In one of these biographies – written by a one-time Manchester radical, James Cheetham, and published soon after Paine's death in 1809 – we are presented with an utterly repugnant human being:

> Paine had no good qualities. Incapable of friendship, he was vain, envious, malignant .... In his private dealings he was unjust, never thinking of paying for what he had contracted, and always cherishing deadly resentments against those who by law compelled him to do justice .... He was guilty of the worst species of seduction; the alienation of a wife and children from a husband and a father. Filthy and drunken, he was a compound of all the vices.[55]

Such characterisations of Paine were not only intended to humiliate the man or stain his reputation, but also provided evidence of the instability of his politics. The public message was to avoid the fiendish ideas of Paine in order to maintain a healthy, stable life. Paine's personal habits were constructed as transgressive behaviours, the objects of disgust and ridicule. This was especially the case when it came to Paine's notoriously luckless marriages and accusations of polygamy. As a sign of natural masculinity, one newspaper suggested 'a man will fight ... for his *children* and his *wife*. But Tom Paine is embarrassed here: he does not know *which wife* he is to fight for.'[56] And one lyrical conservative found Paine gave little consideration to women in both his personal life and in politics:

> In youth, to the fair sex this patriot was supple.
> Of wives, honest Tom, 'tis now said *has a couple*;
> By what means they exist, he cares not a jot.
> In the *new rights of man*, wives are *always forgot*.[57]

Perhaps even more pungent than the criticism of Paine's personal life was his rendering as a dirty human being. As Wagner notes: 'In the 1790s and throughout the following decades, the sobriquet most often attached to Tom Paine's name was "filthy".'[58] His detractors could not emphasise enough the dirtiness of Paine. For an emphatic Cheetham, any description of the 'notorious' filthiness of Paine would be 'very unequal to the reality. Fancy cannot picture an object so offensive to sense.'[59] But this was much more than merely insulting name-calling to defame Paine. There was an underlying pathology to the slander, which conservative writers used as a political imperative: 'Physicians linked dirt and unclean habits with iniquity, apathy, social irresponsibility, irreligion, and political guile. Loyalists tapped into fears about revolution and the burgeoning emphasis on moral probity to forge a tripartite connection between bodily cleanliness, clean politics, and "clean living".'[60] This was also not just about Paine's personal hygiene. His filthy, monstrous body was deviant as well as 'dangerously contagious'[61] – just like his politics. Paine was seen as the 'offspring of malignancy',[62] his ideas and his person like a cancer in society that needed to be eradicated.

One writer envisaged the elimination of Paine one body part at a time: 'I only wonder ... the real Patriots of every nation, do not unite in fond contention, and pull him limb from limb, that each country might proudly say – "Here lies a part of Thomas Paine!".'[63] Others contemplated the death of Paine in a manner more familiar to the eighteenth-century observer. In an engraving called *The End of Pain* (1793) – with the deliberately misspelt pun of Paine's name – Paine dangled on a noose from a lamp-post inscribed with the words 'Rights of this Man' (see Fig. 12.4). Behind him, clinging to the post with his talons, is the Devil looking down on Paine as if in anticipation of his arrival in Hell. But this was to be neither the first nor the last time Paine suffered a figurative death. In 1792, his last dying speech and confession was published in Plymouth after his body was 'hanging the usual time' then 'his Remains were consigned to the Flames', with thousands of spectators exclaiming '*May every Traitor to his King and Country thus perish*'.[64] By the following year, Paine was resurrected in Stoke-upon-Trent where, at his mock execution before a large crowd of spectators, Paine denounced himself in his published last confession: 'never follow the wicked Devices of me THOMAS PAINE for tricks have been dev'lish and I am afraid, I am now going to the Devil for them'.[65]

Occasionally the mock dying speeches and confessions of Paine were distributed during the performances of effigy burnings, as happened at Tottenham in December 1792 when Paine's effigy was seated in a cart before being paraded through the town streets, hanged from a gibbet and burnt before an excitable crowd '*whose acclamations of loyalty*

Figure 12.4 *The End of Pain* (1793). © Trustees of the British Museum

showed their attachment to King and the constitution'.[66] Similar enactments of loyalist effusion and reassurance were to be played out across England between November 1792 and March 1793.[67] These were highly ritualised and predictable performances: the effigy would be paraded around the streets, often before a mock trial followed by its hanging and burning. They were also festive occasions, with fireworks, the ringing of church bells, the singing of songs and the consumption of plenty of alcohol. And they represent a staged drama facilitated by official sanction or, as E. P. Thompson put it, 'carefully fostered demonstrations of loyalty'.[68] However, there was at least one report of an inversion of the script in a village in Suffolk in March 1793. On that occasion, the local rector offered to pay the locals to burn Paine in effigy; but the same people were subsequently given an equal sum of money to burn an effigy of the rector by an 'intelligent gentleman ... to show how little can be learnt, or depended upon with respect to the sentiments of the common people on politics, how little they know of the present disputes, and how easily a sum of money or a little beer will induce them to change sides'.[69] Whether this incident occurred or not, the burnings in general can be 'used to demonstrate popular loyalty to the king, constitution, and government, and also to intimidate any local radicals'.[70]

While the Paine burnings did have these broader political meanings and implications, they were also an attack on the symbolic body of Paine. Symbolically, setting an effigy of Paine alight was about the utter destruction of him, the dispersal of his body and his removal from the community. Fire was not only destructive but in early-modern Western European cultures it also had a significant role in dealing with a folk devil: 'to instill and reinforce fear of purgatory and hell through public burning of witches, heretics, and others presumed deserving of the consequences of God's wrath'.[71] There was also a long legal tradition in Europe that reserved burnings for the most heinous criminals in society, and when the body of that criminal was not available – as was the case with Paine, who had escaped to France in 1792 to avoid trial – then the outlaw would be executed *in effigio*.[72] In this way, as James Frazer stated, effigy burning was 'merely a substitute for burning the wicked' person themselves.[73] On the one hand, burning Paine's effigy was a cathartic and cleansing performance for local communities, allowing loyalists to vent against Paine in a ritualised form of violence and punishment. But, as a form of communal shaming, it also served as a unifying force by making 'unspeakable community grievances and private disputes into matters of community concern'.[74]

IV

Ironically, the Paine burnings to some extent fostered and extended Paine's celebrity status – notorious or otherwise – which was constantly on the rise during the 1790s. He was, as one scholar notes, 'the most widely read theorist in the age of democratic revolutions'.[75] But he was, according to his conservative critics, 'an indigent and illiterate man'.[76] Such a baseless claim ignored its own inherent paradox that Paine sold copies of his major works in the hundreds of thousands. Nonetheless, it did hint at the scurrilous vilification Paine faced as British counter-revolutionary culture in the late eighteenth century constructed an enduring moral panic around him. As Jack Fruchtman notes, Paine believed he was 'a prophet ... a man absolutely certain that he was right because he fought for the cause he believed was just and, ultimately, good'.⁷⁷ Many more, however, insisted Paine was not only wrong but also a danger to society and whose cause was evil. Many would rage against Paine but none better than the American statesman, John Adams, who was inspired by the *Age of Reason* to an unrestrained rant to Benjamin Waterhouse, a physician, in 1805:

> I know not whether any man in the world has had more influence on its inhabitants or affairs for the last thirty years than Tom Paine.... For such a mongrel between pig and puppy, begotten by a wild boar on a bitch wolf, never before in any age of the world was suffered by the poltroonery of mankind, to run through such a career of mischief.⁷⁸

Folk devil or not, even Adams conceded in the end that the late eighteenth century was truly the 'Age of Paine'.

Notes

1 *London Evening Post*, 29 July 1797.
2 Bath Record Office, Coroners' Examinations 1776–98, BC/4/1/1, 'The Information of Witnesses taken at the Guildhall in the City of Bath', 26 July 1797.
3 *Oracle and Public Advertiser*, 1 August 1797. A similar report was circulated in the *True Briton*, 4 August 1797.
4 Mason L. Weems, *God's Revenge against Adultery, Awfully Exemplified in the Following Cases of American Crim. Con.* (Baltimore, 1815), p. 4. For a brief secondary account of Theodore Wilson, see Roger Allen Martin, 'The Wiley-Wilson Murder', *Delaware Lawyer*, 1 (1983), pp. 39–41.
5 Weems, *God's Revenge*, p. 4.
6 Ibid., p. 7.
7 Ibid., p. 10.
8 Ibid., p. 14.
9 Ibid., p. 1.
10 On the homological set of codes used to inform notions of civility, see Jeffrey C. Alexander, 'Citizen and Enemy as Symbolic Classification: On the Polarizing Discourse of Civil Society', in Michèle Lamont and Marcel Fournier (eds), *Cultivating Differences: Symbolic Boundaries and the Making of Inequality* (Chicago and London, 1992), pp. 289–308. Also see Jeffrey C. Alexander, *The Meanings of Social Life: A Cultural Sociology* (Oxford, 2003), pp. 120–54.
11 Roy Porter, *Body Politic: Disease, Death and Doctors in Britain 1650–1900* (Ithaca, 2001), p. 94.
12 Andrew Scull, *The Most Solitary of Afflictions: Madness and Society in Britain 1700–1900* (New Haven and London, 1993), pp. 56–8.
13 Richard Mead, *Medical Precepts and Cautions* (London, 1751), pp. 74–5.

14 Joanna Bourke, *Fear: A Cultural History* (London, 2005), pp. 27, 34, 75.
15 Charles Pigott, *A Political Dictionary: Explaining the True Meaning of Words* (London, 1795), p. 71.
16 Ibid.
17 H. T. Dickinson, 'Thomas Paine and His British Critics', *Enlightenment and Dissent*, 27 (2011), p. 33.
18 Frank Furedi, 'The Objectification of Fear and the Grammar of Morality', in Sean Hier (ed.), *Moral Panic and the Politics of Anxiety* (London, 2011), p. 90.
19 On the sociology of moral panics, see Stanley Cohen, *Folk Devils and Moral Panics: The Creation of the Mods and Rockers* (London, 1972); Eric Goode and Nachman Ben-Yehuda, *Moral Panics: The Social Construction of Deviance* (Oxford, 1994); Kenneth Thompson, *Moral Panics* (London, 1998). On the radical panic in the 1790s, see Michael T. Davis, 'A Reign of Terror: The British Jacobin Panic and the Rule of Law in the 1790s', in David Lemmings and Claire Walker (eds), *Moral Panics, the Press and the Law in Early Modern England* (Basingstoke, 2009), pp. 221–44.
20 Cohen, *Folk Devils and Moral Panics*, p. 9.
21 Ibid.
22 Chas Critcher, 'Moral Panic Analysis: Past, Present and Future', *Sociology Compass*, 2 (2008), pp. 1127–44.
23 Cohen, *Folk Devils and Moral Panics*, pp. 2, 41.
24 Sean Hier, 'Conceptualizing Moral Panic through a Moral Economy of Harm', *Critical Sociology*, 28 (2002), p. 313.
25 Alexander, 'Citizen and Enemy as Symbolic Classification', pp. 296–7.
26 Ibid., p. 294.
27 Kai T. Erikson, *Wayward Puritans: A Study in the Sociology of Deviance* (New York, 1966), p. 13.
28 R. Baumeister, *Evil: Inside Human Violence and Cruelty* (New York, 1997), pp. 73–4.
29 *World*, 21 November 1792.
30 On air ballooning in the late eighteenth century, see Paul Keen, 'The "Balloonomania": Science and Spectacle in 1780s England', *Eighteenth-Century Studies*, 39 (2006), pp. 507–35; Michael R. Lynn, 'Consumerism and the Rise of Balloons in Europe at the End of the Eighteenth Century', *Science in Context*, 21 (2008), pp. 73–98; Michael R. Lynn, *The Sublime Invention: Ballooning in Europe, 1783–1820* (London, 2010).
31 *World*, 21 November 1792.
32 *Evening Mail*, 8 July 1791.
33 David Taylor, *Crime, Policing and Punishment in England, 1750–1914* (Basingstoke, 1998), p. 35. On the crime of arson in the eighteenth century, see Frank McLynn, *Crime and Punishment in Eighteenth-Century England* (Oxford, 1991), pp. 83–7.
34 *The British Chronicle*, 16 May 1792.
35 *The Lincoln, Rutland and Stamford Mercury*, 25 May 1792.
36 *World*, 27 July 1792.

37 *Public Advertiser*, 30 October 1792.
38 H. T. Dickinson, *Liberty and Property: Political Ideology in Eighteenth-Century Britain* (London, 1977), p. 191.
39 *Public Advertiser*, 30 October 1792.
40 Robert Tombs and Isabelle Tombs, *That Sweet Enemy: The French and the British from the Sun King to the Present* (New York, 2007), p. xxiii.
41 Gordon S. Wood, 'Conspiracy and the Paranoid Style: Causality and Deceit in the Eighteenth Century', *William and Mary Quarterly*, 39 (1982), pp. 401–41.
42 Michael Taylor, 'British Conservatism, the Illuminati, and the Conspiracy Theory of the French Revolution, 1797–1802', *Eighteenth-Century Studies*, 47 (2014), p. 299.
43 For visual representations of Paine in association with a demon, see for instance *Specimen of Equality and Fraternity* (n.d.) by John Paget, which shows Paine greeting Priestley who is followed by Nicholas Bonneville portrayed as a demon; *Tom Paine's Nightly Pest* (1792) by James Gillray, showing a demon fleeing through a window from Paine's bedchamber; *Mad Tom in a Rage* (c. 1801), an American print by an unknown artist that presents Paine being assisted by the Devil to pull down the federal government; *The Political Champion Turned Resurrection Man!* (1819) by Isaac Cruikshank, in which William Cobbett rides astride a demon carrying the bones of Paine from America to Europe; and *A Bait for John Bull* (1830) by Charles Jameson Grant, which depicts the Devil attempting to lure John Bull into a trap covered in advertisements for radical works, including those of Paine.
44 *True Blue; or Heart of Oak for Ever* ([London], [1792]), broadside.
45 *Intercepted Correspondence from Satan to Citizen Paine* ([London], [c. 1792]), in Gregory Claeys (ed.), *Political Writings of the 1790s*, 8 vols (London, 1995), V, pp. 412–13.
46 Ralph Sneyd, *Liberty and Equality, Treated of in a Short History Addressed from a Poor Man to His Equals* (London, 1792), p. 6.
47 *Oracle and Public Advertiser*, 18 February 1797.
48 John Barrell, 'Portraits and Caricatures of Paine', unpublished paper presented at 'The Tom Paine Forum: Politics and Revolution', Lewes Town Hall, 4 July 2009. I am grateful to John Barrell for providing a copy of this paper to me.
49 *Morning Post*, 29 May 1794.
50 *Public Advertiser*, 30 October 1794.
51 *Diary of Woodfall's Register*, 13 July 1791.
52 See Corinna Wagner, 'Loyalist Propaganda and the Scandalous Life of Tom Paine: "Hypocritical Monster!"', *British Journal for Eighteenth-Century Studies*, 28 (2005), pp. 97–115; and Corinna Wagner, *Pathological Bodies: Medicine and Political Culture* (Berkeley and Los Angeles, 2013), pp. 129–66.
53 Ibid., p. 133.

54 For an overview of the malicious biographies of Paine, see Dickinson, 'Thomas Paine and His British Critics', pp. 38–43.
55 James Cheetham, *The Life of Thomas Paine* (New York, 1809), pp. 313–14.
56 *World*, 27 July 1792.
57 *World*, 14 July 1791.
58 Wagner, *Pathological Bodies*, p. 139.
59 Cheetham, *The Life of Thomas Paine*, p. 271.
60 Wagner, *Pathological Bodies*, p. 136.
61 Margaret Schildrick, *Embodying the Monster: Encounters with the Vulnerable Self* (London, 2002), p. 68.
62 *Oracle and Public Advertiser*, 18 February 1797.
63 Sneyd, *Liberty and Equality*, pp. 10–11.
64 *The Last Dying Speech, Confession, Behaviour, Birth, Parentage and Education of Thomas Paine* ([Plymouth], [1792]), broadside.
65 *The Last Dying Speech and Confession of Tom Paine, Who was Executed at Stoke-Upon-Trent* ([Stoke-upon-Trent], [1793]), broadside.
66 William Robinson, *The History and Antiquities of the Parish of Tottenham, in the County of Middlesex*, 2 vols (London, 1840), I, p. 73.
67 For a discussion of the Paine burnings, see Nicholas Rogers, 'Burning Tom Paine: Loyalism and Counter-Revolution in Britain, 1792–1793', *Histoire sociale/Social History*, 32 (1999), pp. 139–71; and Frank O'Gorman, 'The Paine Burnings of 1792–1793', *Past and Present*, 193 (2006), pp. 111–55.
68 E. P. Thompson, *The Making of the English Working Class* (London, 1963), p. 123.
69 *Morning Chronicle*, 8 March 1793.
70 Dickinson, 'Thomas Paine and His British Critics', p. 53.
71 Barbara A. Weightman, 'Sacred Landscapes and the Phenomenon of Light', *Geographical Review*, 86 (1996), p. 62.
72 David Freedberg, *The Power of Images: Studies in the History and Theory of Response* (Chicago, 1989), pp. 246–82.
73 James George Frazer, *The Golden Bough: A Study of Magic and Religion* (London, 1967), pp. 851–2.
74 Russell P. Dobash and R. Emerson Dobash, 'Community Response to Violence Against Wives: Charivari, Abstract Justice and Patriarchy', *Social Problems*, 28 (1981), p. 565.
75 Seth Cotler, *Tom Paine's America: The Rise and Fall of Transatlantic Radicalism in the Early Republic* (Charlottesville, 2011), p. 3.
76 *St James's Chronicle*, 9 April 1793.
77 Jack Fruchtman, *Thomas Paine: Apostle of Freedom* (New York, 1994), p. 262.
78 Cited in Craig Nelson, *Thomas Paine: Enlightenment, Revolution, and the Birth of Modern Nations* (New York, 2006), p. 89.

CHAPTER 13

Nelson's Circles: Networking in the Navy during the French Wars

Marianne Czisnik

This essay employs social network analysis to examine the means by which Admiral Horatio Nelson built up a wide range of contacts throughout his career and the ways in which he used the resulting social networks.[1] Nelson's career provides ample evidence for such analysis, not least because the Royal Navy was the largest organisation of its day and a huge network in its own right.[2] Not only did Nelson operate within and rely on this network, he was also one of its major actors whose activities were of major public, and now historical, importance. Moreover, sources which reveal his contacts to people both within and outside the navy are numerous and comparatively accessible.

Nelson's letters form the source base for this analysis. A number of subsequent printed collections supplement Nicolas's seven-volume edition of Nelson's correspondence published in the 1840s.[3] These include three nineteenth-century editions containing Nelson's letters to Lady Hamilton;[4] Naish's edition of *Nelson's Letters to His Wife and Other Documents*;[5] several specialised editions covering particular aspects of his career;[6] and the result of White's lengthy and intercontinental search for undiscovered letters.[7] Each of these works added new material to the impressive 3,774 letters that Nicolas had managed to release into print. In total, 4,838 printed letters have been entered into a database that formed the basis for the analysis contained in this essay.

Nevertheless, this database, though thorough, is necessarily incomplete. During the early years of Nelson's career those to whom he wrote often did not feel any need for or interest in keeping his letters. This started to change gradually when Nelson was posted to the Mediterranean in 1794 and more dramatically when he became famous at the end of 1798, after the battle of the Nile. Even during the campaign leading to the battle of Trafalgar, however, not all of the letters Nelson wrote survived. This is evident from an examination of sources at the National Maritime Museum: a mere sample of forty letters to Nelson in the period 1803 to 1805 from the British ambassador at Madrid (John Holkham Frere), the British consul at Cadiz (James Duff) and the acting governor of Gibraltar (Thomas Trigge) indicates that quite a few of his letters are missing.[8]

I

Despite this caveat, a corpus of 4,838 published letters is more than sufficient to illustrate the links that connected Nelson to many other people, who in turn formed different and varying networks of their own. Nelson represents what sociologists might call a 'node' within a network of 'links'. Taking letters to represent these links, we can give a preliminary impression of how intensely Nelson was woven into the network by looking at how the sheer number of letters changed over the course of his adult life (see Fig. 13.1).

This overview demonstrates that Nelson corresponded more during periods of active service. During his career as a captain in the West Indies (1780–7) the number of letters he wrote increased year by year, while he wrote hardly at all while on half-pay ashore (1788–92). On being given the command of a line-of-battle ship in the Mediterranean at the beginning of 1793, Nelson took up letter-writing at the same rate as he had left off in his last year as a captain on active service. From then until his death his writing activities increased overall, but with

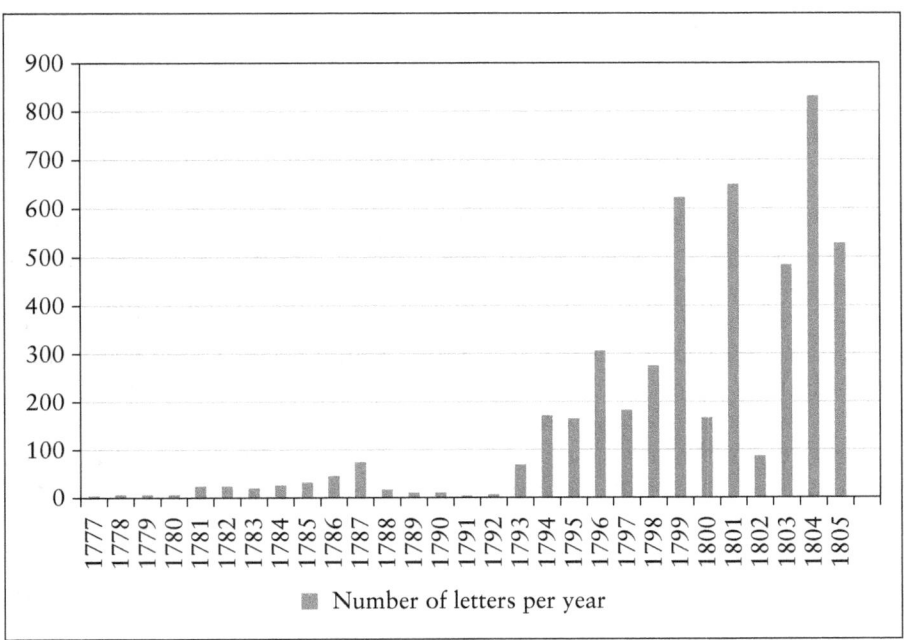

Figure 13.1 Number of letters per year, 1777–1805

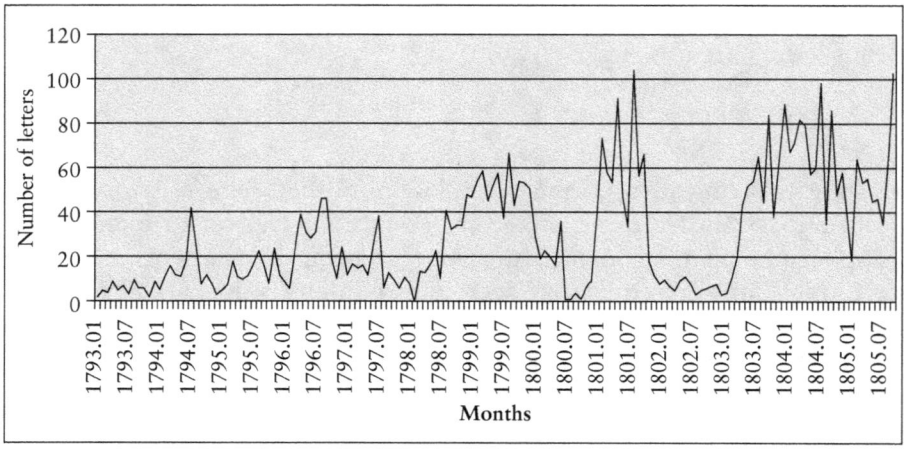

Figure 13.2 Number of letters per month, 1793–1805

some notable troughs: his letter-writing was interrupted by the loss of his right arm and subsequent period of recovery (1797–8), during his overland journey home from the Mediterranean (July–November 1800) and during the peace of Amiens (October 1801 to March 1803). During his last period of active service (May 1803 to October 1805), his writing activity reached an average of two letters per day. This pattern can be seen more clearly in Fig. 13.2, which gives the monthly output of letters for the years 1793 to 1805.

Nelson's correspondence was clearly driven by professional needs rather than by private occasions or even by a simple joy in writing. That professionally motivated letter-writing was central to Nelson's social networking is supported by the fact that Nelson did not become involved in other forms of networking, notably the club, a near-ubiquitous feature of late-eighteenth-century British social life.[9] Nelson does not appear to have made any serious attempts to use clubs as an opportunity for social networking. On the contrary, in letters written during the peace of Amiens he reacted with polite disinterest to approaches from institutions or invitations to events that might have offered such opportunities.[10] He even declined an invitation to the Lord Mayor's dinner at the Guildhall and protested that the City had not honoured 'those brave Captains, Officers, and Men, who so bravely fought, profusely bled, and obtained such a glorious, complete, and most important Victory for their King and Country' at the battle of Copenhagen. He concluded in the third person: 'if Lord Nelson could forget the services of those who have fought under his command, that he would ill deserve to be so supported as he always has been'.[11] Attempts to show that Nelson was a freemason have borne no fruit either.[12]

There is some documentary evidence of Nelson having been a member of the charitable Marine Society, which was founded in 1756. His membership, however, appears to have amounted to no more than occasional financial contributions and he declined an invitation to attend the Society's meeting.[13] Nelson probably regarded such societies as a means to repay obligations to society rather than to meet influential or otherwise useful people. This notion of social obligation is supported by the fact that Nelson also contributed to a war subscription in 1798 and supported the 'Patriotic Fund at Lloyd's Coffee-house', to which he made his captains send lists of killed and wounded so that the wounded and the families of the fallen could receive support.[14]

II

If Nelson did not use clubs, social events or societies as a means of developing his network of contacts, his correspondence was central to achieving these ends. In order to draw conclusions about the identity of his correspondents, the addressees of his published letters have been assigned to the following groups: family, foreigners, government, navy, merchants, Emma Hamilton, others. Some of Nelson's correspondents, of course, belonged to more than one group. His uncles William and Maurice Suckling, for example, were also members of the civil administration and the navy respectively, and the foreigners to whom Nelson wrote were often members of their respective country's navy or government.[15] For those who belonged to more than one group, a primary classification has been assigned.[16] The volume of letters that Nelson wrote to these different groups varied over the course of his life and what follows gives a brief indication of how many letters Nelson wrote and to whom he sent them across eight distinct periods of his career.

In the early years of his career (1777 to 1792), Nelson corresponded mainly with members of the navy (56 per cent of his letters), with members of his family and others (20 per cent and 14 per cent respectively). After France declared war in 1793, during his years as captain, later commodore, in the Mediterranean and during the months after evacuating the Mediterranean, when he was promoted to admiral (1793 to July 1797), the composition of the addressees of his letters changed considerably. Letters to members of the navy still predominated (42 per cent), but Nelson now kept up a busy correspondence with other branches of government (17 per cent) and started to write to foreigners (5 per cent). That the number of letters to his family was considerable (29 per cent of his letters in the period) can be explained by the very active correspondence he maintained with his wife. During the months of convalescence that followed the loss of his right arm (August 1797 to March 1798), Nelson's correspondence naturally dropped to a minimum.

Between being sent out with a squadron to serve in the Mediterranean and Nelson relinquishing his post (April 1798 to June 1800), his correspondence reached unprecedented levels. This was particularly the case after his great victory of the battle of the Nile on 1 August 1798. Of the 1,016 letters he wrote, about half were to members of the navy, and more than a third to members of government and foreigners (15 per cent and 20 per cent respectively), while his private correspondence, particularly to his wife, shrank considerably, in absolute as well as relative terms (sixty-four letters, 6 per cent of his overall correspondence). Nelson was now clearly very much involved on the spot, lost touch with private contacts back home, and entered into new private contacts, with Lady Hamilton in particular. On his way home with Sir William and Lady Hamilton across central Europe (July to November 1800), Nelson fell almost silent in matters of correspondence and even after his return to England at the beginning of November he sent very few letters.

Nelson resumed letter-writing when he was again on active service, first in the Baltic, then in the Channel (January to October 1801). These ten months were not only densely packed with naval activity, but also with emotional upheaval. Consequently, 36 per cent of his letters went to Lady Hamilton, nearly as much as to others in the navy (41 per cent). Being closer to home, Nelson's correspondence to foreigners diminished, as did his links with branches of government other than the navy (notably consuls). His family was relatively neglected (a mere 2 per cent). Nelson's peacetime correspondence, between relinquishing his command during the preparations of the peace of Amiens until renewal of hostilities (November 1801 to April 1803), remained meagre (an average of nine letters a month). Although he now lived with Lady Hamilton, and Sir William Hamilton, most of the time, it is striking that a quarter of his letters in this period were still addressed to her.

From May 1803 to his death at Trafalgar in October 1805, Nelson's letter-writing activity again became very intense. He managed to write an average of two letters a day, as many as during his service in the Baltic and the Channel in 1801. The percentage of his letters to Lady Hamilton, however, sank to just 9 per cent of his overall correspondence. Even so, this still amounted to an average of six letters a month to his mistress. Nelson's professional correspondence as commander-in-chief of the British fleet in the Mediterranean was dominated by contact with members of the navy: 61 per cent of his letters were addressed to them. He also stayed in touch with members of government, foreigners and merchants (17 per cent, 5 per cent and 4 per cent of his outgoing letters respectively).

III

Why did Nelson correspond with the groups of people identified above? As a naval officer on active service, his purpose in creating and making use of what we would now call a social network was threefold. First he wished to keep his subordinates together as an efficient and effective force; secondly, he used his networks to acquire important information that could form the basis for well-balanced decisions and would help him to cooperate with other agents; and lastly, he wanted to be heard in important places to further his own interests and goals. Sociologists like to examine the quality of a network by looking at both ends of those individual links of which it is composed. Do both people benefit from the association, do they share interests, do they even like one another?[17] In this instance, however, the quality of the links Nelson, as the centre of a network, formed with other people can primarily be assessed from his viewpoint alone.

In order to keep his subordinates together as an efficient and effective force it might have been ideal for a leader to be able to choose those subordinates. In his earlier years as a captain in the West Indies, however, Nelson had to take whatever ship and crew were given to him. Only when he was able to put the 64-gun ship *Agamemnon* into commission did he have the opportunity to choose his officers and much of his crew.[18] Even this, however, did not save Nelson from disciplinary problems, which persisted until he gave up the command.[19] Towards the end of his career, as an already famous admiral, he noted in 1804: 'The patronage of Commanders-in-Chief is I fear gone.'[20] Nelson could never, therefore, rely on making his own choices of subordinates.

In order to build a reliable network of subordinates, Nelson had to create an atmosphere of mutual confidence and perhaps even affection. Documentary evidence on personal communication and direct encounters is slim, but suggests that Nelson frequently tried to bring together his subordinates in relatively informal settings and to create a relaxed atmosphere for conversation. He thus invited all those who had taken part in the battle of Cape St Vincent and were now under his command, irrespective of rank, to a commemoration of that battle.[21] He even invited his captains to celebrate the occasion of Lady Hamilton's birthday.[22] In an altogether graver context, about three weeks before the battle of Trafalgar, a dinner on Nelson's flagship, the *Victory*, was conducted in such a relaxed atmosphere that one of the participants recorded in a letter to his wife: 'I dined with his Lordship yesterday, and had a very merry dinner. He certainly is the pleasantest Admiral I ever served under.' A few days later he elaborated further: 'He is so good and pleasant a man, that we all wish to do what he likes, without any kind of orders.'[23]

If Nelson had to deal with his subordinates in a strictly professional context, he could rarely convey his message directly in a meeting on board his flagship. Even in his letters to subordinates, however, he managed to express his appreciation:

> I have very fully to express my approbation of the terms of capitulation, as well as with your conduct personally, and that of the Officers and Men under your command, which I have to request you will be pleased to communicate to them.[24]

It was more important and also more difficult, however, to motivate his subordinates *before* they had achieved something. In such cases, Nelson's letters combined words expressing confidence and trust in his subordinates with an appeal to their sense of duty, obligation and service to a greater cause: 'Relying on your well-known judgment and abilities to act as circumstances may require for the good of His Majesty's Service, it is not necessary for me to be more particular.'[25]

Such passages from Nelson's letters to captains under his command suggest that his links with his subordinates did not only rely on mutual liking and trust, but also depended on their association in a common cause. The fact that Nelson did not feel it 'necessary ... to be more particular' can be explained in part by the trust he had in his subordinates. In a letter to the First Lord of the Admiralty, Nelson explained:

> Much as I approve of strict obedience to orders ... yet to say that an Officer is never, for any object, to alter his orders, is what I cannot comprehend. The circumstances of this war so often vary, that an Officer has almost every moment to consider – What would my superiors direct, did they know what is passing under my nose?[26]

An officer's ability to do exactly this – to exercise his own judgement in an attempt to predict the likely instructions of his superior – presupposed a flow of information and of opinion between him and his superior as well as the sense of being associated in pursuit of a common goal.

It was much more difficult for Nelson to achieve such a sense of close cooperation with those subordinates who never dealt directly with him. It needs to be borne in mind, for example, that during the nearly two and a half years of active service before the battle of Trafalgar, Nelson did not leave his flagship and his subordinates had few if any opportunities to visit him. Beyond the core of Nelson's network of subordinates, namely the commanders of ships belonging to his fleet, he was nevertheless able to keep up some personal contact with other officers, warrant officers and even some petty officers.[27] A letter to the masters of the ships under his command demonstrates that he took care even of 'a most strict and careful survey on the pork, tongues, hog's-lard, pease, and wheat'.[28] Nelson's contact with ordinary sailors was superficial at best and would, in any case, have been conducted orally. One of the few examples that have come down to us is a memorandum for 13 September 1803 'to be read to the respective Companies of His Majesty's Ships and Vessels under my command'. More than a year before Spain declared war on Britain, Nelson appealed to a rough sense of patriotism mixed with some rather practical considerations:

> When British Seamen and Marines so far degrade themselves in time of War, as to desert from the Service of their own Country, and enter into that of Spain; when they leave one shilling per day, and plenty of the very best provisions, with every comfort that can be thought of for them – for two-pence a-day, black bread, horse-beans, and stinking oil for their food ... I blush for them ... A Briton to put himself under the lash of a Frenchman or Spaniard must be more degrading to any man of spirit than any punishment I could inflict on their bodies ... as they have also thought proper to resign all their pay, I shall take care that it is not returned to them, nor their 'R.' taken off ...[29]

This contrasts with Nelson's more positive way of appealing to his sailors' patriotism, immortalised in his signal to the whole fleet (a first in naval history) before the battle of Trafalgar: England Expects That Every Man Will Do His Duty. Notwithstanding such general appeals, personal contact with Nelson appears to have been more effective in creating a feeling of personal loyalty or even affection. A sailor reported after the battle of Trafalgar: 'I never set eyes on him ... for which I am both sorry and glad, for ... the men in our ship who have seen him are such soft toads, they have done nothing but blast their eyes and cry ever since he was killed.'[30]

Whereas all of his subordinates were in some form of contact with Nelson, however superficial or indirect, similar conditions did not apply to his geographically more wide-ranging intelligence network. The people from whom he gained important information and with whom he had to cooperate were usually living in distant places and they were often not personally known to him. His contacts outside the navy to British ambassadors and consuls, merchants of different nations and foreign officials up to heads of state were all in the 'periphery' of his network.[31] These people, who were mostly unknown to Nelson personally, were of value to his network, because of their functions (usually professional, sometimes aristocratic).

In order to create and cultivate a wide-ranging network, Nelson therefore had to find something that would unite him with such heterogeneous and dispersed agents. It was helpful when both ends of a link could offer the other something in exchange, be it information or something else of value. Nelson maintained such relationships with merchants, who on the one hand offered him valuable information and on the other hoped for protection for their trade by means of convoy.[32] Similarly, he tried to maintain a fragile link based on the exchange of information with the Spanish in 1804. Just before Spain declared war on Britain in December 1804, Nelson still kept in touch with the captain-general at Barcelona, whom he could relieve of his fears that 'a bad fever' had broken out at Gibraltar.[33]

When Nelson's sphere of activity stretched into the eastern Mediterranean after the battle of the Nile, he had to build new contacts. His letters of 17 November 1798 to the Russian and Ottoman admirals respectively reveal a distinct difference of tone. He was rather familiar with his Russian colleague:

> I greedily embrace the opportunity of paying my respects, and of assuring you how happy I feel that we are so near each other, and working together for the good cause of our Sovereigns. I shall be proud, when opportunity offers, of paying you my respects in person.

The introduction to his Ottoman counterpart was written in a much more formal style: 'The Grand Signior having condescended to notice my earnest endeavours to serve the cause of humanity against a set of impious men'.[34] In both cases, different as they are in style, he referred to joint interests and thus conjured up a base for mutual support. The fact that Nelson's letter to the Russian admiral made use of a much more cordial tone must not mislead us into thinking that he felt strategically closer to the Russian than to the Ottoman Empire, as he later reported 'a long and friendly conference with Kelim Effendi' and concluded: 'Our ideas have exactly been the same about the Russians.'[35]

In a more extreme way, Nelson veered between attracting the independent-minded Bey of Tunis into cooperating against 'infidels', 'unbelievers', 'enemies of all true Mussulmans', 'French villains' or 'this race of monsters',[36] while at the same time complaining: 'The situation of the poor people taken by the Bey of Tunis is shocking to humanity.'[37] It appears that the less tangible common ground Nelson felt there to be with another agent, the more he resorted to a generalised vocabulary to invoke a common enemy or joint interest. The most extreme example of this kind is probably the message that he sent at the height of the battle of Copenhagen in 1801 to 'the Danes, the brothers of Englishmen' in order to offer negotiations to 'spare Denmark'.[38] It therefore appears that the part of Nelson's professional networking activity that was aimed at receiving information and at cooperating with foreign powers was very much dominated by tactical and sometimes also strategic interests; there was little space for personal approval or affection to play a role.

When Nelson's networking activities were aimed at ensuring he was heard in important places in pursuit of his interests, he faced different challenges. Instead of having to balance other agent's interests in order to achieve his given task, he now had to attract attention and appreciation from influential superiors. In this regard, Nelson was conspicuous in not being attached to a political party or faction. During an important phase, in 1794–5, Nelson's career was even supported by two men who were politically opposed to each other: Lord Hood (Tory) and Gilbert Elliot (Whig).[39] A signal advantage of not being linked to one party, as Roger Knight argues convincingly, was that Nelson stayed out of the major political conflicts within the navy that undid quite a few careers.[40] The disadvantage of such independence was, however, that Nelson lacked a lobby in London. Fifteen months after the battle of the Nile, Nelson remarked in a letter to his wife: 'My task here is still arduous ... I still find it good to serve near home. There a man's fag and services are easily seen. Next to that is writing a famous account of your own action.'[41] Although Nelson took the deeds themselves to be the basis of a good reputation, he recognised the importance of self-promotion.

At times Nelson's independence of mind itself stood in the way of being 'noticed in the world'. Particularly during his West Indian days in the late 1780s, he managed to show a degree of independent thinking that crossed the border into disobedience, alienated some influential superiors and was thus damaging to his career. For example, with an amazing singularity of purpose he defended his own interpretation of the Navigation Laws: 'How the King's Attorney-General conceives he has a right to give an illegal Opinion, which I assert the above is, he must answer for. I know the Navigation Law.'[42] It was partly down to this kind of behaviour that Nelson was only recalled to active service when war with France broke out in 1793 – after five years ashore.

Although Nelson was passionate in maintaining his views, his later conflicts with superiors were less persistent than those in the 1780s. They were either short-lived acts (as was his disobeying Lord Keith's order to join him off Minorca in 1799),[43] could be delegated to lawyers (as was his quarrel over prize-money with Earl St Vincent)[44] or overcome in conversation (as with Sir Hyde Parker in relation to which line of action to follow against Denmark in early 1801).[45] This mellowing may have less to do with age and the passing of time than with the simple availability of means within a wide-ranging social network. As a captain in the West Indies, Nelson was struggling in a narrow naval context with agents that were socially and geographically removed from him. By contrast, as a famous admiral in European waters Nelson could act and indeed had to act within a wide-ranging network. Conflicts as a consequence appeared relatively minor and could be accommodated more easily.

Even this brief exploration of a complex set of relationships allows us to see how Nelson built and made use of a heterogeneous network according to his specific professional needs. He was eminently able to create and maintain the basis for cooperation within and beyond the navy by acknowledging merit and creating a common base of association. This ability in social networking – next to his quality as an outstanding tactician – contributed substantially to his success as a naval officer. Although the efficiency of his network needs to be tested in more detail, it can be claimed that the wider his network grew during the length of his career, the greater his professional success became.

Notes

1 John Scott, *Social Network Analysis* (Los Angeles, 2013), p. 4, considers 'documentary research' of the kind on which this essay relies.
2 N. A. M. Rodger, *The Wooden World: An Anatomy of the Georgian Navy* (London, 1986), p. 11.
3 Nicholas Harris Nicolas (ed.), *The Dispatches and Letters of Lord Nelson* [hereafter *Dispatches*], 7 vols (London, [1844–6] 1997–8).
4 [Anon.], *The Letters of Lord Nelson to Lady Hamilton with a Supplement of Interesting Letters by Distinguished Characters*, 2 vols (London, 1814); Thomas Joseph Pettigrew, *Memoirs of the Life of Vice-Admiral Lord Viscount Nelson, K.B. Duke of Bronté etc.*, 2 vols (London, 1849); [Alfred Morrison], *The Collection of Autograph Letters and Historical Documents formed by Alfred Morrison (Second Series, 1882–1893)*, 2 vols (printed for private circulation, 1893).
5 P. B. Naish, *Nelson's Letters to his Wife and Other Documents, 1785–1831* (London, 1958).
6 H. C. Gutteridge (ed.), *Nelson and the Neapolitan Jacobins: Documents Relating to the Suppression of the Jacobin Revolution at Naples, June 1799* (London, 1903); J. K. Laughton (ed.), *The Barker Collection: Manuscripts of and relating to Admiral Lord Nelson* (London, 1913); Warren R. Dawson (ed.), *The Nelson Collection at Lloyd's: A Description of the Nelson Relics and a Transcript of the Autograph Letters and Documents of Nelson and his Circle and of Other Naval Papers of Nelson's Period* (London, 1932); Geoffrey Rawson (ed.), *Nelson's Letters from the Leeward Islands and other Original Documents in the Public Record Office and the British Museum* (London, 1953).

7 Colin White (ed.), *Nelson: The New Letters* (Woodbridge, 2005).
8 For examples of letters indicating lost letters and replies by Nelson, see National Maritime Museum, Croker Collection, 4/178 and 12/148, 152, 155, 178.
9 For an overview of the development of the culture of clubs in Britain, see Peter Clark, *British Clubs and Societies c.1580–1800: The Origins of an Associational World* (Oxford, 2000).
10 *Dispatches*, V, pp. 31, 33.
11 *Dispatches*, V, pp. 33–4, 8 November 1802.
12 See Leslie A. Gibbons, 'Was Lord Nelson a Freemason?', *The Nelson Dispatch*, 5 (1996), pp. 450–2. Martyn Downer, however, points out that 'Masonic symbolism was pervasive in … medals and in some extraordinary gifts given to Nelson by Davison', see *The Nelson Dispatch*, 8 (2005), p. 561.
13 Dawson (ed.), *Nelson Collection*, p. 175, n. 16.
14 *Dispatches*, III, pp. 4–5 and VII, p. 106; see also III, p. 217; IV, p. 519; VI, pp. 28, 109.
15 To his uncle William Suckling, 'clerk of Foreign Entries' and later deputy collector of customs, Nelson wrote 27 letters. Of the 361 letters Nelson addressed to foreigners, 94 letters were to 27 foreigners who were in their country's navy, 233 letters were addressed to 68 foreigners who were in their country's governments and two letters were written to two foreigners who were merchants. For Suckling, see Roger Knight, *The Pursuit of Victory: The Life and Achievements of Horatio Nelson* (London, 2005), p. 671.
16 The various categories of correspondents have been arranged as follows: all foreigners, whether or not they belonged to navy, government or other group; all members of family, whether or not they belonged to navy, government or other group; members of government who were not foreigners or members of family; members of the navy who were not foreigners, members of family or government; merchants who did not belong in any of the other four groups; others.
17 See, for example, Darwin Cartwright and Frank Harary, 'Structural Balance: A Generalization of Heider's Theory', *Psychological Review*, 63 (1956), pp. 277–93.
18 Knight, *Pursuit of Victory*, p. 145.
19 Ibid., p. 195.
20 Quoted in ibid., p. 477.
21 G. S. Parsons, *Nelsonian Reminiscences: Leaves from Memory's Log* (London, 1843), pp. 246–7.
22 White, *New Letters*, pp. 46–7.
23 *Dispatches*, VII, p. 71.
24 Ibid., VI, p. 450.
25 Ibid., III, p. 473; see also III, pp. 229, 319, 418–19, 432.
26 Ibid., IV, p. 90.
27 For description of these ranks, see Rodger, *Wooden World*, pp. 348–51.

28 *Dispatches*, VI, p. 251.
29 *Dispatches*, V, pp. 201–2. The 'R' (for 'run') referred to the mark placed in the Ship's Books against the names of deserters.
30 Quoted in John Sugden, *Nelson: The Sword of Albion* (London, 2012), pp. 833–4.
31 See Scott, *Social Network*, p. 25.
32 See for examples, *Dispatches*, III, pp. 97, 269–71; V, p. 156.
33 *Dispatches*, VI, p. 237.
34 *Dispatches*, III, p. 173; similar vocabulary can be found in III, pp. 202–4, 265–6, 287–8, 304.
35 Ibid., III, p. 204.
36 Ibid., III, pp. 293–4, 300, 301, 338, 371, 445.
37 Ibid., III, p. 442.
38 Ibid., IV, p. 315.
39 Knight, *Pursuit of Victory*, pp. 635, 645; Nelson acknowledged to Elliot: 'no one has taken more pains to make me noticed in the world than yourself', see *Dispatches*, IV, p. 193.
40 Knight, *Pursuit of Victory*, pp. 551–2.
41 Naish (ed.), *Nelson's Letters to his Wife*, p. 491.
42 Rawson (ed.), *Nelson's Letters from the Leeward Islands*, p. 30.
43 *Dispatches*, III, pp. 408–9.
44 Knight, *Pursuit of Victory*, p. 424.
45 *Dispatches*, IV, pp. 295–8.

CHAPTER 14

The Posthumous Lives of Thomas Muir

Gordon Pentland

> Gerrard [sic], Palmer, Skirving, Thomas Muir and Margarot
> Remember Thomas Muir of Huntershill
> These are names that every Scottish man and woman ought to know
> Remember Thomas Muir of Huntershill
> When you're called for jury service, when your name is drawn by lot
> When you vote in an election, when you freely voice your thought
> Don't take these things for granted, for dearly were they bought
> Remember Thomas Muir of Huntershill
> *Remember Thomas Muir of Huntershill*: words by Adam McNaughton, performed by Dick Gaughan

Dick Gaughan's defiant rendition of Adam McNaughton's song, with its repeated injunction to 'Remember Thomas Muir', is a starkly commemorative act. In presenting a narrative of its subject's life, it plays a consciously didactic role. Like all attempts to recover and reanimate 'hidden' or 'forgotten' pasts, its message rests in part on the idea that there is a likely or existing failure to remember its subject appropriately or with a due sense of his significance. That Muir's life was 'historically significant' has been commemorated in another sense, by his inclusion in the *Oxford Dictionary of National Biography* in a typically lucid essay by Harry Dickinson. This rendering of Muir's life sits neatly within Dickinson's own extensive work on the 1790s. It highlighted the interactions of constitutionalism and the universalism of the French Revolution within the context provided by an increasingly militant loyalism and sought to examine the relationship between political ideas and political actions:

> Muir was never as radical as the fearful government and legal authorities came to believe in the heightened political atmosphere of 1792–3. He believed in the need for moderate political reform, rejected all appeals to force, and advocated change by peaceful, constitutional means. He was, however, intoxicated by the heady atmosphere in Britain and France at this time.[1]

As Dickinson's essay also made clear, the contemporary sources for the life of Muir are limited. Biographies (including a recent and very thoroughly researched biographical novel) have rested on government reports and the account of Muir's trial, a smattering of letters, pamphlets, travel accounts, and French and Spanish records.[2] This combination of a highly visible trial and a globetrotting subsequent career with a paucity of statements generated by Muir himself has allowed him to live a range of posthumous lives. The purpose of this essay is to examine these as a case study of how, when and why revolutionary figures of the 1790s have become politically usable. In Muir's case, these posthumous lives have involved both a narrowing and a widening of his appeal. In the first sense, Muir has moved from being a pan-British figure, the focus of Whig panegyrics and a progenitor of parliamentary reform, to being more exclusively a Scottish figure with a marked presence within nationalist, republican and labour politics. Following a similar chronology, the transnational dimension of Muir's life has been at least partially recovered and his legacy has been shaped and deployed by an emerging Australian nationalism from the end of the nineteenth century.

I

Muir was born in 1765, the son of a prosperous merchant who purchased a small landed property at Huntershill near Glasgow. Later accounts would make much of his political education as a 'student activist' at Glasgow University and a reforming elder within the Church of Scotland. During the French Revolution, Muir became a leading delegate and speaker at the general convention of the Scottish Societies of Friends of the People in Edinburgh in December 1792, before he was arrested in January for the circulation of seditious reading material (principally Thomas Paine's *Rights of Man*) to the populace of Dunbartonshire. Released on bail, Muir elected to travel to Paris to join others in their doomed efforts to intercede for the life of Louis XVI. Realising the dangers that awaited him back in Scotland, Muir shaped to flee to America, but following a flattering reception among the United Irishmen of Dublin he returned to Scotland and was arrested on landing. He had a copy of Paine's pamphlet and a French passport in his pocket.

Declining the assistance of a professional criminal defence, Muir's trial was the great defining moment of his career. Seldom did public opportunities to confront and bloody the nose of established authority come more readily than in the elaborately ritualised space of the High Court of Justiciary. The trial launched Lord Braxfield into notoriety as a hanging judge, the Jeffreys of Scotland, and it cemented Muir's status as a martyr for liberty. Spectators gasped at the severity of the eventual sentence: fourteen years' transportation to Botany Bay. Muir did not spend anywhere near that long in that finishing school of sedition. While the others transported with him thrived, died or returned, he continued his picaresque career as a 'citizen of the world'. He was rescued from New South Wales by an American frigate, *The Otter*, which was, in turn, captured by the Spanish. Muir eventually picked his way back to Paris, part of the flotsam of revolutionary Europe and now disfigured by a wound sustained while in the mid-Atlantic. He spent his final years in the company of exiled United Irishmen, one group among the lobbyists of Paris. He died in Chantilly in 1799.

Muir's self-presentation in court as a martyr for liberty was done with one eye on the future, and later commemorators would make much of his apparent prescience: 'I have devoted myself to the cause of the People. It is a good cause – It shall ultimately prevail – It shall finally triumph.'[3] As an individual and as part of the 'corporate symbol' that would become known as the Scottish martyrs, Muir was immediately important to the reform movement of the 1790s.[4] On the prison hulk *Surprize*, Muir was visited by the republican sculptor Thomas Banks, who took a cast of his head for a portrait bust.[5] An engraved copy of this portrait constituted his revolutionary business card after his escape from New South Wales, which he showed to Spanish officials following the interception of the American frigate on which he had escaped:

> saying that his followers in England had sent it to him, where they were thinking of erecting a marble statue of him, for his firmness and energy shown in the defence of the rights of the Scottish people who had nominated him their deputy.[6]

In the few letters from Muir that survive, this continuing sense of his own self-dramatisation is apparent: 'I have circumnavigated & travelled literally around the Globe. My life is a romance, but a romance of mournful truth ... Well & gratefully I recognise the truth of the lines, put by Mrs Barbauld beneath my Bust'.[7] Muir himself clearly had a sense that his trial, the severity of his sentence and his life following his escape lent themselves to memorialisation. He was not to be disappointed.

II

To understand the recovery and deployment of Muir's legacy in the nineteenth and twentieth centuries requires attention to two types of context. First, the specific political context – what contests were Muir's legacy being mobilised to support and what kind of interpretation did these encourage or require? Second, the commemorative contexts in which his name occurred – who else was being commemorated and in what relation did Muir stand to them? Keeping these two sets of questions in view allows for an assessment of the political usability of Thomas Muir at various points and the way in which he has been 'recruited for a succession of narratives'.[8]

The first, and arguably the most successful, to recruit Muir in this way was his first biographer, the journalist Peter Mackenzie. His own published memoirs are a rich source for the politics and society of Glasgow in the first half of the nineteenth century and delivered a sustained narrative of his own involvement in reform politics.[9] It was the agitation for parliamentary reform after 1830 that really thrust Mackenzie into the limelight, and it inspired a period of incredible productivity. His principal achievement lay in launching the radical newspaper *The Loyal Reformers' Gazette*, the inaugural number of which appeared on 7 May 1831, following the first rejection of Lord John Russell's reform bill in the House of Commons and during the hotly contested general election that followed. Mackenzie claimed a circulation of 20,000 for his newspaper, which government certainly took seriously enough as an opinion former for the Lord Advocate to sustain a correspondence with Mackenzie.[10]

The content of the *Gazette* was in the mainstream of reform-minded popular constitutionalism, as its masthead of a shining crown above the banner 'the King and the People' ostentatiously indicated.[11] It made an appeal to liberties gained in 1688 and proclaimed unbreakable attachment to the patriotic monarch William IV. It was in this context of agitation for parliamentary reform that Mackenzie shaped his life of Thomas Muir. Not only was the history of radicalism in Scotland a constant reference point in his articles, but he also produced inexpensive volumes dealing with the trials of the 1790s and Scotland's postwar experiences.[12] The extraordinary excitement of the reform agitation encouraged similar attempts to link reform to a pre-existing lineage, and efforts were made to commemorate 'founding fathers' of reform, such as Major Cartwright or Thomas Hardy, in the form of monuments and memoirs.[13] Whig identities, especially in Scotland, were premised on a powerful rhetoric of political exclusion during the 1790s, later enshrined in Henry Cockburn's works.[14]

In this context, Mackenzie's Muir had dual significance as both an early advocate of the reform bill and as a hapless victim of Tory persecution, which were themes emphasised in the short biography and trial account, published in 1831, and throughout Mackenzie's journalism. *The Life* was very pointedly dedicated to Francis Jeffrey, the Whig Lord Advocate with responsibility for seeing the Scottish reform act through Parliament, and copies were sent to Jeffrey, Earl Grey and others. This was the company in which Mackenzie saw Muir: a respectable professional man, at ease with aristocratic and professional reformers. This was underlined by his publication strategy for the *Loyal Reformers' Gazette*. Engraved portraits were given away with a number of issues to boost circulation: one of John Kay's profiles of Muir was among them and as such he joined a paper pantheon with Jeffrey, Earl Grey, Lord Brougham, Lord John Russell and William IV.[15] Squeezing Muir into this company involved ignoring the numerous disagreements that would certainly have existed between these very different reformers to produce statements such as: 'his Majesty has echoed again and again, from his place on the Throne, the very sentiments for which Thomas Muir was condemned!' Just as political differences might be subsumed under support for 'the bill, the whole bill, and nothing but the bill', so too Mackenzie's pantheon smoothed over real or potential differences in the vexed context of 1831–2 in favour of a generalised idea of commitment to reform.

It was this interpretation – of Muir as an important, patriotic and persecuted actor in a narrative of reform that reached its apotheosis in 1832 – that Mackenzie, the radical MP Joseph Hume and others sought to carry through into plans for raising monuments to the martyrs of the 1790s. This was in part an exercise in party political contest, in Hume's words 'to keep up a running fire agt. the Tories'.[16] It was also a contest over public space and an attempt on the part of Hume, Mackenzie and others following the 'victory' of reform to put their own stamp on civic spaces that had long been monopolised by Tories. Most pointedly, Edinburgh's statues and monuments had long played a key role in the 'Toryfication' of the urban landscape and were accused of undermining the civic virtue that such public monuments ought to bolster.[17] The result in Edinburgh was a lengthy contest with local Tories for the erection of the monument in the Old Calton burial yard at the foot of Calton Hill. The movement to achieve this monument was, however, a pan-British one, with subscription committees in both Edinburgh and London.[18] Indeed, a shorter version of the austere obelisk was raised in Nunhead cemetery in London in 1851. What both monuments and the ceremonies that launched them found meaningful in Muir (and the other martyrs) was less their specific ideas than their status as pioneers of reform *in general* and their status as victims of a Tory government.

This vision of Muir as a patriotic, persecuted and constitutional reformer has enjoyed a long career after its establishment in the 1830s. It is the Muir implied by Robert Louis Stevenson's unfinished novel, *Weir of Hermiston*, with its brilliant characterisation of Muir's phlegmatic antagonist Lord Braxfield. It is a Muir ever looking forward to the first 'instalment' of reform in 1832, as in the first substantial fictionalised account of Muir's life, E. H. Strain's novel *A Prophet's Reward*. This ends with the narrator, Col. Charles Stirling, assuring Muir that 'such a defeat as yours has in it the elements of a future victory'.[19] This interpretation of Muir was strengthened by further historical research during the twentieth century, most notably by Henry Meikle, which went on to shape further the public image of Muir.[20] In a small flurry of interest around the 150th anniversary of Muir's death, for example, Meikle's radio programme on Muir for Scottish schools in 1948 placed its subject at the beginning of a familiar narrative taking in reform acts and the development of democratic politics.[21] George Pratt Insh's pamphlet of 1949, written at the request of those who sought to commemorate the anniversary, followed suit:

> Of all the trials of the political martyrs his was the one that appealed most strongly to the imagination of the Scottish people. And the memory of those trials was a beacon that gleamed through the encompassing mirk of the long years of repression till the horizon kindled with the promise of the dawn of the great Reform Bill.[22]

III

When Henry Cockburn observed the reform jubilee in Edinburgh in 1832, he noted the memory of Muir being invoked:

> There was one most just black placard ... *It was dedicated to the memory of Muir, Gerrald and Palmer!* I knew that the atrocity of their punishment was deeply remembered among a higher class, and I was delighted to see it understood and proclaimed on the street.[23]

Cockburn himself did much to establish and popularise the constitutional version of Muir outlined above, not least through the posthumous publication of his own celebrated account of sedition trials in Scotland.[24] His observation raises the intriguing question as to whether the Muir that Cockburn saw 'proclaimed on the street' was the same Muir as was 'remembered among a higher class'. While the vision of Muir as a patriotic constitutional reformer aimed at a consensus to match the national movement being generated in support of the reform bills, any such vision necessarily contained enough loose ends to allow for challenges and a certain degree of flexibility.

Muir, alongside other individuals and episodes from the recent past, was an attractive object lesson for Chartists to highlight.[25] Chartists during the 1830s and '40s continued to use Muir's name, and he was especially prominent when legal proceedings against leading Chartists allowed for analogies to be drawn with Muir's own travails. When the Chartist leaders John Collins, Peter McDouall and George White were released from imprisonment in 1840, they embarked on a tour of Scotland. An enormous demonstration met them in Glasgow and press reports noticed two prominent banners featuring Muir. One, 'a faded-looking blue flag', had clearly been used during the reform crisis. Another, which the *Northern Star* attributed to the moulders, bore John Kay's profile portrait of Muir and cited the same epitaph below: 'Illustrious martyr in the glorious cause,/ Of truth, of freedom, and of equal laws'. The banner, however, also featured a much less consensual statement, and tied Muir's image to a political programme that it is far from clear he would have supported: 'Universal Suffrage, vote by ballot, and Annual Parliaments'.[26]

While the essentials of Mackenzie's Muir – the martyr to reform – might have remained intact, the company into which he was placed and the principles with which he was associated could be modified to situate him in a more radical narrative. Such modifications can be seen as part of a wider contest between Glasgow Chartists and Peter Mackenzie himself, whose publications were scathing of Chartist leadership and advocated more moderate reform. Indeed, the procession for the 'political martyrs' of 1840 carrying the Muir banners identified above made a point of halting outside the offices of Mackenzie's paper, the *Reformers' Gazette*, to give three loud groans. Similar efforts to annex Muir's legacy to the cause of radical reform were apparent in the efforts to raise a monument. There was considerable controversy at the original 1837 meeting at the Crown and Anchor Tavern, when Fergus O'Connor, later the pre-eminent physical force Chartist, moved an amendment:

> That this meeting ... is of the opinion that the above mentioned gentlemen are victims to an unjust and cruel law, which would not have disgraced the statute book if the rights of universal suffrage had been conceded to the people.[27]

Chartists thus tried to appropriate Muir for their own more radical reform programme, which stood in contrast to Hume's more consensus-building model.

There is some evidence that a different idea of Thomas Muir altogether appealed to at least some Chartists. The resurgent but embattled movement of 1848 was apt to draw analogies between its own bleak situation and the repression of the 1790s. The government raid on the offices of the *North British Express* and the arrest of a number of prominent Chartists in Edinburgh and Glasgow allowed just such comparisons.[28] The trial of one of these Chartists, the ageing shoemaker James Cumming, suggests another narrative to which Muir could be recruited and which would see him in very different company. In a letter intended for the Glasgow Chartist James Smith, but which had fallen into official hands, Cumming gave the names and numbers of armed insurrectionary clubs in Edinburgh. The names demonstrated the protean influences on Scottish radicals: the Irish influence was apparent in the Mitchell and Emmet Clubs; the Washington Club looked even further back and further afield; and the Baird and Hardie club, with twenty members, enrolled the memory of the men of 1820 in the cause of armed insurrection. The largest of these insurrectionary cells, however, with two hundred members, was the Muir Club.[29]

IV

If some Chartists thus saw a different role for Muir, and sought to recover his insurrectionary credentials, such imaginings became more prominent in the twentieth century alongside other altered presentations of Muir's legacy. Three important contexts help to explain both revived interest in Muir and changed interpretations of his political significance. One was provided by two global conflicts. The political and social turmoil before, during and after the First World War, in particular, made the 'age of revolutions' between 1790 and 1848 a fruitful one for those who sought historical comparisons. The second context was provided by the success of the Labour movement in the West of Scotland. Socialists, even more than Chartists, faced the challenge of making a middle-class martyr relevant to a working-class movement, whose diagnosis of society's ills rested less heavily on radical *political* explanations. A final context was provided by the continuing debate over the 'Scottish question' following the political emergence of Home Rule as an issue from the 1880s. This coincided with a growing cultural nationalism and a keen interest in the distinctiveness of Scottish history and culture. Contests over the Scottish past were both omnipresent and politically charged, and became more acute following the Second World War.[30] Within this long and uneven politicisation of national identities, Muir became more and more decidedly a *Scottish* martyr.

Perhaps the most active force in mobilising the potential of the eighteenth-century age of revolutions during the early twentieth century was the Independent Labour Party (ILP). It played a crucial role in broadening socialism's appeal, organising grassroots support and in focusing attention on key issues such as housing.[31] Some part of the ILP's success, however, can also be attributed to its cultural politics, including its commemorative activities, through which it attempted to shape its own version of the Scottish past and annex to its cause the powerful symbols of radical and liberal traditions. Prominent in this regard was William Stewart, a prolific contributor to *Forward*. His *Fighters for Freedom in Scotland* and numerous articles in the press dwelt on the period from the 1790s to the 1820s with the conviction that 'history repeats itself, with variations'.[32] The book was originally published in 1908 and in that context the parallels came easily: Stewart, for example, could claim that Muir 'had been transported for doing what Maxim Gorky and his comrades are now doing in Russia'. Muir was to be rescued from oblivion as an inspiration for workers whose historical imaginations had been deadened by the iniquities of capitalism and as a pioneer in that 'struggle between privilege and democracy ... which can only be fully realised in Socialism'.[33] This perspective on Muir was largely shared by Thomas Johnston, whose influential *History of the Working Classes in Scotland* (1920) substantially reimagined Muir's role as that of the bourgeois political activist and emphasised his attempts to mobilise the working classes.[34]

Such historical work on the left cleared the way for commemorations initiated by the Edinburgh federation of the ILP. These became annual events into the 1930s under the auspices of the ILP and, latterly, the Scottish Socialist Party (SSP).[35] An SSP banner from 1938, now in the People's Palace Museum in Glasgow, bears the slogan 'Thomas Muir, Baird and Hardie died that you should be free to choose your government. Workers in Spain are dying because they dared to choose their own government. Unite for the Struggle!' As this indicates, however, Muir was not alone in this pantheon derived from the revolutionary era and in some ways he remained an awkward fit. For both the Chartists and the ILP, more promising material was to be found in the events surrounding the 'general rising' of 1820 and the commemoration of its unassailably working-class martyrs.[36] A similar pecking order was apparent in other contexts as well. The emergence of an 1820 Society at the end of the 1960s concentrated on establishing the systematic commemoration of the working-class martyrs of 1820, while commemorations of Muir remained isolated rather than annual events.[37] The 1820 Society latterly sought to expand its activities to take in Muir, and at an Edinburgh event in 1982 made plain his place within the pantheon of the radical nationalist left: 'Muir's goals were not limited to parliamentary reform but embraced, like the martyrs of 1820 and John McLean, the creation of a Scottish republic.'[38]

As the above should make clear, while Muir was increasingly claimed as relevant to socialist and revolutionary republican movements in the twentieth century, he became at the same time a more obviously nationalist figure. This had longer roots. The ILP, for example, retained a very public support for Home Rule into the 1920s, and the *Forward* could lament that Muir and other exemplars of Scottish nationality did not feature in school history lessons.[39] This 'nationalising' of Muir was apparent in other early twentieth-century contexts. In 1915 the *Scottish Review* identified the age of Burns and Muir as 'strangely resembling our own', presented Muir's trial as the decisive catalyst for Burns' nationalism and thus appropriated both men as far-seeing pioneers of Scottish Home Rule.[40]

Such appropriations rose and fell in tandem with the political presence and success of nationalism from the 1960s. The preface to Michael Donnelly's 1975 pamphlet on Muir, for example, was penned by Oliver Brown, a prominent nationalist and radical republican from the 1930s onwards and a prolific contributor to the *Scots Independent*. His characterisation of Muir described his own perspective very neatly: 'Muir was just as enthusiastic a Scottish nationalist as he was a citizen of the world.'[41] Frequently this nationalism was tied with revolutionary republican (and sometimes explicitly socialist) politics, as it was in the commemorations of the 1960s and 1980s and in Peter Arnott's 1986 play, which began with activists attacking George III's garden party with shouts of 'Down with the English. Free Scotland', and has as Muir's impassioned plea to the French Directory:

> I call upon the French army to invade my country, set us free, help us rise and be a nation, and together we will defeat the British Empire. I ask that you join with me in establishing a Free Scottish Republic.[42]

A similar radical republican nationalism is apparent in another playwright's interpretation of Muir in a recent biography.[43]

Just as nationalism itself is amenable to a wide range of political positions, so too the 'nationalist' Muir has not been the exclusive property of the radical left. Indeed, more recent invocations of his name have returned to the more consensual ground of regarding Muir as a forefather of democratic reform rather than a committed republican insurrectionary. This was the significance of Muir as he appeared in a party conference speech by Alex Salmond and in a recent petition to commemorate Muir in statue form in or near the Scottish Parliament, which disclaimed any partisan intentions: 'While his legacy might be construed by some as that of a "left wing" revolutionary, such a tag is inappropriate to the period he lived through.' The nationalist inflection in both cases, nevertheless, remained clear: 'This petition asks the Scottish Parliament to support the process by which Muir joins the pantheon of Scottish historical heroes whose actions were selfless and motivated for the general good of the nation.'[44] Whatever other political positions Muir's memory is annexed to, he is almost invariably presented now as a nationalist of some description. There was little doubt which way the Twitter account set up in Muir's name before the 2014 Scottish independence referendum would lean.

V

As befits the restless internationalism of his life, however, some of Muir's posthumous lives have been passed outside of Great Britain. There was some interest in Muir in the United States, though the nineteenth-century myth that it was George Washington who sent *The Otter* to rescue Muir from New South Wales has long since been scotched.[45] Though interest in and familiarity with his life story did not long outlive Muir, immortality of a sort was assured by the inclusion of part of his defence speech in a very widely read rhetorical primer, *The Columbian Orator*, whose principal contemporary fame derives from its formative role in the self-education of the radical abolitionist and former slave Frederick Douglass.[46] In France, some relative celebrity among the émigré community under the Directory did not seem to outlive Muir himself. Where he has continued to be 'politically usable' has been in the place of his brief confinement, Australia.

The rediscovery of Muir and the more muted mobilisation of his political legacy followed a similar chronology to the increasingly nationalist and radical uses of his name in Scotland.[47] The heightened visibility of questions of nationality within Australian politics and culture from the 1880s provided a context in which Muir's story was revisited. Historians of Australia have long grappled with the difficulties of Australian beginnings and in the nineteenth century the 'convict stain' presented especial problems in narrating self-consciously national origins. In particular, the centenary of white settlement in 1888 prompted a frequently uncomfortable engagement with this issue.[48] In the context of an emerging radical republicanism, a more assertive imperial patriotism and the ongoing discussions around Australian Federation from the late 1880s, the question of these 'old' beginnings at the end of the eighteenth century was closely linked to the question of 'new' ones at the end of the nineteenth.

One man who took a particular interest in both Thomas Muir and the other 'Scottish martyrs' in this context was George Burnett Barton, whose brother, Edmund, was intimately involved in the movement for Federation and would become the first prime minister of Australia. George Barton's career as a journalist, editor and sometime English literature academic had afforded plentiful opportunities to consider the vexed question of Australian nationality. In the 1860s this had featured in his efforts to present an account and a collection of 'indigenous' (by which he meant white Australian) literature for the Paris Exposition Universelle of 1867.[49] In the 1880s he became involved in government attempts to provide an official history of New South Wales and was responsible for its first published volume, in which he pieced together 'the history of an infant nation'.[50]

It was almost a natural extension of these literary and historical interests when, from 1896, he began to write a series of features in the Sydney *Evening News*, which later came under the title of 'Celebrities of Botany Bay', and which offered serialised histories of famous early convicts. The longest series, which ran from August 1896 until March 1897 (and thus ran during the excitement of the 'People's Convention' at Bathurst, organised by the Australasian Federation League), focused on the Scottish Martyrs, with Thomas Muir receiving the greatest attention.[51] Long before Barton put pen to paper, correspondents in the Australian press had mooted the historical rehabilitation of convicts such as Muir, one querying why there was no monument or memorial to him in Sydney 'as an example for Australians'.[52] Barton's portrayal was a sympathetic one and, in line with Barton's own political views, Muir was explicitly rescued from the obloquy of contemporary spy reports, which lumped him with insurrectionary United Irishmen. He was instead presented as a persecuted constitutionalist and democrat.[53] Barton evidently intended to publish the series as a book (as happened posthumously with his articles on Margaret Catchpole) and the draft manuscript for this expanded on some of the anti-republican themes of the articles.[54] As such, Muir was the focus of an early attempt, in the midst of debates around Federation and nationality, to rescue Australian origins from the psychological baggage of the 'convict stain'.

Interest was sustained from that point onwards. Various newspapers ran biographical features on 'Australia's Greatest Martyr', and when the ILP held its commemorations in Edinburgh these were widely reported in the Australian press.[55] In parallel with Meikle's endeavours in Scotland, historians became interested in the Australian aspects of Muir's story, with the researches of Marjorie Masson of Melbourne constituting an important early example.[56] John Earnshaw worked in a similar direction and undertook dogged research work in the 1940s to reconstruct Muir's globetrotting, assisted in some respects by a prolonged correspondence with Meikle. His research finally appeared in published form in 1959, with the express rationale of achieving 'a clear picture of perhaps the most celebrated convict ever transported to the shores of Australia'.[57] This vision of Muir as an early national hero reached its widest audience when it became the central theme of a volume by the travel writer and indefatigable chronicler of the Australian 'outsider', Frank Clune.[58]

Earnshaw's research was rigorous, but in part his interest in Muir was spurred by a nationalist impulse to uncover (white) Australian beginnings. The presence in Sydney of the manuscript of the anti-Jacobin satire *The Telegraph*, purportedly by Muir himself, was tantalising not least because 'it would appear to be the first poem to be written in Australia that had been preserved'. Once research and his correspondence with

Meikle demonstrated that it was not by Muir's hand, Earnshaw dutifully reported this to the judge and bibliophile John Ferguson for inclusion in his mammoth *Bibliography of Australia*.[59] Later authors found the prospect of Muir's dual role in the paternity of Australian democracy and Australian literature all too tempting, with Muir's authorship repeated again in Robert Hughes' *Fatal Shore*.[60] And while Muir's role as Australia's inaugural poet is now safely exploded, his role as a pioneer democrat continues to grow. Indeed, his story inaugurates a recent engaging account, one of whose objectives is to ensure 'that twenty-first century readers, especially younger Australians, might learn the stories of the rebels, radicals and protestors who sacrificed their own freedom to help achieve the liberty, democracy and egalitarianism we enjoy today.'[61]

VI

It is entirely appropriate that the locations of the two copies of a bust of Muir by the sculptor Alexander Stoddart should reflect at least some of the diversity of Muir's associations. One is held as part of a permanent exhibition at Bishopbriggs library, near the former Huntershill estate. Part of this is now occupied by Huntershill Village, a cross between a local shopping centre and a heritage attraction. It has become central to recent efforts to commemorate Muir, in the form of an annual Thomas Muir Festival and various built memorials, including a Thomas Muir cairn and the Thomas Muir Coffee Shop. The other bust is in the Museum of Australian Democracy located within the old Parliament building in Canberra.

While frequently acknowledging the cosmopolitanism and internationalist outlook of Muir himself and, of course, the transnational context of his career, the temptation to place him within national narratives is all too evident. His claimed paternal involvement in both Scottish and Australian democracy are but two faces of an ever-shifting series of roles into which Muir has been placed and, sometimes, squeezed. The ambiguities inherent in his own statements, the transformative nature of the times in which he lived and the sheer romance of his own compelling life story have all contributed to the malleability of his legacy. Since his death, Muir has proved to be politically usable at various points and has lived a number of posthumous lives: as a constitutional reformer, herald of the reform acts and the house martyr of a gradualist approach to political change; as an advanced radical democrat committed to universal manhood suffrage; as a radical republican insurrectionary; as a kind of vanguardist bourgeois intellectual, committed to the politicisation of the working class; and as a modern nationalist and pioneer of Home Rule and/or Scottish independence. Thomas Muir's voyage continues.

Notes

1. H. T. Dickinson, 'Muir, Thomas (1765–1799)', in H. C. G. Matthew and Brian Harrison (eds), *Oxford Dictionary of National Biography* (Oxford, 2004). See also idem, 'Thomas Muir and the "Scottish Martyrs" of the 1790s', *The Historian*, 86 (2005), pp. 23–31.
2. The most reliable biography remains Christina Bewley, *Muir of Huntershill* (Oxford, 1981); Murray Armstrong, *The Liberty Tree: The Stirring Story of Thomas Muir and Scotland's First Fight for Democracy* (Edinburgh, 2014).
3. This phrase, which appears on the Edinburgh monument, is from the edition of the trial with the John Kay portrait of Muir as frontispiece, *Trial of Thomas Muir, Esq. Younger of Huntershill* (Edinburgh, 1793), p. 130. Other versions give alternative (and less eloquent) renditions of Muir's closing words.
4. David S. Karr, '"The Embers of Expiring Sedition": Maurice Margarot, the Scottish Martyrs Monument and the Production of Radical Memory across the British South Pacific', *Historical Research*, 83 (2013), p. 642.
5. William McCarthy, *Anna Laetitia Barbauld: Voice of the Enlightenment* (Baltimore, 2008), pp. 344–5; John Barrell, 'Thomas Banks and the Society for Constitutional Information', in Sarah Monks, John Barrell and Mark Hallett (eds), *Living with the Royal Academy: Artistic Ideals and Experiences in England, 1768–1848* (Aldershot, 2012), pp. 131–52.
6. National Library of Australia [hereafter NLA], Papers of Sir John Ferguson, MS 3626, Antonio Bonilla to Marquis de Branciporte, 26 September 1796.
7. NLA, Papers of Sir George Murray [microform], Mfm G 7672, Thomas Muir to Theophilus Lindsey, 14 July 1796.
8. Thomas Laqueur, 'In and Out of the Panthéon', *London Review of Books*, 23:18 (2001), p. 3.
9. Peter Mackenzie, *Reminiscences of Glasgow and the West of Scotland*, 3 vols (Glasgow, 1865–8); James Maclehose (ed.), *Memoirs and Portraits of One Hundred Glasgow Men*, 2 vols (Glasgow, 1886), II, pp. 199–202.
10. William Patrick Library, Kirkintilloch [hereafter WPL], Peter Mackenzie Papers, GD 185/7.
11. James Epstein, 'The Constitutional Idiom: Radical Reasoning, Rhetoric and Action in Early Nineteenth-Century England', *Journal of Social History*, 23 (1990), pp. 553–74.
12. P. Mackenzie, *The Life of Thomas Muir, Esq., Advocate, younger of Huntershill, near Glasgow* (Glasgow, 1831); idem, *An Exposure of the Spy System*; idem, *The Trial of James Wilson for High Treason, with an Account of his Execution at Glasgow, September, 1820* (Glasgow, 1832).
13. 'The Memory of Major Cartwright', *Cobbett's Weekly Register*, 73:4 (23 July 1831), pp. 218–25; Thomas Hardy, *Memoir of Thomas Hardy, Founder of, and Secretary to, the London Corresponding Society* (London, 1832).
14. See especially Henry Cockburn, *Memorials of his Time* (Edinburgh, 1856).
15. Muir's portrait appeared in *Loyal Reformers' Gazette*, 31 December 1831.

16 WPL, Peter Mackenzie Papers, GD 185/4/18, Joseph Hume to Peter Mackenzie, 20 December 1836.
17 For a discussion of the monument, see A. Tyrell with M. T. Davis, 'Bearding the Tories: The Commemoration of the Scottish Political Martyrs of 1793–4', in Paul Pickering and Alex Tyrell (eds), *Contested Sites: Commemoration, Memorials and Popular Politics in Nineteenth-Century Britain* (Aldershot, 2004), pp. 25–56.
18 Though not without some tensions over where the monument should be located, Karr, '"Embers of Expiring Sedition"', p. 659.
19 E. H. Strain, *A Prophet's Reward* (Edinburgh, 1908), p. 342.
20 H. W. Meikle, *Scotland and the French Revolution* (Glasgow, 1912).
21 National Library of Scotland [hereafter NLS], Papers of H. W. Meikle, Acc. 3421/81, Lectures on Historical Subjects, [typescript] 'Scottish Heritage 2. Summer Term 1958. "Thomas Muir"'.
22 George Pratt Insh, *Thomas Muir of Huntershill (1765–1799)* (Glasgow, 1949), p. 19.
23 Henry Cockburn, *Journal of Henry Cockburn: Being a Continuation of the Memorials of his Time*, 2 vols (Edinburgh, 1874), II, p. 34.
24 Henry Cockburn, *An Examination of the Trials for Sedition which have hitherto occurred in Scotland*, 2 vols (Edinburgh, 1888).
25 For examples, see Gordon Pentland, '"Betrayed by infamous spies"? The Commemoration of Scotland's "Radical War" of 1820', *Past and Present*, 201 (2008), pp. 141–73; Matthew Roberts, 'Chartism, Commemoration, and the Cult of the Radical Hero, c. 1770–1840', *Labour History Review*, 78 (2013), pp. 3-32.
26 *Northern Star*, 26 September 1840.
27 *Scotsman*, 25 February 1837; Karr, '"Embers of Expiring Sedition"', pp. 653–4.
28 *The Scotsman*, 29 July and 2 August 1848; *Glasgow Herald*, 31 July 1848.
29 The letter is reproduced in L. C. Wright, *Scottish Chartism* (Edinburgh, 1953), pp. 229–30.
30 For an excellent recent overview, see James Mitchell, *The Scottish Question* (Oxford, 2014); R. J. Finlay, *A Partnership for Good? Scottish Politics and the Union since 1880* (Edinburgh, 1997), chs 1–3.
31 A. McKinlay and R. J. Morris (eds), *The ILP on Clydeside, 1893–1932: From Foundation to Disintegration* (Manchester, 1991).
32 *Forward*, 15 February 1919.
33 William Stewart, *Fighters for Freedom in Scotland: The Days of Baird and Hardie* (London and Glasgow, 1908), pp. 5, 8.
34 Thomas Johnston, *The History of the Working Classes in Scotland* (2nd edn, Glasgow, 1929), pp. 218–22.
35 *Scotsman*, 23 September 1929, 16 June 1934, 29 August 1938. The SSP comprised largely those members of the ILP who wished to continue affiliation to the Labour Party.
36 Pentland, '"Betrayed by Infamous Spies?"'.

37 For an example, see 'Thomas Muir of Huntershill and the Scottish Martyrs: Commemoration Meetings Arranged by the Workers' Party of Scotland', *Scottish Vanguard*, 2:8/9 (August/September 1968), pp. 6–9.
38 *1820 Society Newsletter*, 1982. Speech by Dave Leadbetter of the Scottish Republican Socialist Club.
39 *Forward*, 5 April 1919.
40 Luath, 'Robert Burns as a Poet of Scottish Nationalism', *Scottish Review*, 38:80 (December 1915), pp. 504–26.
41 Michael Donnelly, *Thomas Muir of Huntershill, 1765–99* (Bishopbriggs, 1975).
42 British Library, MPS 3045, [playscript] Thomas Muir's Transportation Show.
43 Hector MacMillan, *Handful of Rogues: Thomas Muir's Enemies of the People* (Glendaruel, 2005).
44 http://www.snp.org/media-centre/news/2011/mar/alex-salmond-addresses-snp-conference; http://archive.scottish.parliament.uk/business/petitions/pdfs/PE1325.pdf [both accessed 8 August 2014].
45 See, for examples, *Aurora General Advertiser*, 25 January 1797, *Albany Register*, 4 December 1797, *Porcupine's Gazette*, 6 May 1797, 2 and 6 March 1798.
46 Caleb Bingham, *The Columbian Orator: Containing a Variety of Original and Selected Pieces* (Boston, MA, 1797), pp. 43–4; Frederick Douglass, *Narrative of the Life of Frederick Douglass, an American Slave, written by Himself*, ed. by Robert B. Stepto (Cambridge, MA, [1845] 2009), pp. 49–51.
47 See the excellent account of the Australian engagement with Muir in the *Dictionary of Sydney* http://dictionaryofsydney.org/entry/muir_thomas [accessed 12 September 2014].
48 Mark McKenna, 'The History Anxiety', in Alison Bashford and Stuart Macintyre (eds), *The Cambridge History of Australia*, 2 vols (Cambridge, 2013), II, pp. 561–80; Lyn Spillman, *Nation and Commemoration: Creating National Identities in the United States and Australia* (Cambridge, 1997), ch. 3; Mark McKenna, *The Captive Republic: A History of Republicanism in Australia, 1788–1996* (Cambridge, 1996), pp. 160–3.
49 G. B. Barton, *Literature in New South Wales* (Sydney, 1866); idem, *Poets and Prose Writers of New South Wales* (Sydney, 1866).
50 G. B. Barton, *History of New South Wales from the Records. Vol. I – Governor Phillip, 1783–1789* (Sydney, 1889), p. vi.
51 *Evening News*, 15 August 1896 to 6 March 1897.
52 *South Australian Advertiser*, 23 June 1869; *Australian Town and Country Journal*, 28 September 1878.
53 *Evening News*, 6 February 1897.
54 State Library of New South Wales, George Burnett Barton papers and correspondence, DLMSQ 107/61, 'The Scottish Martyrs'; G. B. Barton, *The True Story of Margaret Catchpole* (Sydney, 1924).

55 *Brisbane Courier*, 24 April 1908; *Australasian*, 29 December 1923; *Windsor and Richmond Gazette*, 25 January 1929; *Queenslander*, 15 February 1939.
56 Marjory Masson and J. F. Jameson, 'The Odyssey of Thomas Muir', *American Historical Review*, 29 (1923), pp. 49–72.
57 John Earnshaw, *Thomas Muir, Scottish Martyr: Some Account of his Exile to New South Wales, his Adventurous Escape in 1796 across the Pacific to California and thence, by way of New Spain, to France* (Cremorne, NSW, 1959).
58 Frank Clune, *The Scottish Martyrs: Their Trials and Transportation to Botany Bay* (Sydney, 1969).
59 NLS, MS 3829, Letters between Henry Meikle and John Earnshaw, 25 February 1948 and 16 March 1949.
60 For discussion of the poem and its authorship, see Nigel Leask, 'Thomas Muir and *The Telegraph*: Radical Cosmopolitanism in 1790s Scotland', *History Workshop Journal*, 63 (2007), pp. 48–69.
61 Tony Moore, *Death or Liberty: Rebels and Radicals Transported to Australia 1788–1868* (Millers Point, NSW, 2010), p. 12.

Appendix: Selected List of H. T. Dickinson's Publications, 1964–2015

No attempt has been made to include forthcoming works. Where articles have been translated into another language, this is indicated in square brackets following the title.

Authored Books

Bolingbroke (London, 1970).
Walpole and the Whig Supremacy (London, 1973).
Radicalism in the North-East of England in the Later Eighteenth Century (Durham, 1979).
Liberty and Property: Political Ideology in Eighteenth-Century Britain (London and New York, 1977) [paperback edition (1979) and translations into Spanish (1981) and Japanese (2006)].
British Radicalism and the French Revolution 1789–1815 (Oxford and New York, 1985) [translation into Chinese (2015)].
Caricatures and the Constitution 1760–1832 (Cambridge, 1986).
The Politics of the People in Eighteenth-Century Britain (London and New York, 1994) [paperback edition (1996) and translation into Chinese (2015)].

Edited Collections

Britain and the French Revolution 1789–1815 (London and New York, 1989).
Britain and the American Revolution (London, 1998) [with Michael Lynch], *The Challenge to Westminster: Sovereignty, Devolution and Independence* (East Linton, 2000).
A Companion to Eighteenth-Century Britain (Oxford, 2002) [paperback edition 2006]
[with Ulrich Broich, Eckhart Hellmuth and Martin Schmidt], *Reactions to Revolutions: The 1790s and their Aftermath* (Munster, 2007).

Editions of Texts and Source Collections

The Correspondence of Sir James Clavering 1708–1740 (Durham, 1967).
Politics and Literature in the Eighteenth Century (London and Totowa, NJ, 1974).

Bernard Mandeville, *The Mischiefs that ought justly to be Apprehended from a Whig Government* (Los Angeles, 1975).
The Political Works of Thomas Spence (Newcastle upon Tyne, 1982).
Lord Hervey, *Ancient and Modern Liberty Stated and Compar'd* (Los Angeles, 1989).
William Pulteney, *A Proper Reply to a Late Scurrilous Libel; Intitled, Sedition and Defamation Display'd (1731)* (New York, 1998).
Constitutional Documents of the United Kingdom 1782–1835 (Munich, 2005).
British Pamphlets on the American Revolution, 8 vols (London, 2007–8).
Ireland in the Age of Revolution 1760–1805, 6 vols (London, 2012–13).

Journal Articles

'Peterborough and the Capture of Barcelona, 1705', *History Today*, 14 (1964), pp. 705–15.
'The Capture of Minorca, 1708', *Mariner's Mirror*, 51 (1964), pp. 195–204.
'The Mohun-Hamilton Duel', *Durham University Journal*, 57 (1965), pp. 159–65.
'The Attempt to Assassinate Harley, 1711', *History Today*, 15 (1965), pp. 788–95.
'The Earl of Peterborough's Campaign in Valencia, 1706', *Journal of the Society of Army Historical Research*, 45 (1967), pp. 35–52.
'The Poor Palatines and the Parties', *English Historical Review*, 82 (1967), pp. 464–85.
'The Tory Party's Attitude to Foreigners', *Bulletin of the Institute of Historical Research*, 40 (1967), pp. 153–65.
'Henry St John: A Reappraisal of the Young Bolingbroke', *Journal of British Studies*, 7 (1968), pp. 33–55.
'Letters of Bolingbroke to James Grahme', *Transactions of the Cumberland and Westmorland Antiquarian and Archaeological Society*, 68 (1968), pp. 117–31.
'The Richards Brothers: Exponents of the Military Arts of Vauban', *Journal of the Society of Army Historical Research*, 46 (1968), pp. 76–86.
'The Recall of Lord Peterborough', *Journal of the Society of Army Historical Research*, 47 (1969), pp. 175–87.
'Henry St John, Wootton Bassett, and the General Election of 1708', *Wiltshire Archaeological and Natural History Magazine*, 64 (1969), pp. 107–11.

'Bolingbroke's attack on Alexander Pope in 1746', *Notes and Queries*, 16 (1969), pp. 342–4.

'Bolingbroke and the Idea of a Patriot King', *History Today*, 20 (1970), pp. 13–19.

'The October Club', *Huntington Library Quarterly*, 33 (1970), pp. 155–73.

'The Correspondence of Henry St John and Thomas Erle', in three issues of the *Journal of the Society of Army Historical Research*, 48 (1970), pp. 205–24 and 49 (1971), pp. 3–9, 77–8.

[with K. J. Logue], 'The Porteous Riot, 1736: Events in a Scottish Protest against the Act of Union with England', *History Today*, 22 (1972), pp. 272–81.

'Walpole and His Critics', *History Today*, 22 (1972), pp. 410–19.

'The Rodneys and the Brydges', *Mariner's Mirror*, 59 (1973), pp. 313–16.

'Benjamin Hoadly, 1676–1761: Unorthodox Bishop', *History Today*, 25 (1975), pp. 348–55.

'The Letters of Henry St John to the Earl of Orrery', *Camden Society Miscellany*, 26 (1975), pp. 137–99.

'Bernard Mandeville: an Independent Whig', *Studies on Voltaire and the Eighteenth Century*, 152 (1976), pp. 559–70.

'The Eighteenth-Century Debate on the Glorious Revolution', *History*, 61 (1976), pp. 28–45.

'Party, Principle and Public Opinion in Eighteenth Century Politics' [review article], *History*, 61 (1976), pp. 231–8.

[with K. J. Logue], 'The Porteous Riot: A Study of the Breakdown of Law and Order in Edinburgh, 1736–1737', *Journal of the Scottish Labour History Society*, 10 (1976), pp. 21–40.

'The Eighteenth Century Debate on the Sovereignty of Parliament', *Transactions of the Royal Historical Society*, 5th series, 26 (1976), pp. 189–210.

'The Politics of Edward Gibbon', *Literature and History*, 4 (1978), pp. 175–9.

'The Hexham Militia Riot of 1761', *Bulletin of the Durham Local History Society*, 22 (1978), pp. 1–6.

'Whiggism in the Eighteenth Century' [Japanese], *Asia University Law Review*, 19 (1985), pp. 331–55.

'Politics and the People in the Reign of George III' [review article]', *Journal of British Studies*, 24 (1985), pp. 508–16.

'Popular Politics in the Age of Walpole' [Japanese], *Asia University Law Review*, 21 (1986), pp. 221–44.

'The Politics of the People in Eighteenth-Century Britain' [Chinese], *Nanjing University Journal*, (1987), pp. 52–63.

'How Revolutionary was the "Glorious" Revolution of 1688?', *British Journal for Eighteenth Century Studies*, 11 (1988), pp. 125–42.

'How Revolutionary was the "Glorious" Revolution of 1688?' [Chinese], *World History*, 6 (1988), pp. 83–93.

'The Impact of the French Revolution on Britain', *Contemporary Review*, 254 (1989), pp. 20–6.

'Counter-revolution in Britain in the 1790s', *Tijdschrift Voor Geschiedenis*, 102 (1989), pp. 354–67.

'Pressure Groups and Vested Interests in Eighteenth-Century Britain' [Chinese], *Nanjing University Journal*, (1989), pp. 25–37.

'Letters of Bolingbroke to the Earl of Orrery 1712–13', *Camden Society Miscellany*, 31 (1992), pp. 349–71.

'The Rights of Man from John Locke to Thomas Paine' [Chinese], *Developments in World Studies*, 1 (1993), pp. 34–44.

'Thomas Paine' [review article], *History*, 81 (1996), pp. 228–37.

'Irish Radicalism in the Late Eighteenth Century' [review article], *History*, 82 (1997), pp. 266–84.

'Sovereignty and Empire: The British Case against the American Colonists', *Douglas Southall Freeman Historical Review*, 4 (1997), pp. 3–29.

'Our American Brethren: British Sympathizers with the American Colonists', *Douglas Southall Freeman Historical Review*, 4 (1997), pp. 30–58.

'Britain and the American Revolution' [Polish], *Klio*, 5 (2004), pp. 97–117.

'Thomas Muir and the "Scottish Martyrs" of the 1790s', *The Historian*, 86 (2005), pp. 23–31.

'Britain and the American Revolution' [Chinese], *Clio at Beida*, 11 (2005), pp. 46–66.

'L'Irlande à l'époque de la Révolution francaise', *Annales historiques de la Révolution française*, 342 (2005), pp. 159–83.

'The Jacobite Movement 1688–1788' [Polish], *Wiadomosci Historyczne*, 6 (2006), pp. 5–11.

'British Reaction to the American Revolution' [Chinese], *Historical Monthly*, 236 (2007), pp. 85–97.

'Modern Constitutional Ideas and Developments and the Challenge posed to the British Constitution', *EurAmerica*, 38 (2008), pp. 31–64.

'Public Opinion and the Abolition of the Slave Trade', *Revue française de civilisation britannique*, 15 (2008), pp. 121–40.

'Britain and the American Revolution' [Polish], *Wiadomosci Historyczne*, 2 (2009), pp. 15–22.

'The Ideological Debate on Democracy in Britain, 1768–1848' [Chinese], *Clio at Beida*, 14 (2009), pp. 258–99.

'Civilization, Prosperity and Harmony: From the perspective of an Historian' [Beijing Forum Address, 2008], *Journal of Philosophy and Social Sciences: Peking University*, 46 (2009), pp. 15–18.

'The Failure of Conciliation: Britain and the American Colonies 1763–1783', *The Kyoto Economic Review*, 79 (2010), pp. 91–109.

'The Debates on the Rights of Man in Britain: From the Levellers to the Chartists (1640s–1840s)', *Valahian Journal of Historical Studies*, 15 (2011), pp. 11–41.

'The Modern British Constitution: Reformed or Undermined?' [Chinese], *Journal of Nanjing University*, 48 (2011), pp. 19–31.

'George III and Parliament', *Parliamentary History*, 30 (2011), pp. 395–413.

'The Debates on the Rights of Man in Britain: From the Levellers to the Chartists (1640s–1840s)' [Chinese], *Academic Research*, 8 (2011), pp. 96–108, 160.

'Debates on the Rights of Man' [Chinese], *Xinhua Digest*, 24 (2011), pp. 138–43.

'British Reactions to the American Revolution', *The Annals of the Ovidius University of Constanta: The History Series*, 8 (2011), pp. 51–69.

'The Debates on the Rights of Man in Britain: From the Levellers to the Chartists (1640s–1840s)' [Chinese], *World History*, 11 (2011), pp. 30–42.

'The Modern British Constitution: Reformed or Undermined?', *Valahian Journal of Historical Studies*, 16 (2011), pp. 177–97.

'The Glorious Revolution of 1688: the First Modern Revolution?' [Chinese], *Chinese Journal of British Studies*, 3 (2011), pp. 9–23.

'Thomas Paine and His British Critics', *Enlightenment and Dissent*, 27 (2011), pp. 19–82.

'The Debates on the Rights of Man in Britain: From the Levellers to the Chartists (1640s–1840s)' [Japanese], *Waseda Journal of Political Science and Economics*, 383 (2012), pp. 3–21.

'The Westminster Parliament within the British Constitution: From the Glorious Revolution to the Present Day' [Japanese], *Waseda Journal of Political Science and Economics*, 385 (2013), pp. 2–19.

'Why did the American Revolution not spread to Ireland?', *Valahian Journal of Historical Studies*, 18–19 (2012–13), pp. 155–80.

'British Democratic Politics: From the Wilkesites to the Chartists' [Chinese], *Chinese Journal of British Studies*, 5 (2013), pp. 10–35.

'British Reactions to the American Revolution' [Japanese], *Seiyoshi Ronso*, 35 (2013), pp. 75–90.

'Scotland and the French Revolution' [Chinese], *Chinese Journal of British Studies*, 6 (2014), pp. 1–15.
'Lesser British Jacobin and Anti-Jacobin Writers during the French Revolution', *Enlightenment and Dissent*, 29 (2014), pp. 1–41.
'British Visual Propaganda and the French Revolution' [Chinese], *Chinese Historical Review*, 6 (2015), pp. 31–56.
'Britain and the Ideological Crusade against the French Revolution' [Chinese], *Sichuan University Journal*, (2015), pp. 34–45.
'How Democratic were British Politics from the Wilkesites to the Chartists (1760s to the 1840s)?', *Intellectual History*, 5 (2015), pp. 225–73.

Chapters and Contributions to Edited Collections

'The Duke of Newcastle', in Herbert van Thal (ed.), *The Prime Ministers*, 2 vols (London, 1974–5), I, pp. 75–91.
'The Politics of Bernard Mandeville', in Irwin Primer (ed.), *Mandeville Studies* (The Hague, 1975), pp. 80–97.
'The Rights of Man from John Locke to Thomas Paine', in O. D. Edwards and G. A. Shepperson (eds), *Scotland, Europe and the American Revolution* (Edinburgh, 1976), pp. 38–48.
'John Wilkes' and 'Thomas Paine', in J. O. Baylen and N. J. Gossman (eds), *A Biographical Dictionary of British Radicals*, 3 vols (Sussex and New Jersey, 1979–88), I, pp. 359–64, 529–34.
'The Debate on "The Achievement of Stability"' and 'Whiggism in the Eighteenth Century', in John Cannon (ed.), *The Whig Ascendancy* (London, 1981), pp. 23–6, 28–44, 49–50.
'Popular Politics in the Age of Walpole', in Jeremy Black (ed.), *Britain in the Age of Walpole* (London and New York, 1984), pp. 45–68, 214–15, 229–32.
'Government and Politics in England 1701–1783', in Christopher Haigh (ed.), *The Cambridge Historical Encyclopaedia of Great Britain and Ireland* (Cambridge, 1985), pp. 205–9.
'Political Ideas and Political Reality in Eighteenth Century Britain', in Michael Sutton (ed.), *History of Ideas Colloquium. Occasional Papers no. 1* (Newcastle upon Tyne, 1986), pp. 5–21.
'The Precursors of Political Radicalism in Augustan Britain', in Clyve Jones (ed.), *Britain in the First Age of Party 1680–1750* (London, 1987), pp. 63–84.
'The Rights of Man from the Levellers to the Utopian Socialists', in G. Birtsch (ed.), *Grund- und Freiheitsrechte von der ständischen zur spätbürgerlichen Gesellschaft* (Göttingen, 1987), pp. 67–87.

Entries on 'Bolingbroke', 'Namier', 'J. H. Plumb' and 'E. P. Thompson', in John Cannon (ed.), *The Blackwell Dictionary of Historians* (Oxford, 1988).

'The Politics of Pope', in Colin Nicolson (ed.), *Alexander Pope: Essays for the Tercentenary* (Aberdeen, 1988), pp. 1–21.

'The Politics of the People in Eighteenth-Century Britain' [Chinese], in Wang Juefei (ed.), *The Political, Economic and Social Modernisation of Britain* (Nanjing, 1989), pp. 253–79.

'Popular Loyalism in Britain in the 1790s', in Eckhart Hellmuth (ed.), *The Transformation of Political Culture: England and Germany in the Late Eighteenth Century* (Oxford, 1990), pp. 503–33.

'Radicals and Reformers in the Age of Wilkes and Wyvill', in Jeremy Black (ed.), *British Politics and Society from Walpole to Pitt 1742–1789* (London and New York, 1990), pp. 123–46, 230, 254–8.

'Britain and the Ideological Crusade against the French Revolution', in L. Domergue and G. Lamoine (eds), *Après 89: la révolution modèle ou repoussoir* (Toulouse, 1992), pp. 153–74.

'The French Revolution and the Counter-Revolution in Britain', in Hans-Christoph Schröder and Hans-Dieter Metzger (eds), *Aspekte der Französischen Revolution* (Darmstadt, 1992), pp. 231–63.

'Die Kultur der Radikalen', in Celina Fox (ed.), *Metropole London: Macht und Glanz einer Weltstadt 1800–1840* (Recklinghausen, 1992), pp. 209–24.

'Radical Culture', in Celina Fox (ed.), *London: World City 1800–1840* (London, 1992), pp. 209–24.

'The Rise and Fall of the Theory of Natural Rights in late Eighteenth and early Nineteenth Century Britain', in Otto Dann and Diethelm Klippel (eds), *Naturrecht - Spätaufklärung - Revolution* (Hamburg, 1995), pp. 23–47.

'The Contract Theory and Natural Rights: from John Locke to Thomas Paine', in Jean-Louis Breteau (ed.), *Le contrat dans les pays anglo-saxons: théories et pratiques* (Toulouse, 1995), pp. 127–56.

'Democracy' and 'Elections', Iain McCalman (ed.), *The Oxford Companion to The Romantic Age: British Culture 1776–1832* (Oxford, 1999), pp. 34–42, 494–5.

'The Ideological Debate on the British Constitution in the late eighteenth and early nineteenth centuries', in Andrea Romano (ed.), *Il Modello Costituzionale Inglese e la sua Recezione nell'area Mediterranea tra la fine del 700 e la prima metà dell'800* (Milan, 1998), pp. 145–92.

'"The Friends of America": British Sympathy with the American Revolution', in Michael T. Davis (ed.), *Radicalism and Revolution in Britain 1775–1848* (London and New York, 2000), pp. 1–29.

'Alexander Davison', 'Thomas Muir', 'Henry St John', 'Thomas Spence', 'Christopher Wyvill' and 'Sir Wiliam Yonge', in H. C. G. Matthew and Brian Harrison (eds), *Oxford Dictionary of National Biography* (Oxford, 2004).

'Richard Price on Reason and Revolution', in William Gibson and Robert G. Ingram (eds), *Religious Identities in Britain, 1660–1832* (Aldershot, 2004), pp. 231–54.

'The Politics of the People in an Industrializing Society: Britain c.1760–c.1850', in *Evolution of Civilizations: Historical Experiences in the Modern Times of the East and the West, Proceedings of the Beijing Forum, 2006* (Beijing 2006), pp. 756–88.

'John Trenchard', in Duncan Brack and Ed Randall (eds), *Dictionary of Liberal Thought* (London, 2007), pp. 402–4.

'The Representation of the People in Eighteenth-Century Britain', in Maija Jansson (ed.), *Realities of Representation: State Building in Early Modern Europe and European America* (Basingstoke and New York, 2007), pp. 19–44.

'Thomas Gordon', in Ellen J. Jenkins (ed.), *Dictionary of Literary Biography, vol. 336: Eighteenth-Century British Historians* (Farmington Hills, MI, 2007), pp. 153–9.

Twenty-five essays in Gregory Fremont-Barnes (ed.), *Encyclopaedia of the Age of Political Revolutions and New Ideologies, 1760–1815*, 2 vols (Westport, CT, 2007).

'Politique britannique et luttes de partis dans les négociations du traité d'Utrecht', in Jean-Pierre Jessenne, Renaud Morieux and Pascal Dupuy (eds), *Le négoce et la paix: les nations et les traités franco-britanniques (1713–1802)* (Paris, 2008), pp. 15–46.

'The Ideological Debate on Democracy in Britain 1768–1848', in *Traditions and Modernity: State-structures and Political Cultures: Proceedings of the Beijing Forum, 2008* (Beijing, 2008), pp. 140–72.

'History, Academics and the Progress of Society', in *Selected Papers of the Beijing Forum 2008 on The Harmony of Civilizations and Prosperity for All* (Beijing, 2009), pp. 31–8.

'The Political Context', in Pamela Clemit (ed.), *The Cambridge Companion to British Literature of the French Revolution in the 1790s* (Cambridge, 2011), pp. 1–15, 207–8.

'Periodization in British History', in Qian Chengdan and Gao Dai (eds), *New Explorations in British History* (Beijing, 2011), pp. 403–25.

'Burke and America', in D. W. Dwan and C. Insole (eds), *The Cambridge Companion to Edmund Burke* (Cambridge and New York, 2012), pp. 156–67.

'The Impact of the War on British Politics', in Edward Gray and Jane Kamensky (eds), *The Oxford Handbook of the American Revolution* (Oxford and New York, 2013), pp. 355–69.

'The Society of the Friends of the People' and 'The Society for Constitutional Information', in Lawrence Goldman (ed.), *The Oxford Dictionary of National Biography* (online edn, Oxford, 2014).

Notes on the Contributors

David Allan is Reader in Scottish History at the University of St Andrews and has held visiting fellowships at Yale, Harvard and Brown. His books include *Virtue, Learning and the Scottish Enlightenment* (1993), *Philosophy and Politics in Later Stuart Scotland* (2000), *Scotland in the Eighteenth Century* (2002), *Adam Ferguson* (2006), *A Nation of Readers* (2008), *Making British Culture: English Readers and the Scottish Enlightenment* (2008) and *Commonplace Books and Reading in Georgian England* (2010).

Marianne Czisnik completed her PhD at the University of Edinburgh. Her publications include *Horatio Nelson: A Controversial Hero* (2005) and several essays and articles. She is currently preparing an edition of Nelson's letters to Lady Hamilton for the Navy Records Society, while working as Head of Finance in the Brandenburg State Office for the Environment.

Michael T. Davis is Lecturer in the School of Humanities at Griffith University. His publications include *Radicalism and Revolution in Britain, 1775–1848* (2000), *The London Corresponding Society* (2002), *Newgate in Revolution: An Anthology of Radical Prison Literature in the Age of Revolution* (ed. with I. McCalman and C. Parolin, 2005), *Unrespectable Radicals? Popular Politics in the Age of Reform* (ed. with P. A. Pickering, 2008) and *Terror: From Tyrannicide to Terrorism in Europe, 1605 to the Future* (ed. with B. Bowden, 2008).

Frances Dow CBE was formerly a Senior Lecturer in History at the University of Edinburgh where she taught and published on seventeenth-century British History. Her work includes *Cromwellian Scotland 1651–1660* (1979) and *Radicalism in the English Revolution 1640–1660* (1985). Having served successively as Dean, Provost and Vice Principal at the University of Edinburgh, she retired in 2003.

Rémy Duthille is Senior Lecturer in English studies at the Université Bordeaux–Montaigne. His work focuses on political ideology and sociability in eighteenth-century Britain.

Matthew P. Dziennik completed his PhD at the University of Edinburgh and is currently Kent Postdoctoral Fellow at the University of Saskatchewan. He has published widely in academic journals and his first book, *The Fatal Land: War, Empire, and the Highland Soldier in British America*, is under contract.

Martin Fitzpatrick was formerly Senior Lecturer and Senior Research Associate at the Department of History and Welsh History, the University of Wales, Aberystwyth. His publications have been concerned with the lives and thought of Joseph Priestley and Richard Price, Rational Dissent (especially its relationship with radicalism), the theme of toleration and the nature of the Enlightenment. He was co-founder with D. O. Thomas of the *Price-Priestley Newsletter* (subsequently *Enlightenment and Dissent*).

Matthew Grenby is Professor of Eighteenth-Century Studies in the School of English Literature, Language and Linguistics at Newcastle University. His publications include *The Anti-Jacobin Novel: British Conservatism and the French Revolution* (2001), *Children's Literature* (2007), *Popular Children's Literature* *in Britain* (ed. with Julia Briggs and Dennis Butts, 2008), *The Cambridge Companion to Children's Literature* (ed. with Andrea Immel, 2009) and *The Child Reader 1700–1840* (2011). He is editor of the *Journal for Eighteenth-Century Studies* and Vice-President of the British Society for Eighteenth-Century Studies.

Eckhart Hellmuth is Professor Emeritus of Modern History at the University of Munich. He has specialised in the intellectual and cultural history of eighteenth-century Britain and Germany. His authored and edited publications include *Naturrechtsphilosophie uns bürokratischer Werthorizont* (1985), *The Transformation of Political Culture: England and Germany in the Late Eighteenth Century* (1990) and *Rethinking Leviathan: The Eighteenth-Century State in Britain and Germany* (ed. with J. Brewer, 1999).

Joanna Innes is Professor of Modern History at the University of Oxford. She has been editor of *Past & Present* (1990–2000) and Vice-President of the Royal Historical Society (2008–11). Her publications include *Inferior Politics: Social Problems and Social Policies in Eighteenth-Century Britain* (2009), *Charity, Philanthropy and Reform in Europe and North America 1690–1850* (ed. with H. Cunningham, 1998), *Rethinking the Age of Reform: Britain 1780–1850* (ed. with A. Burns, 2003) and *Re-imagining Democracy in the Age of Revolutions: America, France, Britain, Ireland 1750–1850* (ed. with M. Philp, 2013). She has also written many articles on social problems and policies in the British Isles, 1688–1850.

Stephen M. Lee has degrees from the Universities of Edinburgh and Manchester. His first book, *George Canning and Liberal Toryism, 1801–1827* (2008), was awarded the Royal Historical Society's Whitfield Prize. He currently works as a Deputy Headteacher at Torquay Boys' Grammar School.

Emma Macleod is Lecturer in History at the University of Stirling. Her publications include *A War of Ideas: British Attitudes to the Wars Against Revolutionary France, 1792–1802* (1998), *British Visions of America, 1775–1820: Republican Realities* (2013) and a large number of contributions to edited collections and scholarly journals.

Shin Matsuzono teaches modern and contemporary Western History at Waseda University in Japan. He completed his PhD on 'The House of Lords and the Godolphin Ministry, 1702–10' at the University of Leeds and has published widely on eighteenth-century British parliamentary history.

Gordon Pentland is Reader in History in the School of History, Classics and Archaeology at the University of Edinburgh. His publications include *Radicalism, Reform and National Identity in Scotland, 1820–1833* (2008), *Spirit of the Union: Popular Politics in Scotland, 1815–1820* (2011) and a large number of journal articles on the political and cultural history of Britain since the French Revolution.

Atle L. Wold is Senior Lecturer of British Civilisation Studies at the University of Oslo. He completed his PhD thesis 'The Scottish Government and the French Threat, 1792–1802' at the University of Edinburgh. In recent years, his main research interest has been privateering and diplomacy during the period of the French Revolutionary and Napoleonic Wars.

Index

Note: *italic* signifies table, **bold** signifies figure

Aberdeen, Colleges, 103, 104, 105, 106
Acts *see specific names of acts*
Adams, John, 77, 78, 152, 190
Addington, Henry, 44, 49
agrarian socialists, 3, 103
air balloons, 180
Alexander, Jeffrey, 179
Alien and Sedition Acts (1798), 158
America, 73, 77–8, 81, 91, 149–58, 217; *see also* Revolution, American
Anderson, Benedict, 77
Anglicanism, 10–12, 14–17; *see also* church/Church
Anne, Queen of England, 18, 33
antiquity, 20, 105, 108, 113
Argyll, John Campbell, 2nd duke of, 32, 33, 62
arms, ban on, 59–60, 62, 64, 67
army, armies *see* military, the
Arnott, Peter, 216
Asgill, John, 22
atheism, 90
Atterbury, Francis, 11
Atwood and Wilson narratives, anti-Paine sentiments, 176–8
Australia, and Muir, 217–19
authoritative writings, 164, 165–6, 170

Ban MacIntyre, Duncan, 61
Banks, Thomas, 209
Baptists, 156
Barlow, Joel, 122, 152
Barrell, John, 185
Barrington, bishop, 46, 52
Barton, George Burnett, 217–18
Beattie, James, 103, 104
Belknap, Jeremy, 152
Bible, 19, 107, 141
Birmingham, 92, 151
bishops, 42, 43, 45, 48, 50, 51, 90; *see also* individual names of bishops
Blair, Robert, 165, 168, 169
Blake, William, 139
Bland, Humphrey, 62
Blount, Charles, 10, 11, 13, 17
Bonnet, Alistair, 133–4
Bonwick, Colin, 153
Bordeaux (France), 78, 82
Boston Post-Boy (newspaper), 75–7
Botany Bay, 209, 218

Bourdieu, Pierre, 74
Braxfield, Lord, 164, 169, 208, 211
Brissot, Jacques Pierre, 152, 153
Britain, toasting in, 73, 76, 77, 78, 82
Brown, Oliver, 216
Burdett, Francis, 51
Burke, Edmund, 89–99
  hostility to Dissenters, 94–9
  infamous phrase of, 131, 142
  Reflections (1790) and other works, 80, 94, 96, 97–8, 185
  toleration for Dissenters, 89–93
Burnett, John, 172–3
Burns, Robert, 76, 216

Cadiz, 194
Campbell, George, 103
Cape St Vincent, battle of, 199
caricaturists, 73, 185; *see also* Cruikshank, Isaac
Carmichael, Gershom, 106
Cartwright, John, 151, 210
Catholics and Catholicism, 11, 45, 48, 92, 157
censorship, 11, 12, 13–14, 16
Chaimbeul, Mairearad, 61
Champion, Justin, 9
Chartists and Chartism, 131, 212–14
Chase, Malcolm, on Spence, 118, 121–2, 124, 138
Cheape, Hugh, 60
Cheetham, James, 186, 187
Chesterfield, Philip Stanhope, 4th earl of, 63
children's literature (Spence and Newbery), 3, 131–42
church buildings, 40, 50
church/Church
  and Dissenters, 10–13, 14, 15, 44, 46, 94
  reform, 39–53
  and the state, 14, 16–17, 91, 96, 97–9, 157
civic humanism *see* humanism
civil liberty, 9, 91, 152; *see also* liberty; toleration
clans, Highland, 58, 59, 67
clergy, 39
  acts, 40
  and Dissent, 47, 89–90
  incomes, 45, 49, 50, 51
  non-residence, 41–2, 46, 48, 49, 50
Clerk, John of Penicuik, 2nd Baronet, 29, 30, 31–3

clothing, Highland *see* Highland dress
clubs and societies, 75, 125, 196, 197
    radical, 77–81, 94, 103, 163, 208, 214
Cockburn, Henry, 168, 173, 210, 212
coffee-houses, 80, 197
Cohen, Stanley, on moral panic, 178–9
Coleridge, Samuel, 99
Collins, Anthony, 10, 19–21, 22
Columbian Orator, The (primer), 217
common law, 164, 165, 165–6, 168
Commons, House of, 30–1, 50, 181, 181
Congress, US, 154
conservatism, popular, 2, 176–90; *see also* loyalism; Tories
constitutionalism, 63, 68, 93–4, 207, 210
Convocation, 10–11, 39
Copenhagen, battle of (1801), 202–3
Corsica, 75
country party, ideology, 121, 124
Craftsman (journal), Tindal's Letter, 14
Craigie, Robert, 64
Cruikshank, Isaac, 181–2, 181, 182, 183–4, 184
Crusonia, 118, 131–2, 136, 139, 141, 142
Cumberland, William Augustus, duke of ('Butcher'), 61–2, 63–4, 65
Cumming, James, 213–14
curates, 43, 48, 50, 51, 52, 53

debate, 16, 20–1, 125
    Parliamentary, 26–36, 51, 53; *see also* sedition, trials
Defoe, Daniel, 139
deism, 11, 14, 17, 90
Denmark, and Nelson, 202–3
Denton, William, 10, 13
devils and demons, 183–5, 184, 187, 188
Diary or Woodfall's Register, 185–6
Dickinson, H. T., 5, 178
    edition of Spence's writings, 3, 118, 124, 131–2
    Muir essay, 207–8
    other works, 1, 4, 59, 121, 149, 183
Dickinson, William, 41, 43, 49
Disarming Acts (1716 and 1725), 59, 62
Dissenters
    on Church and state, 39, 41, 44, 96–7, 157
    'new dissent', 39, 43, 46–7, 52
    and reform/regulation, 41, 48, 52
    Relief Bill, 89, 90
    republicanism and revolution, 93–4
    and toleration, 89–92, 97, 98
    see also Winterbotham, William
Donnelly, Michael, 216
Douglass, Frederick, former slave, 217

drinks and drinking vessels, 73–4, 76
Dundas, Henry, 80
Dundas, Robert, 80, 164, 167
Durey, Michael, 150, 152, 155, 156

Earnshaw, John, 218–19
Edinburgh, 163, 208, 212
    Chartists in, 213, 214
    Muir legacy, 211, 215, 218
    University of, 2, 104–5
education, radicals on, 131–42, 152, 217, 219; *see also* schools
Edwards, Bryan, 153
Elliott, Gilbert (*later* Lord Minto), 203
emigration, 153, 155, 158
enclosure, 125, 133
English language, reform, 136, 138, 141
Epstein, James, 73
Erskine, John, 166, 167–9, 170
ethnic hostility, 58, 59, 61, 63, 137; *see also* slavery
evangelism, 39, 43, 46–7, 51, 52

fables, 132, 133–4, 139
Feathers Tavern Petition, 89, 98
Federalists and federalism, 81, 152, 153, 155, 217, 218
Ferguson, Adam, 105, 108, 109, 110, 114
festivals, revolutionary, 78, 79, 81–2
Findlater, earl of, 65
First World War, 214
Fletcher, Archibald, 168
Fletcher of Saltoun, Andrew, 27
folk devils, 179, 189
Forbes of Culloden, Duncan, 61
Forward (newspaper), 215
Fox, Charles James, 92–3, 94–5, 97, 98
France
    French wars, 44, 46, 82, 183, 197, 203
    see also naval networking; Paris; Revolution, French
Francis, Philip, 96
Franklin, Benjamin, 152
Frazer, James, 188
Frederick, Prince of Wales, 135, 138
freedom *see* liberty
Friends of the People (society), 163, 208
Fruchtman, Jack, 189–90
Furedi, Frank, 178

Gaelic Scotland, and post-Culloden acts, 58–69
George, Prince of Wales (*later* George III), 135, 137; *see also* George III, King of England

INDEX

George I, King of England, 34
George II, King of England, 135, 137, 138
George III, King of England, 48, 216
Gerrald, Joseph, 163, 167, 169
Gibraltar, 195, 202
Gillies, Adam, 167, 169
Glasgow, 104–5, 208, 210, 213–14
Glasites, 124–5
Glenure, Duncan Campbell of, 64, 66, 68
Glorious Revolution *see* Revolution, Glorious (1688)
Godolphin, Sidney, 1st earl of, 28–9, 30, 32
'Golden Age', education for, 139–40, 141
Greece, ancient, free debate, 20
Gregory, Francis, 14, 14–16, 22
Grenville, William Wyndham, 1st Baron, 41, 44, 45–6, 47–8, 49, 51, 52
Grey, Charles, 2nd Earl Grey, 210, 211

Hall, John, 123, 123, 126–8
Hamilton, Emma, 194, 198, 199
Hamilton, James, 4th duke of, 32–3, 36
Hamilton, Sir William, 198
Hardwicke, earl of, 63, 65
Hardy, Thomas, 210
Harley, Robert *see* Oxford, Robert Harley, Earl of
Harrington, James
  Oceana and other works, 3, 108, 118–28, 123, 126–8
  see also Spence, Thomas
Hearnshaw, F. J. C., 115
Henderland, Lord, 169–70
heresy, 10–11, 15–16; *see also* sedition
Hickeringhill, Edmund, 10, 13
Highland dress, ban on, 59–61, 63–4, 65–7, 69
HMS *Victory* (Nelson's flagship), 199–200
Hobbes, Thomas, 106, 109
Hodgson, William, 80
Home Rule, Scottish, 214, 215–16
Hood, Lord, 203
Hughes, John Roydon, 66
Hughes, Robert, 219
humanism, 107–8
Hume, David, 104, 170–2
Hume, Joseph, 211
Huntershill, 219
Hutcheson, Francis, 106, 108–9, 111

income tax, 44, 45
Independent Labour Party (ILP), 214–15, 218
'influence', case study of, Harrington/Spence, 118–28
inheritance, laws of, 120

insanity, observations on, 176–8
Insh, George Pratt, 212
institutional writings, 165
Ireland and the Irish
  Church reform, 45, 48, 50
  peerage, 32
  toasting in, 77, 78
  United Irishmen, 82, 208, 209
Italy, 46, 81

Jacobite rebellions, 35, 58, 62, 135
Jacobites and Jacobitism, 33, 58, 60–1, 63, 65, 66
James II, King of England, 14, 151
Jay Treaty (1795), 155
Jefferson, Thomas, 81, 152, 153, 155, 156
Jeffrey, Francis, 210, 211
Jeffreys of Scotland, 208
Jellinek, Georg, 9
'Jew Bill' (1753), 137
Jewell, B. Frank, 63
Jewish world (ancient), Old Testament, 107
Johnston, Thomas, 215
journals, 14; *see also Lilliputian Magazine* (Newbery); Spence, *Pig's Meat*
'jubilee', 138–9, 142
judiciary, US, 154; *see also* law
jurisprudence, 105, 106, 107, 109

Kay, John, Muir profile, 211, 213
Knight, Roger, 203
Knox, Thomas R., 119, 124

Labour movement, 214–15; *see also* socialism
land ownership
  Church and, 45, 50–1
  Ogilvie's *Essay* on, 103, 106–15
  and post-Culloden acts, 58, 64, 65, 69
  Spence and Harrington on, 118, 120–1, 122, 123–5, 133, 138–9
  see also property
land tax, 30–1, 45, 48
law
  civil, 16–17, 47, 63, 65–8, 154
  and land rights *see* land ownership
  science of *see* jurisprudence
  on sedition, 163–73
  see also magistrates; *specific names of treaties and bills*
leasing-making, 168, 169, 170–1, 172
letters, Nelson's, 194–204
Levy, Leonard W., 21–2
liberty, 75–6, 82–3, 154, 157–8
  of conscience and press, 9–22
  see also civil liberty; rights

licensing system, 10, 17, 19
Lilliputian Magazine (Newbery), 132, 134, 135, 137, 139, 140, 142
Lincoln (city), 47
Lindsey, Theophilus, 89, 90, 92, 151
Locke, John, 10, 13, 111, 141, 155
Lockhart, George, 28, 31, 33
London, 30, 31, 77, 122, 134, 187
Lords, House of, 27–36, 42, 50
Louis XVI, King of France, 208
Loyal Reformers' Gazette (newspaper), 210, 211, 213
loyalism, 2, 63, 78, 80; *see also* conservatism, popular
Luim, Iain, 60

Mackenzie, George, 166–7, 168, 169
Mackenzie, Peter, 210–11, 213
Mackintosh, James, on *Essay* (Ogilvie), 114
McNaughton, Adam, 207
Madrid, 194
magazines, 41, 58, 114; *see also Lilliputian Magazine* (Newbery)
magistrates, 13, 16, 47, 63, 65–8
Mairearad Chaimbeul, 61
Margarot, Maurice, 163–4, 165
Marlborough, John Churchill, 1st duke of, 32
marriage, laws of, 120
Marseille, toasting in, 78–9
martyrs, Scottish *see* Muir, Thomas
Marxism, 115, 131
Masson, Marjorie, 218
materialism, 108
medicines, 133
meeting houses, 48, 69
Meikle, Henry, 212, 218, 219
merchants, 201, 202
'The Mercolians' (story), 132, 136–9
Methodism, 46, 47
military, the, 62, 64–5, 66, 67–8, 137, 154; *see also* naval networking
militias, citizen, 108
Milton, John, 10, 17
monarchy, 96, 112, 151, 153–4, 155, 170–2
Montgomery, James William, 169
Montrose, James Graham, 1st duke of, 34
More, Thomas, 118
Mortmain Act (1736), 50–1
Muir, Thomas, 207–23
  commemorations and portraits, 207, 209, 211–12, 216, 219
  legacy, posthumous, 209–19
  trial and transnational career, 82–3, 151, 208–9
Murray, Rev. James, 124, 125

Naish, P. B., 194
Namier, Lewis, 1, 69
Napoleon Bonaparte, 73, 82
National Maritime Museum, 194
nationalism, 214, 215–16, 217–19
naval networking, 194–204
Navigation Laws, 203
Nelson, Horatio, Viscount Nelson, 194–204
  letters, letter-writing: correspondent groups and patterns, 197–8; editions, 194–5; numbers of, 195–6, 195, 196; for professional networking, 196, 199–204
Netherlands, 20, 81
New South Wales, 209, 217
Newbery, John, children's literature, 3, 132–42
Newcastle, Thomas Pelham-Holles, 1st duke of, 30–1, 61, 62–3
Newcastle upon Tyne, 122, 124, 125, 132–3
Newgate prison, political prisoners, 149, 150, 151, 153, 155, 158
newspapers, 9–22, 134
  and moral panics, 178–9
  on Paine, 176, 180–1, 183, 184–5, 186
  political toast lists and writings, 75–7, 78, 79, 81
  on reform and Muir, 82–3, 213, 215, 218
  see also specific names of newspapers
Nicolas, Nicholas Harris, 194
Nile, battle of, 194, 198
North, Lord, 77, 90
Nottingham, Daniel Finch, 2nd earl of, 27

O'Connor, Fergus, 213
Ogilvie, William, *Essay*, 103–15
Ottoman Empire, and Nelson, 202
Oxford, Robert Harley, earl of, 32, 33

Paine, Thomas, 77, 176–93
  Atwood and Wilson narratives and, 176–8
  caricatures of, 181–2, 181, 182, 183–5, 184, 187, 188
  conservatives on character and appearance of, 186–7, 189
  and other radicals, 103, 151, 153, 155
  works, 140, 157, 158, 176–7, 180, 185–6
Paley, William, 46, 48
Palmer, Thomas Fysshe, 151, 172
Paris, 81, 208, 209, 217
parishes, Church reform, 40, 43, 46–8, 52
Parliament, British
  church/Church reform, 39–53
  Paine caricature, 181, 181
  reform, 209, 210–14
  Scots peerage in, 26–36
patriotism, 75, 77, 201, 217

patronage, 42–3, 48, 65
Peerage Bills crisis, prelude to, 26–36
Pelham, Henry, 62, 63, 65, 137
Pennsylvania, popular rule, 152
Perceval, Spencer, 44, 51, 53
periodicals *see* journals
Pigott, Charles, 80, 178
Pig's Meat (journal) *see* Spence, Thomas, *Pig's Meat*
piracy in publishing, 133, 151–2
Pitt, William (Pitt the Younger), 39–41, 42, 43–5, 46, 48–9, 53, 92
Place, Francis, 132
plagiarism, 151–2, 158
plaid, belted (*breacan-an-fhèilidh*), 60, 63, 66, 67
Plekhanov, Georgi, on Ogilvie, 115
Plumptre, Anne, 78–9
Plymouth, Paine's mock 'death', 187
Pocock, J. G. A., 58, 120, 126–8
poor, the, 45, 63, 67
Porter, Roy, 177
Porteus, bishop, 46
Powell, Martyn, 78
President, US, 154
press freedom, 9–22; *see also* newspapers
Pretyman, George, bishop of Lincoln, 45, 46, 47, 52
Price, Richard, 79, 91, 93–5, 98, 150–1, 158
Priestley, Joseph, 92–3, 96–7, 151, 184
Printing Act (1662), 10, 17, 19
property, and political rights, 152, 183; *see also* 'jubilee'; land ownership
Proscription, Act of (1746), effects of, 59–69
Protestantism, 11, 12–13; *see also* church/ Church; Dissenters
Pufendorf, Samuel, 106

Quakers, anti-toasting laws, 78
Queensberry, duke of, 32

Raynall, Abbé, 152
reason, 14–15
reform, Church, 39–53
reform, Parliamentary, 209, 210–14
Reformation, English, 11, 12, 18, 42, 49
Regiam Majestatem (legal text), 165–6, 168
Reid, Thomas, 103, 104, 108, 109
religious liberty, 9–22; *see also* toleration
republicanism, 73, 81–3, 93, 150, 151; *see also* nationalism; Winterbotham, William, *View of America*
Revolution, American, 77–8, 93–4; *see also* America
Revolution, French

attacks and fears of, 150, 152, 158, 183, 189, 208
effects on Church and state, 39, 44, 52, 93–4
transnational toasting, 79–82
Revolution, Glorious (1688), 14, 79, 93–4, 113, 150–1, 210
rights
British, 62, 69
natural, 13, 15, 17–18, 20, 21–2, 109–10
political, and property, 152, 183
see also land ownership
Rights, Bill of, 125, 154
rioting and riots, 44, 92, 151, 171–2
'Rise and Progress of Learning' (story), 132, 134–6, 138, 139, 141
Robertson, William, 152
Rome, ancient, 20, 113
Rousseau, Jean-Jacques, on lost rights, 110
Roxburghe, John Ker, 5th earl of, 27, 35
Russell, Lord John, 210, 211
Russia, 202, 215
Ryder, Sir Dudley, 63

Sacheverell, Henry, 98–9
Saint, Thomas, 132, 133, 141
Salmond, Alex, 216
satire and satirists, 80, 178, 185, 218–19; *see also* Cruikshank, Isaac
Savile, Sir George, 92
schools, 46, 52, 212, 215; *see also* education
Scots law, and sedition, 163–73
Scott, Sir William, 43, 48, 49–51
Scottish martyrs *see* Muir, Thomas
Scottish peerage question, 26–36
Seafield, James Ogilvy, earl of, 28, 29
Second World War, and Scottish nationalism, 214
sedition, 74, 75, 96, 149
trials, 118, 122, 152, 158, 163–73, 210, 212
Senate, US, 154
servants, and post-Culloden acts, 66, 67
Sheridan, Richard Brinsley, 92, 95, 96, 181
ships, 199–200, 209, 217
Sinclair, Charles, 167, 168
Skinner, Quentin, 119–20, 121–2
Skirving, William, 163, 164
slavery, 137, 152–3, 156, 158, 217
Smart, Christopher, 134, 135, 137
Smith, Adam, 105, 106, 109, 110
social equality, 155–6
social networking, 194–204
socialism, 3, 103, 115, 214–15, 218
societies *see* clubs and societies
society, evolution of (Ogilvie), 109

Socinianism, 14, 94
Somers, John, 1st Baron, 27–8
Spain, declares war on Britain (1804), 201, 202
spelling reform, 136, 138, 141
Spence, Thomas
  and Harrington, 118–28
  'Land Plan', 121, 122, 123–5, 133
  and Ogilvie, 103, 113
  Pig's Meat (journal), 118, 122, 123, 124, 126–8, 131, 132
  as radical educationalist, 3, 131–42
Stair, James Dalrymple, 1st Viscount, 106, 165, 166
Stanhope, James, Earl (later Viscount Stanhope), 34, 36
state, the
  and church/Church, 16–17, 91, 96, 97–9, 157
  and rights, 17–18, 62, 69, 111–12
  see also reform, Church; sedition, trials
statute law, 163–4, 165, 168
Stewart, Dugald, reviews *Essay* (Ogilvie), 114
Stewart, William, 214–15
Stoddart, Alexander, 219
Stoke-upon-Trent, Paine's mock 'death', 187
Stowe, Temple of Ancient Virtue (1737), 138
Strain, E. H., 211–12
Suckling, Maurice, 197
Suckling, William, 197
Suffolk, effigy burning, 188–9
Sunderland, Charles Spencer, 3rd earl of, 34, 36
Supplement/S'upl'im'int (Spence), 131–2, 136, 141; *see also* Crusonia
Swift, Jonathan, 139

tartan *see* Highland dress
Tattersfield, Nigel, 133
taxation, 30–1, 33, 44–5, 48, 77, 152
Taylor, Michael, 183
tenant farmers, and post-Culloden acts, 66, 67
Test and Corporation Acts (1787 and 1789), 44, 51, 93, 94, 97, 157
Thirty-Nine Articles, doctrine of, 89, 91
Thompson, E. P., 125, 188
Thompson, Peter, 74
Tindall, Matthew, 11–14, 18, 21–2
tithes, 44, 45, 48
toasting, political (1765–1800), 73–83
Toland, John, 10, 11, 17
toleration, 15, 89–92, 94, 98; *see also* freedom
Tories, 99, 211

Townshend, Charles, 2nd Viscount, 35, 36
Trafalgar, battle of, 194, 198, 199, 201
trials for sedition *see* sedition, trials
Triennial Act, 35
Troeltsch, Ernst, 9
Twomey, Richard, 153

Union (England and Scotland) negotiations (1706–16), 26–36
Unitarianism, 92, 94, 98, 99, 151
United Irishmen, 82, 208, 209, 218
United States of America *see* America
utilitarianism, 108
utopian texts, 118, 134, 136–9, 152

Valentine's Gift (Anon.), 132, 133
Verhoeven, Wil, 150, 152, 155, 158
Victory, HMS (Nelson's flagship), 199–200

Wagner, Corinna, 186
Waldstreicher, David, 77
Walpole, Robert, 36, 62
War of the Austrian Succession (1740–8), 135, 137
Washington, George, 77, 155
weaponry, in the *Gàidhealtachd*, 59–60, 64, 67
Wedell, William, 94, 95
West Indies, 195, 203, 204
Whigs, 79, 94–5, 151, 210
  on Church, 44, 50–1, 92–3, 97, 98
  and post-Culloden acts, 60–3, 65, 68, 69
  and Scots peerage question, 27–8, 32–3, 34, 36
Whiston, William, 19
White, Collin, 194
Wilberforce, William, 46–7, 51
Wilkes, John, 75–6, 77, 125
William IV, King of England, 210, 211
Wilson, Theodore, 176–8
wine and wine trade, 74, 76
Winterbotham, William
  sources for works, 152–3
  two sermons (1792), 149, 150–1, 155, 156, 158
  View of America, 149–58
women, 74, 75, 76, 78, 186
World (newspaper), Paine and balloon analogy, 180

'Zigzag' fables, 132, 133–4

EU representative:
Easy Access System Europe
Mustamäe tee 50, 10621 Tallinn, Estonia
Gpsr.requests@easproject.com

www.ingramcontent.com/pod-product-compliance
Lightning Source LLC
Chambersburg PA
CBHW050850230426
43667CB00012B/2232